STRUCTURE AND

IMAGERY IN

ANCRENE WISSE

The University Press
of New England

MEMBER INSTITUTIONS
Brandeis University
Clark University
Dartmouth College
The University of New Hampshire
The University of Rhode Island
The University of Vermont

STRUCTURE AND

IMAGERY IN

ANCRENE WISSE

JANET GRAYSON

Published for The University of New Hampshire

by The University Press of New England

Hanover, New Hampshire 1974

249.6
An 22 Yg

189820

PREFACE

The idea of producing a study of the structure and imagery of this great Middle English work originated in a Columbia University seminar when, at the encouragement of Professor Howard Schless, I ventured a serious look at the devotional content of Part One. My hope of finding some material of literary interest beyond the devotional matter was both satisfied and stimulated at once, even where there had seemed to others so much piety, so little art. It was Geoffrey Shepherd's illuminating introduction to his edition of Parts Six and Seven that suggested to me that the spiraling images of which Part Seven is built could be the structural 'mechanism' of the whole Rule. I was already convinced that the arrangement of devotions in Part One followed a circular progression. The problem remained to trace the movement of the images when each motif did not possess an entirely independent life, but served to carry other motifs forward at the same time. Moreover, closely bound up with the selection and placing of images was the author's distinction of outer and inner Rule. The division is clear enough in the overall partition of 'distinctions' but is less obvious and more vital in the author's use of literal and allegorical modes, where the one so often develops into the other.

The difficulties of extricating threads without violating the fabric were immense, for I had before me the danger of disfiguring the imprint of order which inheres in a medieval work. The remarkable emotional effect of the Rule is cumulative, and the image motifs that create this effect must be studied as integrated members of the stage of spiritual growth attained by the anchoress. Since the author's chapters are records of these stages, it seemed best (and least disruptive to the essential order of the Rule) to stay with the author's arrangement and follow his progress chapter by chapter.

For their many suggestions and wise counsel, which made possible the preparation of my original manuscript, I thank Howard Schless and the late Elliot V. K. Dobbie. Also remembered are Marjorie Coogan Downing and Roderick Dhu Marshall, who showed me the possibilities of literature and instilled a deep affection for the Middle Ages. Their influence extends into this book.

Finally, special thanks are due to Search Press, London, for permission to quote extensively from the M. B. Salu translation, *The Ancrene Riwle*. I am grateful also to the Council of the Early English Text Society for their permission to use the J. R. R. Tolkien edition of CCCC 402, *Ancrene Wisse*, as the basis of my study.

Chesterfield, New Hampshire   J.G.
May 20, 1973

CONTENTS

ABBREVIATIONS

ALMA   *Arthurian Literature in the Middle Ages*

AR   *Ancrene Riwle*

AW   *Ancrene Wisse* (MS. cccc 402, first revised version of *AR*)

BM   British Museum

EETS   Early English Text Society

Nero   MS. Cotton Nero A.xiv, edited by Mabel Day for *EETS*

PL   Migne's *Patrologia Latina*

Regula   *De vita eremitica* of Aelred of Rievaulx

STRUCTURE AND

IMAGERY IN

ANCRENE WISSE

INTRODUCTION

The Author and His Rule of Living

At some point early in the thirteenth century, a cleric of apparent distinction and considerable learning responded to the gentle pleading of three sisters, young women already dedicated to serving Mary's part in an unnamed anchorhold in England, and put together for their daily use a guide for the regulation of the inner and outer life. This Rule of Anchoresses, the *Ancrene Riwle*[1] is based firmly in the traditional materials of the time: Scripture and patristic literature.

To these basic sources the author added his knowledge of the techniques of medieval devotional prose, such as etymology, exegesis, amplification, allegory and symbolism—and, it might be added, the benefit of experience and an understanding of human nature. The author was a man of eclectic tastes, well trained in Bible studies, at home equally in the Old Testament and the New. He was a student of the works of the Church Fathers (especially Saints Augustine, Gregory, and Bernard) and of the rhetorical devices of composition current in the late twelfth century.[2] Out of the index of his learning comes whatever is known of him, for he is all but silent on the subject of personal biography.[3]

1. The name (corrected from *Ancren Riwle*) designated by James Morton for the untitled work he translated from MS. Cotton Nero A.xiv for the Camden Society in 1853. Hereafter, *AR* or the Rule: texts cited by page/line.

2. See Geoffrey Shepherd's introduction to his edition of Parts VI and VII, *Ancrene Wisse*, Nelson's Medieval and Renaissance Library (London, 1959), for details of the range of the author's reading and sources.

3. In the Nero MS. there are references to 'Vre leawede breþren' (10/25) and 'ure ordre' (11/5), which point to a monastic order. However, these are probably interpolations. In tone and subject matter the author is unmonastic. Joseph Hall conjectured that the author was advanced in years because of the expression of weariness at the end of the Rule: 'Me were leouere godd hit wite do me toward rome, þen forte biginnen hit eft forte donne.' *Selections from Early Middle English* (Oxford, 1920), II, 375. However, relief and exhaustion might well be expected in the man at the end of this undertaking.

The general format of the Rule as a document of benevolent counsel for female recluses was provided by the *De vita eremitica* of Aelred of Rievaulx (1109–1167), composed under circumstances similar to those of the *AR*, for Aelred admits in his prologue that his sister had often asked him to write a rule of living for her as a recluse.[4] Had the author of *Ancrene Riwle* been satisfied to follow the pattern of the usual *regula*, he would have produced a pious, articulate treatise for the edification of these three young sisters who had taken on the dour hardships of enclosure and whose spiritual life was of first importance to him. But copying out old script was not to his taste. The conventional tools and precepts of the formal *regula* or more casual epistle undergo vital renewal in his hands; and the emergent creation, the Rule, though the echoes of Aelred are strong, stands apart as a work of high artistic merit and profound religious faith.

The popularity of the Rule in its own time is attested by the number of manuscripts that have survived, eight in English (of which five were written in the thirteenth century, three in the fourteenth); two in French; four in Latin (the earliest belonging to the end of the thirteenth century).[5] The author, in fact, seems to expect a wider circulation, since he makes allowances for physical tolerances different from those of the

4. The *De vita eremitica ad sororem liber*, PL 32, cols. 1451–1474, incorrectly inserted among St. Augustine's works; also called *Regula ad sororem*, *De institutione inclusarum* and *Informacio ad sororem*. Aelred's prologue states that his sister had urged him to compose such a rule for many years: 'Jam pluribus annis exigis a me, soror, ut secundum modum vivendi quem arripuisti pro Christo, certam tibi formulam tradam, ad quam et mores tuos dirigere, et vitam religionis, et vitae religiosae possis exercitia ordinare.' Col. 1451. The point is repeated in the epilogue. Many devotional pieces were written at the request of a dear friend or spiritual brother, but always the author had a larger audience in mind. Nowhere in Aelred's *Regula* does the personality of his sister emerge. She is there to provide the occasion for his work.

5. English MSS. of the thirteenth century are BM Cotton Nero A.xiv, edited by Mabel Day for EETS (1952); Corpus Christi College, Cambridge, 402, edited by J. R. R. Tolkien for EETS (1962): BM Gonville and Caius College, Cambridge, 234, edited by R. M. Wilson for EETS (1954); BM Cotton Titus D.xviii; BM Cotton Cleopatra C.vi., edited by E. J. Dobson for EETS (1972). Belonging to the fourteenth are BM Royal 8 C.i, edited by A. C. Baugh for EETS (1956); Bodleian Library Vernon MS.; Magdalene College, Cambridge, Pepys, 2498.

three sisters. The most interesting of the English MSS. are the Cotton Nero A.xiv, British Museum, and the Corpus Christi College, Cambridge, 402, known as the *Ancrene Wisse*, the title given to the Rule by the scribe in a marginal note of CCCC 402 and the only manuscript so designated.[6] The Corpus Christi MS. (1225–1230) is somewhat earlier than Cotton Nero and is the best version of the Rule in terms of closeness of language and date to the original and in consistency of dialect and orthography. However, the *AW* differs from the original version of the Rule in an important respect. It represents a revision (possibly the first) of the Rule for use by a community of anchorites rather than for the three sisters alone; as well, it adds a number of details, such as the reference to the Dominicans and Franciscans in England, which could not have appeared in the original,[7] and eliminates some of the biographical material (including the reference to the author's lay brothers). The Nero MS. contains these personal details, omitted in the *AW*, and so has been regarded in some respects as closer to the original. But whichever has the greater claim to this distinction, the durability of the Rule in adaptation, revision, and translation is indisputable. Writers continued to draw upon it in the fourteenth century, incorporating sections into devotional prose of their own and, in some cases, into other rules.[8]

While the publication in 1853 of James Morton's edition of the Nero MS. made the work available to readers, it was not until this century that scholars recognized it as 'undoubtedly the most influential and

6. 'I þe feaderes & i þe sunes & i þe hali gastes nome her biginneð ancrene wisse.' The Corpus MS. of the *Ancrene Wisse*, ed. J. R. R. Tolkien, EETS, No. 249 (Oxford, 1962) is the source text of this study. Except where noted, all subscript page and line numbers refer to CCCC 402.

7. The writer mentions these orders twice, first in 36/13 as 'Vre freres prechurs & ure freres meonurs' and again in 213/11–12 as 'freres preachurs & meonurs.' The Dominicans came to England in 1221, the Franciscans in 1224.

8. See Hope Emily Allen, 'Some Fourteenth Century Borrowings from the *Ancren Riwle*,' *MLR*, 18 (1923), 1–8; 'Further Borrowings from the *Ancren Riwle*,' *MLR*, 24 (1929), 1–15; 'Wynkyn de Worde and a Second French Compilation from the *Ancren Riwle*,' *Essays in Honor of Carleton Brown* (London, 1940), pp. 182–219. Portions of the Rule appear in the fourteenth century *Chastising of God's Children*, *Gratia Dei*, *Adam and Eve*, *The Poor Caitiff*, and the fifteenth century *Treatise of Love*.

important of the prose works of the early ME period.'[9] The obvious quality of the Rule has engaged the interest of such scholars as R. W. Chambers, Hope Emily Allen, G. G. Coulton and J. R. R. Tolkien, among many others; and their studies have yielded some answers to the question of provenance.[10]

The Three Sisters

Although the author reveals practically nothing of himself, he occasionally comments on the condition and habits of the sisters, and from this we can compose a picture of the kind of life they lead. They are young women of gentle birth, 'sisters of one father and of one mother,' who, 'while in the blossom of their youth' forsook the world to become anchoresses. Unlike many recluses, they are not concerned about food or clothing, their needs being provided by a friend.

Each anchoress has a maidservant who remains within the anchorhold, and possibly a second who attends to errands on the outside. The servants receive as wages food and only 'enough to live on.' The sisters live in separate cells 'under the eaves of a church' and communicate with their servants by means of a parlor window built into the wall that joins their cells. Through this window they might occasionally glance out at a visitor who has come to dine in the servants' quarters. A second window enables the anchoress to watch the celebration of the Mass; thus one wall of the anchorhold is attached to the side of the church from which the altar is visible. A third window, unglazed but equipped with shutters, opens onto the courtyard or the road. A black curtain embroidered with a white cross covers this window, which is drawn back when a visitor comes to make inquiries. If he grows troublesome, the shutters are closed. It is this window of which we read so much in the Rule.

Each cell is simply but comfortably furnished. Each anchoress has a small bed, a table for dining, at least two chairs or a chair and a stool,

9. Bruce Dickins and R. M. Wilson, *Early Middle English Texts* (London, 1951), p. 89.

10. A summary of research appears in Shepherd, *AW*, pp. xiv–xxv.

sewing materials, and possibly an embroidery frame. There is a crucifix on the wall, a font for holy water, a small altar containing relics, an image of the Virgin, and 'other images.' Nearby are her books, English and French and Latin. One of the English books is the life of St. Margaret. There is a Psalter, a missal and breviary of some kind, a book of saints' lives, the *Vitae Patrum*, and, of course, they are soon to have the *Ancrene Riwle*.

Much of their day is spent in prayer and meditation, and between devotions they occupy themselves with reading passages from their French, English, or Latin books; or they may mend church vestments and make simple garments for the poor. They are not to embroider lace without permission, for elaborate needlecraft is to be avoided. Nor can they make gifts for friends.

They are to be hospitable to guests, but not liberal, for their provisions are donated by a benefactor and must not be squandered in 'lavish entertainments.' They must not teach school at the window, keep a cow, or engage in business enterprises. The face must be veiled before the eyes of men, whether by a headdress or by a wall or 'a curtain over a firmly-closed window.'

They are not to wear rings, brooches, striped girdles or gloves; their shoes and gowns should be comfortable and appropriate to the season. No linen is to touch the skin unless it is coarsely made, and the night-gown is to be belted at the waist, but not tightly. The head should be covered by a wimple or by a cap with white or black veil:

> Wummon, seið þe apostle, schal wreon hire heaued. Wrihene,
> he seið, nawt wimplin.   (215/24–25)

White or black, color is unimportant, for religion is 'nawt i þe wide hod, ne i þe blake cape, ni i þe hwite rochet, ne i þe greie cuuel' (10/17–19).

The women may wash themselves and their things whenever they wish. The hair may be cut, or shaved (if they prefer) four times a year, or merely trimmed. Blood-letting is permitted but not encouraged, and for the three days following each operation they are to do nothing more strenuous than exchange edifying stories with their maidservants.

They lead hard lives, the author says, harder than he wishes them to. Often, they must bear the arrogance of 'those who once might have been your serfs,' and suffer the insolence of Slurry, the cook's boy. As for their food, they are to abstain from meats and fat and are to observe fast-days, but their diet is already so small that the author worries about their health. He often expresses concern that immoderate neglect of the body may embitter them and alter their dispositions. That would be the worst offense.

He asks that they make profession in three matters: first, obedience, chastity, and constancy of abode; then, that they follow the advice of their confessor; and finally, that they abide strictly by all solemn vows. Everything else, including the counsels of the exterior Rule, may be adjusted to changing circumstances. His Rule is interested mainly in the 'governance of the heart,' for the sisters 'do already fulfill all the demands of the outer Rule.'

The Structure of the Ancrene Wisse

Considering the amount and quality of scholarly activity inspired by the Rule, there has been comparatively little examination of structure or style. However relative and shifting may be the definition of 'style,' there exist certain patterns within an overall design in the Rule which can be traced, dismantled, and reconstructed in order to understand better the characteristic effect of the work on readers.

The most penetrating summary of the author's skill in the art of composition belongs to Geoffrey Shepherd, in his introduction to Parts Six and Seven.[11] Under subheadings that cover most of the range of the literary merits of the Rule, Shepherd discusses the structural components of the work as a whole; aspects of method, uses of metaphor, manner of presentation, and effect. Among his conclusions on the 'highly artificial and carefully calculated' style of the *AW* is the point that the author's intention is 'not to prove but to move . . . AW is thus written with a practical end in view. Its words are intended to be fully

11. Shepherd, *AW*, pp. lix–lxxiii.

commotiva'; the Rule 'was planned as a whole . . . the parts were adapted and fitted to form a unified treatise. "Notice," we are bidden, "how each Part leads on to the next"'; structural and verbal repetitions occur so frequently in the Rule 'that we must conclude that symmetry, parallelism, and antithesis are habits' of the author's thought. The author's interest in simile is very slight, but metaphor 'is a condition of the thought and expression of this writer . . . a metaphorical cast of thinking underlies all the amplifications and interpretations.'[12]

A careful reading of the imagery of *AW* simply proves that the work is as spirited and articulate as its admirers have claimed. The author's deep religious conviction is indisputable. We may add to our image of the man the gift of unusual literary ability and consider him twice blessed. His *is*, as Shepherd says, astonishing prose.

This study of the Rule will examine those parts of the work which show a systematic attention to style. My intention is to describe the organization of the argument by (1) studying the structural affinities of image, method of elaboration, and transition; and (2) showing how by artful selection and positioning of figures the author of *AW* is able to animate the fundamental concept of 'outer and inner' in order to create the kind of vibrating upward movement within the images and (in a larger sense) the chapters that gives 'a curious spiral quality to the structure of the *Ancrene Wisse*.'[13]

The *AW* is divided substantially into two parts, described by the author in his introduction as the inner Rule and the outer Rule:

Þe an riwleð þe heorte & makeð efne & smeðe wið ute cnost & dolc of woh inwit . . . Þeos riwle is eauer inwið & rihteð þe heorte.   (5/15–18)

Þe oþer riwle is al wið uten & riwleð þe licome & licomliche deden; þe teacheð al hu me schal beoren him wið uten, hu eoten, drinken, werien, singen, slepen, wakien.   (6/3–6)

12. Ibid.
13. Ibid., p. lxxiii.

The one governs the heart and keeps it untroubled and free from the wounds and tumours of an unhealthy conscience . . . This rule is always interior, guiding the heart.

The other is completely external, and governs the body and its actions. It gives directions about all outward behaviour, about eating and drinking, dress, singing, sleep, and vigil.

The outer Rule, he continues, exists only to serve the inner. The one is the handmaid and the other the lady she serves; all that is ever done in the outer Rule is meant only to serve, to perfect the heart within.

This is no incidental distinction by which the ordinary duties of every-day life are separated from contemplative withdrawal. Discerning at once the analogy of heart and anchorhold, inner spirituality and outer (or physical) enclosure, the author exposes this correspondence to every kind of amplification, relegating the body, the outer life, to a secondary place as servant, guardian, ancilla of the heart—the seat or 'nest' of the inner life. The nature of the physical contacts and experiences of the anchoress determines the quality of her spiritual growth, just as the physical walls and windows of the anchorhold are the custodians of her seclusion and religious development. The progress of the anchoress is meticulously graduated to the point of contact with Christ and is described not only by the passage of the chapters from the discipline of the senses to the reception of Love, but organically by a series of cumulating images, each building upon its predecessor in a spiral-like ascent.

Nor is the linear division of the two Rules ever static (as it would appear from the author's statement on the purpose of Parts One and Eight, the outer Rule). The interaction of outer and inner aspects of experience is built into the fabric of the whole work, shifting alternately from one to the other according to the level of meaning of the metaphor or analogy under discussion at the moment. So the author may illustrate a precept with an appropriate image, as, for instance, a bird (the pelican) striking down its own young birds, killing them. The common-place 'anger kills' is rendered in the literal (outer) act of murder. But as the full dimensions of the precept are explored and applied to the experience of the anchoress, the didactic elements slowly distend, and the images assume a moral and intensely spiritual character (inner). The

bird's act is made analogous to the anchoress' hurting all possibilities of
bringing forth good and finally to her smiting Christ Himself. But in
purging herself of anger, the anchoress restores her good, as the bird
revives its young with its blood; she grows spiritually, as the bird begins
its upward flight; and ultimately she finds refuge in Christ, as the bird
(now, the dove) creeps into the sanctuary of the rocks (Christ's wounds).
Once the mystical sense has been conveyed, the author may reverse the
process quite suddenly and return to the original precept or rule (outer).
What began as an important but unimaginative counsel has taken on
the complexities of anagogue, and the literal application to the life of
the anchoress is now much more meaningful than it would have been
had the author merely set down a series of caveats or thou-shalt-nots.

Another example of this interpenetration of outer-inner pattern in
images, though more limited in range, is the figure of the *hands*
in Part Two, 'Custody of the Senses.' The anchoress is warned to
keep her hands inside the window to avoid physical contact with male
visitors:

> Hwen se ȝe moten to eani mon eawiht biteachen, þe hond ne
> cume nawt ut, ne ower ut, ne his in.   (34/2–4)

This simple caution is a regulation of the outer Rule in the sense of its
directness. It is repeated later in stronger terms when she is told to shut
the window on the man who reaches for the curtain: 'Ȝef ei wurðeð
swa awed þet he warpe hond forð toward te þurl clað, swiftliche
ananriht schutteð al þet þuel to & leoteð him iwurðen' (51/10–13). The
outstretched hand that reaches after flesh (a literal, or outer figure)
becomes transformed radically into the nailed hands of Christ in the
concluding section of the chapter, in a meditation on the Passion. The
movement of images has been inward from the physical-literal outer
image of the hands of anchoress and the male to the spiritual-tropo-
logical inner figure of Christ's hands:

> Godes honden weren ineilet o rode. Þurh þe ilke neiles ich halsi ow
> ancres, nawt ow, ah do oþre, for hit nis na neod, mine leoue
> sustren: haldeð ower honden inwið ower þurles.   (62/6–9)

God's hands were nailed to the cross. By those nails, I adjure you anchoresses—(not you, my dear sisters, for there is no need)—but you others: keep your hands inside your windows.

Regulations bring the Rule outward as the author continues his warning that touching with the hands brings trouble, entices the man, leads to sin and, what is worst, angers God. These hands, which some vain anchoresses look upon as beautiful, should be digging up dirt 'out of the grave in which they will rot':

Ha schulden schrapien euche dei þe eorðe up of hare put þet ha
schulien rotien in.   (62/23–24)

The mingling of levels belonging to the inner and outer life reinforces the need for careful scrutiny of the sense of touch, and the reinforcement is stronger than had the author relied only on a rule governing 'handling'.

In a much more pronounced way, the collective inner Rule (Parts Two through Seven), undergoes conversion from concern with the physical world to the spiritual, from preoccupation with the means to achieve Love to the actual reception of Love. Just as the individual image-motifs and distinctions move inward toward a settling in Christ, so the inner Rule moves relentlessly inward toward its center: the heart, Love, grace, Christ. As each part gives way to the next, the spiritual *affectus* by which the soul is drawn to God grows at the expense of physical things; the anchoress passes through graduated stages of purification or trial which prepare her for the advent of Christ, who comes to her as a knight bound by Love to sacrifice Himself in her behalf.

And within the broad range of each distinction minor but palpable changes in meaning are taking place—all moving inward toward the heart, which is the 'seat of the soul.' It is precisely this resilience of movement that creates the tension in the work, that lends the effect of 'perpetual' motion laboring toward an end, a goal. The outer-inner activity depends on shifts in the 'sense' of an idea from literal and allegorical levels to moral, symbolic, and anagogic, each of these being inner-directed and more expressive of deeper spiritual growth than the last. So Part Two begins with a detailed discussion of the senses, their responsibility as custodians of the heart, the assaults upon them by temptations from the outside. It ends with an account of the delights reserved for the senses in the mystical nuptials, and finally the suffering of Christ's senses in the Passion. In Part Three ('Regulation of the Inward Feelings') the sins of anger and pride are expunged from the heart to prepare it, as the bird prepares the nest, for Christ. In Part Four ('Temptations') the allegorized battle with the animal-sins is taken up at the end by the anchoress' champion, Christ, who then offers her refuge in His wounds. The sinner of Part Five ('Confession'), moved to a full confession by the grim threats of final judgment, wins forgiveness as had the penitent thief from Christ Himself. In Part Six ('Penance') the path chosen by the anchoress in her journey to heaven proves to lead to the cross, which she is to share with Christ as part of her penitential life. Her resurrection from the tomb is assured, since she has died with Christ. The Christ-knight who, in Part Seven ('Love'), comes to save her does so almost against her will, but having given his life, he leaves her free—and free to love him though she has only the memory of his sacrifice.

These examples suggest the bare shell of progress within the individual chapters. Yet there is rarely an arrangement of images so clumsily contrived that what results is no more than a mechanical exercise in the four-fold modes of Christian experience. The gradual development of meanings and perceptions out of literal truths and commonplace events is what the author is after, but he refuses to sacrifice the intelligible world of physical matter. The one must serve the other, as the handmaiden serves the lady, as regulation of the outer life serves the inner. Thus, after having developed the allegorical potential of an idea or image, the author will often let go this 'inner' probing and return his prose to practical application of a rule or precept (now very much enlarged by allegory and symbol). With this knowledge, which is indeed a deeper wisdom, the anchoress may govern her life and so grow inwardly. Although they are all by definition parts of the inner Rule—that which governs the heart—Parts Two through Seven rely heavily on sense and matter, intermingling these where necessary with spirit. Like a human life, *AW* participates in both worlds.

The *heart* is the symbol of spiritual life in the Rule. Here, the love of God is nurtured and good works are born. The 'nest of the heart' is inviolable, a sacred place of retreat for the Bridegroom and spouse. The concept of heart as center (physically, in relation to the body; spiritually, relation to Love) is an important organizational device in the Rule, and belongs, as might be expected, to the inner Rule. The direction of the inner Rule is indicated by the chapter headings, as given by Miss Salu: Custody of the Senses, Regulation of the Inward Feelings, Temptations, Confession, Penance, Love. These areas embrace the consecutive steps of attitude and act leading to communion. The anchoress works her way up through ever-diminishing attachments to the body's needs and unworthy spiritual defects until she is ready for the visitation by Christ. But He comes as no sweeping descent of glorious light; there is no instant of mysterious transport into contemplation, as we might expect if this were a mystical work. Instead, in an ingenious and totally unexpected reversion to allegory and romance, He comes as the Christ-knight to press His suit for the love of a regal but imperious lady. Within a courtly frame, the crucifixion is reenacted—the sacrifice of the knight that lifts the siege from the lady's castle. The crucifixion is handled masterfully, as if it were a unique moment in the composing of the Rule—all the more striking since every part of the Rule to Part Seven has treated a particular aspect of the crucifixion, often in great detail, from the abuse of Christ's senses (Part Two) to His anxiety at the death and dishonor about to befall Him (Part Six). The passages are highly emotional but always controlled, always moving toward a center—that point in Part Seven when Christ and anchoress (the lady) personally confront each other and strike a bargain: His life for her love. The allegorical meeting, the exchange of vows, the death of the knight are made possible by the love of the knight. That love finds its abode in the 'nest of the heart.'

The point of ultimate convergence of image 'spirals' in *AW* is Part Seven. 'Spiral' is a convenient term to designate the effect of 'piling up' of cumulating imagery within individual chapters and their recurrence from chapter to chapter. The author's habit of returning to an idea or image which has again become pertinent to the discussion, adding a detail or uncovering a fresh nuance, creates the semblance of circularity. More specifically, the dynamic movement of a theme follows a spiral-like pattern; the images begin to accumulate, are suddenly pulled together in a summary statement, and veer off into a new series, related to the original spiral but not dependent upon it. The spirals, however, are only partially resolved in the summary statement, for quite often they reappear later in the text, having accumulated additional meanings during the course of the discussion. The author's ability to reuse themes and motifs without suffocating the reader with endless verbal and image repetitions rests on his control of spirals, certainly one of the unique structural achievements of *AW*.

Encircling the inner Rule, like a protective band of tougher fiber, is the outer Rule, Parts One and Eight, 'an invention of man, instituted solely to serve the other.' It stands in attendance on the inner Rule 'like the handmaid,' serving the lady in the governance of the heart. But the author's fondness for analogy extends beyond the subtle enclosing of one set of rules within another. The sense of outer-inner relationship pervades the Rule: the world and the anchorhold; the anchorhold enclosing the recluse; the body enclosing the heart; spiritual beauty within carnal matter; the outer Rule holding within it the inner Rule. This 'little world made cunningly' is a God-centered microcosm; physical and spiritual experience are opposite sides of a single perception. The readiness is all.

To approach the *AW* as a reader about to probe the components of structure and imagery is to be rewarded to the point of surfeit, for one of the major difficulties of close study of the Rule is its extraordinary density. Scores of men, women, animals, birds, devils, and saints make an appearance in various religious and social contexts. The five senses, Seven Deadly Sins, nine comforts, eight vigils, six remedies (the list is endless) pass through the pages attended by exempla, homilies, and biblical precepts. Wars rage, castles are stormed, hell opens its jaws, Elijah is caught up in the fiery chariot, Christ is anointed with spices— these are a handful of the colorful activity of medieval life and thought that enlivens the serious moral message of the Rule.

Method of This Study

The eight chapters of the present book cover the eight parts (or distinctions) of *AW*. Although the inner Rule is to receive the largest share of attention, Parts One and Eight (the outer Rule), of considerable interest as documents of contemporary religious practice, are examined insofar as they yield imagery that contributes to the understanding of the whole work. Chapter One on 'Devotions' deals briefly with liturgical prayers and private devotions recommended by the author but considers in detail the devotion on the Five Joys of Mary, which has certain structural affinities with the whole of the inner Rule. Chapter Eight on 'External Rules' summarizes the author's advice on the regulation of the outer life.

It is not within the scope of this book to examine scrupulously every image and metaphor. The imagery is limited to whatever designs contribute materially to the structure and progress of the Rule. Thus incidental legends and illustrations, though interesting in themselves and peripherally related to the subject at hand, have been omitted. Occasionally it was necessary to pass over even some relevant details of the text because including them would have made the argument unmanageable. What reads well in the original can collapse and disintegrate under fastidious analysis, as we know. Indeed, any study of *AW* that picks apart the matrix or disrupts the unity (even for the sake of showing off the special talents of the unknown author) does violence to the work. Hopefully, the compensations outweigh the risks.

The Tolkien edition of CCCC 402 has been used throughout except where missing passages are supplied by Nero. Modern English translations that accompany the Middle English excerpts (the modern English altered occasionally in punctuation to conform to the original, as used) are provided by the M. B. Salu translation of *Ancrene Wisse*.

ONE 'DEVOTIONS'

In the ordering of the outer life, with which the *Ancrene Wisse* begins, lies the possibility of perfecting the inner life, of purifying the heart. This, says our author quoting St. Paul, is the end of the law.[1] If we can accept that the author conceived his book to reflect a slowly expanding spiritualization that starts with formula and ends in anagogue, we have a clearer understanding of 'Devotions,' its introductory position and, indeed, its inclusion in the Rule.

Using fully the possibilities laid open by analogy, the author imposes the same outer-to-inner structure on his Rule that the anchoress must study in perfecting her life—moving gradually inward to the heart, the seat of the soul. This is the design of the Rule; it is repeated in the organization and, implicitly, in the texture, so that form and content are integrated to show growth. The reader experiences the *growing*.

The Rule is enclosed by matters that can be considered external—that is, not dealing directly with the inner Rule. At least, of Part Eight there is no question. The advice, precepts, strictures, last-minute reminders are common in regula of this period and provide interesting historical commentary on conditions in religious communities, though in terms of the overall purpose of the Rule the final section is far less interesting than that which has come before. Part One, which deals with daily devotions, is not, it would seem, an integral part of the progress of the Rule proper, the 'leafdi riwle,' as it moves deliberately toward its center, the heart, Love. Yet even within the mass of instructions and repetitions that seem at best merely preparatory to spiritual growth there is careful attention to arrangement of parts, not only in the precedence of one set of devotions over another, but in the placing centrally of the longest and most impassioned set of devotions, the Five Joys of Mary. In this

1. A pivotal point of Part Seven: 'Schirness of heorte is godes luue ane. I þis is al þe strengðe of alle religiuns, þe ende of alle ordres.' (197/15–17.)

arrangement there is a design that duplicates the general organization of the whole work—that is, an interaction of outer-and-inner movement that focuses gradually on Mary, on the centrality of the Virgin's role as woman, maiden, and mother.

The *AW* is a document intended to instruct religious women; as such considerable time and space given over to prayer and study is to be expected. The middle position of the Joys among prayers addressed to the Father, the Son, the Trinity—male figures—attests to the growing prestige of Mary and to recognition of her privileged role as mediatrix and vehicle of the Incarnation. It is in the spirit of the time that part of the day's prayer should be dedicated to Mary, though the choice of five Joys rather than seven or fifteen (the usual number on the Continent) reflects the English tradition of Marian worship.[2] In *AW*, moreover, we have the first full treatment of the Joys in English. The coincidence of an elaborate devotion to Mary and the insertion of devotions between prayers to the Godhead tells us something of the author's intention in the plan of his book and suggests that his idea, at least in Part One, came from a reading of the work of Stephen, abbot of Sawley.

Dom André Wilmart made a brief study of the Five Joys as they developed from an eleventh-century antiphon, the *Gaude, dei genetrix*, a 'poetic echo' of the Ave Maria. The occasion of this historical review was the publication of an early prose meditation of Stephen, about whom little is known other than his tenure as abbot of Sawley from 1200 to 1230.[3] What seems clear, however, is his debt in inspiration to Aelred's *Regula* as he describes with mounting emotion the Fifteen Joys of Mary from the moment of her selection to the enthronement in heaven. Stephen's meditations are of interest and relevance to the *AW* because they embody an expanded, traditional version of the Joys found in the *AW*; and they contain parts, prayers and formulae similar in kind and

2. Two early lyrics on the Five Joys are found in *English Lyrics of the XIIIth Century*, ed. Carleton Brown (Oxford, 1932), pp. 27, 65, 179n. The few verbal similarities in lyrics and *AW* result from conventionalized vocabulary.

3. 'Les Méditations d'Etienne de Sallai,' ed. André Wilmart, *Revue d'Ascétique et de Mystique*, 10 (1929), 368–415. Stephen's name appears in a list of abbots connected to Sawley (founded in 1148 and again ca. 1190) and in the register of the Archbishop of York.

arrangement to those of the *AW*, particularly the *Gaude, dei genetrix*, which to Dom Wilmart was the important link in the *AW* connecting the Five Joys to the early antiphon.

The body of the meditations follows the plan set forth in the prologue, where Stephen makes clear the care he has taken in arranging parts. The work is divided into three sections, he tells us, each containing five parts, each followed by a pause. The first section (*quinarius*) deals with events from the birth of the Virgin to the birth of Christ; the second from the Nativity to the Crucifixion; the last from the Passion to the Assumption of the Virgin.[4] The meditations are lengthy but uncomplicated in organization. They begin with the meditation proper on an event in Mary's life; next there is the *gaudium*, beginning in all cases, 'Gaude gloriosissima dei genetrix et sanctissima uirgo semper Maria'; finally, the *peticio*, again consistent in formula, which asks the boon of spiritual perfection. Each meditation concludes with an *ave*; each series of five (*quinarius*) is set off by a pause (*pausatio*), the first pause celebrating the singularity of the Virgin and the second the miracles wrought by the Son. Stephen's choice of fifteen Joys is arbitrary, but his preoccupation with form is evident in the rigid symmetry and repetition of phrase, formula, prayer.[5]

4. The copyist's *incipit* gives a more exact breakdown, stressing symmetry of parts: 'Et continet quelibet ipsarum quindecim: primo, meditacionem gaudii; secundo, expressionem eiusdem gaudii uirgini directam; tercio, peticionem meditantis; quarto, salutacionem angelicam per quedam uerba deuota auctam. Et in fine primi et secondi quinarii, post quintam et decimam peticiones, ante subsequentes meditaciones, sunt due pausaciones recapitulantes actum meditantis.' Stephen's divisions are concerned equally with substance and parts: 'In tres quinarios diuidamus prerogatiuas gaudiorum beate uirginis, ut si non uacauerit omnes simul persoluere, post quemlibet quinarium possimus pausam facere; et sit primus quinarius a natiuitate beate uirginis usque ad natiuitatem saluatoris, secundus a natiuitate saluatoris usque ad passionem crucis, tercius a tempore passionis usque ad assumptionem eiusdem beate uirginis.' Wilmart, pp. 391–393.

5. Classifications of this kind, if not so precise, are common in the Middle Ages. The author of *AW* ends his introduction with a summary of each distinction to follow, advising the reader what to expect, emphasizing the progression of parts set down according to a specific design: 'Nu, mine leoue sustren, þis boc ich todeale on eahte destinctiuns, þet ȝe cleopieð dalen; & euch wið ute monglunge spekeð al bi him seolf of sunderliche þinges, & þah euchan riht falleð efter oðer, & is þe leatere eauer iteiet to

The exceptional treatment of the Five Joys in *AW*, unprecedented in English devotional literature, may well have been inspired by just such a prose meditation as that of Stephen of Sawley. There are stylistic and substantive similarities that point to influence, the glaring exception being the Rule's use of five Joys instead of fifteen. Five reflects a growing national preference on one hand and a sense of proportion on the other, since a heavier distribution of Joys amid the other prayers of Part One would have greatly upset the purpose of the devotions, to set down a daily regimen of prayers and duties for many intentions. As it stands, prayers on the Five Joys of Mary are the longest segment in Part One, and like Stephen's meditation, show the strength and intensity of Marian worship, already stirring up new currents in medieval devotion.[6] As part of the growing body of literature honoring and exalting the Virgin, the Joys expressed the need of the faithful to systematize their devotion into a series of vocal praises that could be repeated daily. No doubt popular legends and, particularly, the steady proliferation of miracles of

---

þe earre. Þe earste dale spekeð al of ower seruise. Þe oðer is hu ȝe schulen þurh ower fif wittes witen ower heorte, þet ordre & religiun & sawle lif is inne. I þis destinctiun aren chapitres fiue, as fif stuchen efter fif wittes þe witeð þe heorte as wakemen hwer se ha beoð treowe . . . ' and so on until the eight parts are dealt with (11/19–12/15). But the *AW*'s attention to arrangement of whole parts as well as details is no mere show of rhetoric. The author is a craftsman conscious of style, wholly in control of his materials, who allows his book to be neither strangled by form nor vitiated by disorder.

6. The Veneration of the Virgin, inspired largely by the new direction of religious piety that stressed the humanity and suffering of Christ, produced a body of literature often so passionate in utterance that it is difficult to ignore the erotic element. Stephen's meditations, though falling short of art, do achieve a certain sustained pitch in ardor. The dangers of 'misinterpreting' the nature and purpose of devotion are anticipated by André Wilmart in the prefatory comments to 'Les Méditations': 'Il est évident que Marie est honorée, invoquée non point tout d'abord pour elle même, mais, exactement, à cause de ses relations privilegiées et incomparables avec le Fils de Dieu fait homme.' Wilmart's next line touches the real issue: 'Les textes n'expriment, au fond, pas autre chose, même si certains le font maladroitment' (p. 381).

In a related study, Wilmart strives to discourage misreading the place of the Virgin in the divine plan, as if to correct modern exaggerations of medieval Mariolatry: 'Marie représente Jésus et . . . l'on ne doit point distinguer l'une de l'autre, "la très douce dame" n'ayant d'autre rôle, dans l'accomplissement du plan divin, que celui de produire Jésus.' 'Le Triple Exercise d'Etienne de Sallai,' *Revue d'Ascétique et de Mystique*, 11 (1930), 361.

the Virgin, in which Mary personally intervened to save the life or reputation of the sinner for no other reason than that he had faithfully sung her praises every day, provided the vital energy in propagating the Joys.

A further point of possible influence of Stephen's work upon our author in the compilation of the Five Joys is the existence in two of the surviving manuscripts of the meditations of a shorter, untitled three-part meditation. The 'Triple Exercise' (as Wilmart called it) has a simple plan: a brief introduction is followed by a meditation on the Trinity, a second on the Virgin, a third on the New Jerusalem.[7] The parts of the exercise are so arranged as to reflect the theological view of Mary's special place in the history of the world. Wilmart observed:

> Il est notable que la seconde partie de l'exercice, le deuxième acte de la trilogie, censée complète, a pour objet direct la personne de Notre-Dame, là où notre logique, après les développements con-sacrés à la Trinité dans la première partie, attendrait l'exposé du mystère de l'Incarnation. Tel est bien aussi, si je ne me trompe, le dessein de l'auteur à savoir de placer devant l'esprit de son disciple, entre la Trinité et l'Eglise, l'oeuvre proprement évangé-lique. Or c'est par une méditation sur les privilèges de Marie qu'il prétend atteindre son but. Ce choix délibère du moyen permet de comprendre la nature spéciale, vraiment profonde, de la dévotion du moyen âge envers la Sainte Vierge, depuis le XIIe siècle environ.[8].

By placing the meditation on Mary in the middle of the 'Triple Exercise' so that she is flanked on one side by the Trinity and on the other by the New Jerusalem, Stephen incorporates into the structure of the work the actual role of the Virgin in the divine plan—that is, her centrality in the mystery of the Incarnation and Redemption. The Virgin (through Christ, whom she brought into the world) is the human link between Trinity and Church. The middle position serves also to reinforce (implicitly) her role as mediatrix between man and the Godhead.

Of the several similarities that exist in the devotional prose of Stephen

7 'Le Triple Exercice,' pp. 355–374.
8. Ibid., p. 360.

of Sawley and the *Ancrene Wisse*, none is so striking as this concentration on Mary's centrality, which, in the form of the Five Joys, constitutes the basic structure of Part One of the Rule. If the author of the Rule had access to both the meditations on the Joys and the 'Triple Exercise,' he would have a very respectable precedent for the integration of form and content in his own presentation of the devotion.[9] The 'Triple Exercise' is conventional in all other respects, sincere and unpretentious in approach to its subjects. The divisions are obvious and well-defined (there is no overlapping), its prose is uncomplicated, its sentiment genuine and lacking in surprises. The arrangement of the 'exercises' is functional and successive; Mary stands between outer sections.

In *AW* devotions are less patently defined. They converge at the Five Joys, the culmination of Part One toward which prayers, versicles, and *gaudia* move, building finally into the impassioned praises of the Virgin. Prayers, hymns, and gestures are especially heavy midpoint in 'Devotions,' when the elevation of the Host in the Mass initiates a series of salutations to the Trinity and to the Cross, followed immediately by the Five Joys of Mary. The Joys deserve special attention, for the prayers are so arranged that, growing upon the crest of its predecessor, each rises to increased fervor. This is especially marked in the variations on the *ave* appended to the Joys—25/24–26/10, beginning 'Leafdi, swete leafdi, swetest alre leafdi. Leafdi, leouest leafdi, lufsumest leafdi'—which, like many of the meticulously wrought exhortations to come which purport to be guides to spiritual perfection, seem to be the immediate personal experience of the author himself.

The Five Joys, which commemorate the most significant events of Mary's life from the Annunciation to the Assumption, occupy the middle portion of Part One. The devotion appeals, says the author, to the 'interior comfort' (the 'froure me inwið' of 23/1), a spiritual peace attainable through physical denial and imitation of Mary. The communi-

9. The meditations and 'Triple Exercise' are addressed to the same person apparently and probably circulated together; but the earliest MS. containing the meditations (second half of thirteenth century) does not contain the 'Triple Exercise.' Stephen's work may be intermediate between Cistercian piety (as influenced by Aelred) and the movement toward formalism represented by the *Ancrene Riwle*.

cation of the pure flesh of Mary (the clean vesicle) that gave flesh and blood to Christ is posited as a reality reaching down into the anchorhold, at least by analogy. Apart from their strictly devotional use, the Joys show a dynamic inward movement as Mary draws nearer to her destiny in heaven. She remains remarkably passive throughout, resigned to serve the powerful forces at work through her. Each Joy develops naturally, linked to the others by common and recurrent themes—the most obvious one that of maidenhood, miraculously preserved or restored. The tight construction of the segment suggests independence from neighboring offices in Part One, but the devotion is very much a development if not an outgrowth of the earlier Mass and *Cruces* passages and, of course, is the direct source of the intensely active meditation that follows in 24/15–26/18. Motifs begun in prayer during Mass recur. There is continued reference to physical things (the body, limbs) and human situations—but negatively, so that these are transformed into spirit while remaining corporeal in fact and image. The effect produced is tension, the immediacy of matter and spirit, polarity reduced as worthiness increases. The prototype of change and ascent is Mary. The Joys chart her progress.

To the elaboration of the Joys the author has brought his power in handling paradox, allusion, and many subtleties of language unequaled at this early period. He has full control over traditional materials, and he accommodates the art of composition to religious themes, creating a dynamic interplay of form and content—the characteristic achievement of the Rule. The Joys are disassembled and examined below with this in mind.

The Five Joys are connected by the chanting of *aves* and psalms told in series of five, the number symbolically relevant to the Virgin and the Passion (in the five wounds). Prayers for the adoration of the Cross (*Cruces*) had served to establish the importance of this number. The sequence follows a regular pattern. Each of the five Joys begins with the invocation 'Leafdi seinte Marie, for þe ilke muchele blisse þet tu hefdest' and is followed by a brief meditation and petition related to the Joy. Each is concluded by a fivefold repetition of *Ave Maria* as far as the words *dominus tecum*; a psalm; the *ave* throughout. The first Joy contains the

Magnificat in place of a psalm. The psalms of the remaining four Joys begin with letters that, together with the M of the *Magnificat*, spell out the acrostic Maria ('Þe salmes beoð inumene efter þe fif leattres of ure leafdis nome, hwa se nimeð ȝeme,' 25/16–17).

THE FIRST JOY: ANNUNCIATION (*theme, to cleanse*)

Leafdi seinte Marie, for þe ilke muchele blisse þet tu hefdest inwið þe i þet ilke time þet iesu, godd, godes sune, efter þe engles gretunge, nom flesch & blod in þe & of þe, underfeng mi gretunge wið ilke aue & make me telle lutel of euch blisse utewið, ah froure me inwið & ernde me þeo of heouene. Ant ase wis as i þe ilke flesch þet he toc of þe nes neauer sunne, ne i þin, as me leueð efter þe ilke tacunge, hwet se biuore were, clense mi sawle of fleschliche sunnen.   (22/26–23/7)

O Lady, St. Mary, because of the great joy that thou hadst within thee when Jesus, God, God's Son, after the angel's greeting, took flesh and blood in thee, and of thee, receive my greeting with the same Ave, *and make me account for every outward joy but little. But give me interior comfort, and let me have the joys of heaven through thy merits. And as surely as there was never any sin in that flesh that He took from thee nor in thine own, as we believe, after that taking flesh, whatever there may have been before, cleanse my soul of fleshly sins.*

The first prayer asks for purification, that the fleshly sins be cleansed away. The Joy relies on juxtaposition of opposites in a literary as well as functional sense to show the interaction of body and spirit, the phenomenon initiated by Christ's very act in the conception ('i þet ilke time þet iesu, godd, godes sune . . . nom flesch & blod in þe & of þe'). Reducing the opening clause to essential parts, we see that the author's phrases emphasize the polarities of outer and inner: *the great joy that thou hadst within thee . . . make me account every outward joy but little . . . give me interior comfort.*

To pare further, the 'interior comfort' emerges as the central condition of the Joy and the basis of an impressive analogy: 'for þe ilke muchele blisse þet tu hefdest inwið þe . . . froure me inwið.' This is more than a plea for spiritual peace; it encompasses (symbolically) the implanting of Christ, especially when read together with the next clause, 'froure me inwið & ernde me þeo of heouene,'[10] which asks Mary's intercession and implies that by emulating the Virgin—that is, the life of the model anchoress—it is possible to receive Christ. This idea is expanded into the motif of bird and nest in Chapter Three. The incidental reference in the Joy to the disputed doctrine of the Immaculate Conception seems a needless addition here unless—considering the author's fondness for analogy—it can be applied to his audience, the anchoress, to whom the cries of Augustine of a house in ruins, recited during the elevation of the Host, are still fresh: '*The house of my soul is too narrow for Thee to enter. Let it be enlarged by Thee. It is in ruins. Repair it. I confess and know that it contains what is offensive to Thine eyes, but who shall cleanse it? Or to whom but Thee shall I cry?*

THE SECOND JOY: NATIVITY *(theme, to heal)*

Leafdi seinte maria, for þe ilke muchele blisse þet tu hefdest þa þu sehe þe ilke blisfule bearn iboren of þi cleane bodi to moncunne heale, wið uten eauer euch bruche, wið ihal meiðhad & meidenes menske, heal me þet am þurh wil tobroken, as ich drede, hwet se beo of dede, & ȝef me in heouene seon þi blisfule leor & bihalde lanhure meidenes menske, ȝef ich nam wurðe forte beon iblisset in hare ferredden. (23/11–18)

O Lady, St. Mary, because of the great joy that thou hadst when thou sawest the blessed Child born of thy pure body for the salvation of mankind, without any breaking of virginity, in complete maidenhood and maiden honour, heal me that am broken, as I fear, in my will, however I stand in deed, and grant that I may see in heaven thy blessed face, and at least look upon the glory of those who are virgins, even if I am not worthy to be blessed in their company.

10. Nero reads 'ernde me þe blisse of heouene' (16/19). Salu translates 'the joys of heaven through thy merits,' p. 15.

Thematically, this second Joy is divided into the following rising rhythms:

(a) for þe ilke muchele blisse þet tu hefdest þa þu sehe þe ilke blisfule bearn iboren
(b) of þi cleane body to moncunne heale wið uten eauer euch bruche
    (b¹) wið ihal meiðhad & meidenes menske
(b) heal me þet am þurh wil tobroken, as ich dred, hwet se beo of dede
(a) ȝef me in heouene seon þi blisfule leor & bihalde
    (b²) lanhure meidenes menske

The conditions here come full circle from the Virgin's joy at the sight of the 'blisfule bearn' to that of the anchoress at Mary's 'blisfule leor.' The Nativity provides the occasion for the Joy, but the real issue is repair, restoration of a state of innocence (the 'house in ruins' to the 'clean vesicle') through Mary as *dei genetrix*. The appeal midpoint of 'heal me' releases, springlike, the upward thrust of emotion and throws a personal coloring over the concluding phrases. Adding to the effect is the sound value of 'heal me,' arrayed with the associations of 'moncunne heale' and 'ihal meiðhad & meidenes menske.'

THE THIRD JOY: RESURRECTION *(theme, to share)*

Leafdi seinte Marie, for þe ilke muchele blisse þet tu hefdest þa þu sehe þi deorewurðe sune, efter his derue deað, arisen to blisful lif, his bodi seueualt brihtre þen þe sunne, ȝef me deien wið him & arisen in him, worltliche deien, gasteliche libben, dealen in his pinen feolahliche in eorðe, forte beon i blisse his feolahe inheouene. For þe ilke muchele blisse þet tu hefdest, leafdi, of his blisful ariste efter þi muchele sorhe, efter mi sorhe þet ich am in her, lead me to þi blisse.   (23/20–28)

O Lady, St. Mary, because of the great joy that thou hadst when thou sawest thy dear and precious Son, after His grievous death, risen to joyful life, His Body sevenfold brighter than the sun, grant me to die with Him and to rise in Him, to die to the world and to live spiritually, to share His sufferings as a companion, on earth, that I may be His companion in happiness, in heaven. Because of the great joy that thou hadst, O lady, in His blessed resurrection, after thy great sorrow, lead me, after the sorrow in which I live here, to thy happiness.

To the themes of the first two Joys can be added that of the third, to share, or participate *imitatio dei* in the divine. Alliteration is strong; repetition of phrase and image creates a sense of increased urgency; verbal and rhetorical devices vitalize the language, as, for example:

> *derue deað . . . blisful lif*
> *deien wið him & arisen in him*
> *wortliche deien, gasteliche libben*
> *dealen in his pinen feolahliche in eorðe forte*
> *beon i blisse his feolahe inheouene*

This middle Joy is pivotal in the reconciliation of body and spirit. The tension of opposites begins to dissipate. Contradictions of maidenhood and marriage, light and darkness, death and life fade away.

THE FOURTH JOY: ASCENSION (*theme, to rise*)

Leafdi seinte Marie, for þe ilke muchele blisse þet tu hefdest þa þu sehe þi brihte blisful sune, þet te giws wenden forte aþrusmin i þruh, se wurðliche & se mihtiliche on hali þursdei stihe to his blisse in to his riche of heouene, ȝef me warpe wið him al þe worlt under fet, & stihen nu heorteliche, hwen ich deie gasteliche, o domesdei al licomliche to heouenliche blissen. (23/1–24/8)

O Lady, St. Mary, because of the great joy that thou hadst when thou sawest thy fair and blessed Son, whom the Jews had thought to shut away in the tomb, rising on Ascension Thursday, in such glory and power, to His happiness in His heavenly kingdom, grant that I may, with Him, cast all the world underfoot and rise now in heart, at my death in spirit and at the day of judgement all bodily, to the joys of heaven.

The fourth Joy repeats the pattern of the others by concluding with the hope for 'blisse,' just as they begin with the fact of Mary's 'blisse.'

The contrast of the two worlds is struck in the casting away of one kingdom for another, the leaping up from this world into the next. What remains adds force with its verbal plays: '3ef me warpe wið him al þet worlt under fet, & stihen nu heorteliche, hwen ich deie gasteliche, o domesdei al licomliche . . .'

The ascension is of the pure through the corrupt—the Son out of the tomb, the triumphant spirit out of the world, the heart out of the body. But the reconciliation of body and soul, which is to come on Judgment Day, presupposes a clean body, a reminder of the special role of physical realities in the divine plan.

THE FIFTH JOY: ASSUMPTION (*theme, to reign*)

Leafdi seinte Marie, for þe ilke muchele blisse þet fulde al þet eorðe þa he underueng þe in to unimete blisse, & wið his blisfule earmes sette þe i trone, & cwene crune of heaued brihtre þen þe sunne, heh heouenliche cwen, underueng þeos gretunges of me swa on eorðe þet ich mote blisfulliche grete þe in heouene. (24/9-14)

O Lady, St. Mary, because of the great joy that filled all the earth when He received thee into eternal happiness and with His blessed arms set thee in thy throne, and set a queen's crown on thy head brighter than the sun; O high, heavenly Queen, receive these greetings from me here on earth that I may greet thee in happiness in heaven.

In this fifth Joy—the purification is now complete—Christ and the soul are joined in the vibrant imagery of Mary's coronation in a heaven brighter than the sun. The assumption of the Virgin, the embrace by Christ and the enthronement complete the spiritual passage which took its humble beginnings 'efter þe engles gretunge.' Although her demesne is heavenly, the Virgin's role has become passive once again; she is received ('he underueng þe') into heaven, set in her throne ('sette þe i trone') by the Son who, in the first Joy, *took* flesh and blood in and of her.

The transformation described by the Five Joys of Mary can be sketched briefly as beginning with moral stain and possibility of renewal, and

ending with a positive resolution—a union of opposites. Christ and Mary
are joined in each Joy devotionally, in the last, physically: 'his blisfule
earmes' set her in her throne. The lesson of the devotion is the life and
afterlife of Mary. The petitions seek spiritual comfort from the Virgin
whom the anchoress has chosen to follow by withdrawing from the
world and studying the love of God. The hope is that just as Christ and
handmaiden have been reunited, so the anchoress will be received, since
ideally she is by definition and analogy *ancilla Dei*.

The inclusion of the Joys in Part One is appropriate and orthodox, but
beyond their merits as devotional matter, they present in miniature the
kind of spiritual advance, step by step, that characterizes all of the inner
Rule to come.

The Joys are followed by the *Gaude, dei genetrix*, the eleventh-century
antiphon;[11] and then comes the incantation of *aves*, beginning with an
intense and repetitive invocation to Mary, which, though ostensibly
instructional, reveals the author's very deep personal involvement in
prayer. We expect the devotion to end at 25/20 with the following
uninspired cadence:

> Þe ureisuns þet ich nabbe buten ane imearket beoð iwriten ouer
> al wið ute þe leaste. Leoteð writen on a scrowe hwet se ʒe ne
> kunnen.

> *With the exception of the last one, the prayers which I have only in-
> dicated are written in all the books. Whichever you do not know, have
> written on a scroll.*

But the prose springs off into a new meditation, the more striking for its
highly emotional, almost frenzied, chanting of praises. This is a rare
moment in the Rule, for the author is not given to lapses in restraint; but
midway in the progress of *aves*, he moves abruptly to Latin repetitions
of the English phrases, and then retards in a formula ending:

> Leafdi, swete leafdi, swetest alre leafdi, leafdi, leouest leafdi,
> lufsumest leafdi, O pulcherrima mulierum, leafdi seinte Marie,
> deorewurðe leafdi, leafdi, cwen of heouene, leafdi, cwen of are.
> Leafdi do me are. Leafdi, meiden, moder. Meiden, godes moder.

11. The *Gaude* is appended, pp. 231–232.

Iesu cristes moder. Meiden of milce. Moder of grace. O uirgo uirginum, Maria, mater gratie, mater misericordie, tu nos ab hoste protege & hora mortis suscipe, per tuum uirgo filium per patrem paraclitum, assis presens ad obitum nostrumque muni exitum. Gloria tibi, domine, qui natus es de uirgine, & cetera.   (25/22–26/5)

Thus, while the *O uirgo uirginum* carries the chant forward, it serves to brake the prose to coherent, orderly praise, that echoes the petition of the Joys.

From this point, devotions become increasingly physical in the motor sense, with growing attention to bending, kneeling, prostrating the body, etc. Without disturbing the emotional quality or continuity of forward movement, the Rule turns slowly outward from the meditation on the Virgin to the Trinity, psalms, prayers, and vernacular texts. Instructions on religious and household duties follow—external matters remote in kind and degree from the supremely spiritual meditation that had been the center of the chapter, but just such routine observances as fill out the anchoress' day and the first 'distinction.' Part One ends as it began, with remembrance of the Trinity and the Holy Cross.

Keeping in mind the special standing of the Joys as the central and most intense meditation, we will look at the other devotions in this chapter which throw light on the author's intentions.

'Devotions' open with morning duties and Our Lady's Matins, vocal prayers and postures, and instructions on when and how they are to be recited.[12] Except for the early antiphons on the Cross, beginning *Ave, principium nostre creationis* (13/4 ff.), which are lengthy, prayers and gestures are quickly described. There is an interesting expansion of prayers to the Trinity beginning with *Paternosters*, which the sisters are urged to repeat often during the day, though the author suggests an alternate of the traditional version: 'O þis wise ȝe mahen, ȝef ȝe wulleð, seggen ower pater nostres' (17/26). *Paternosters* include commendation of the Trinity, reinforced by the repetition of triplets:[13]

12. Dom Gerard Sitwell's summary of semiliturgical and private prayers as they occur in the Rule are included in the Salu translation, pp. xxi–xxii.

13. Stephen of Sawley's plan in the tripartite 'Triple Exercise' is to reproduce the Trinity humerically.

Almihti godd, feader, sune, hali geast, as ȝe beoð þreo an godd,
alswa ȝe beoð an mihte, an wisdom, & an luue; & þah is mihte
iturnd to þe in hali writ nomelich, þu deorewurðe feader, to þe
wisdom, seli sune, to þe luue, hali gast. Ȝef me, an almihti godd,
þrile i þreo hades, þes ilke þreo þinges, mihte forte serui þe,
wisdom forte cweme þe, luue & wil to don hit, mihte þet ich mahe
don, wisdom þet ich cunne don, luue þet ich wulle don aa þet te
is leouest. (17/28–8)

*Almighty God, Father, Son, and Holy Ghost, even as You Three
are one God, even as You are one Power, one Wisdom, and one Love,
and yet in Holy Scripture power is especially attributed to Thee,
Beloved Father, wisdom to Thee, Blessed Son, love to Thee, O Holy
Spirit; give me, O one Almighty God, threefold in three Persons, these
same three things, power to serve Thee, wisdom to please Thee, love
and will to bring these into action, strength that I may act, wisdom that
I may know how to act, love that I may desire to perform always what
is most pleasing to Thee.*

After the prayers to the Father there follow prayers to the Son and commemoration of the five wounds; and then, completing the Trinity,
prayers on the seven gifts of the Holy Ghost. In their fullness and duration, these prayers depart from the more incidentally presented devotions of the opening, for as Part One moves 'inward,' prayers grow more
elaborate, more emotional, and more excited.

When the author has dealt with the Trinity (and the symbolic numbers
of the three Persons), he continues with prayers in praise of the ten
commandments, twelve apostles, six works of mercy, four gospels, and
nine orders of angels; but the order of presentation of numbers has no
apparent significance beyond the author's wish to include whatever
numbers he can in this limited format. Special prayers for the sick, the
imprisoned, and the sorely tempted Christian close this segment and
bring Part One to the first highly impassioned address to the Godhead—
rapid Latin phrases combined with the tormented utterances of St.
Augustine from *Confessions*. At moments of intense concentration—
during the elevation of the Host ('hwen þe preost heueð up godes
licome'), the meditations on the Cross, or devotions on the Five Joys of

Mary—there is active movement toward spiritual enlightenment; a
striving upward toward union, peace; an ascent that begins in struggle
and ends in triumph as the Virgin (in whose devotion all these forces
converge) is assumed into heaven and crowned. In a small but essential
way, the progress corresponds to the allegorical history of the anchoress
as it is charted in the inner Rule.

The first marked indication that the author has imposed a design upon
the material occurs at the elevation of the Host (20/19). The entire passage
is rather long, for it starts with the 'raising up of God's body,' continues
with a series of prayers in Latin (*orationes ad elevationem*), and the excerpts
from the *Confessions*, and ends with the aftermath of the Mass-kiss,
which returns the prose to Middle English. The text in modern English
is given here:

> At Mass, when the priest elevates the Body of God, stand and say
> this verse: Behold the salvation of the world, the Word of the
> Father, a true sacrifice, living flesh, the whole Godhead, true Man,
> and then fall to your knees with these greetings: Hail, cause of our
> creation! Hail, price of our redemption! Hail, consolation of our
> time of waiting! Be Thou our joy who art to be our reward; let
> our glory be in Thee throughout all ages for ever, Amen. *O Lord,*
> *be always with us. Glory be to Thee, O Lord. But what place is there*
> *in me into which my God may come, and remain in me, God, who made*
> *heaven and earth? Is there, O Lord my God, that in me which may*
> *receive Thee? Wilt Thou come into my heart and inebriate it, and shall*
> *I embrace Thee, my only good? What art Thou to me? Pity me, that I*
> *may speak. The house of my soul is too narrow for Thee to enter. Let it*
> *be enlarged by Thee. It is in ruins. Repair it. I confess and know that it*
> *contains what is offensive to Thine eyes, but who shall cleanse it? Or to*
> *whom but Thee shall I cry? Cleanse me, O Lord, from my secret faults,*
> *and from other sins spare Thy servant. Have mercy, have mercy,* and so
> on to the end of the psalm, with the *Gloria Patri, Christ hear us,*
> twice, *Lord have mercy on us, Christ have mercy on us, Lord have mercy*
> *on us. Paternoster* and *Credo . . . the resurrection of the body and life*
> *everlasting. Amen. Oh my God, save Thy servant, who trusts in thee.*
> *Teach me to do Thy will because Thou art my God. Lord, hear my prayer*

and let my cry come unto Thee. Let us pray. Grant, we beseech Thee,
Almighty God, that Him whom we see darkly and under a different
form, on whom we feed sacramentally on earth, we may see face to face as
He is, and that we may be worthy to enjoy Him truly and really in heaven
through the same Jesus Christ Our Lord. Amen.

After the kiss of peace in the Mass, when the priest communicates,
forget the world, be completely out of the body, and with burning
love, embrace your Beloved who has come down from heaven
to your heart's bower, and hold Him fast until He has granted
you all that you ask.

(Salu, pp. 13–14; *AW* 20/19–21/23)

There is subtle progression here from ordinary instruction to high
emotional tension, ending in satisfaction that exceeds physical participation in communion. The section is a contained unit alternating physical
(outer) and spiritual (inner) levels of devotion; and the intoning of
prayers and formulae, the chanting repetition of holy names, open the
way to the materialization of Christ.

The gradual movement toward union with Christ can be traced with
the help of a few key lines:

A   I þe measse hwen þe preost heueð up godes licome . . .
    (At Mass, when the priest elevates the Body of God . . .)

[Bridge: Salutations] Ecce salus mundi, uerbum patris, hostia uera
    (Behold the salvation of the world, the Word of the Father, a
    true sacrifice)

B   Quis est locus in me quo ueniat in me deus . . .
    (But what place is there in me into which my God may come . . .)

A   Concede, quesumus, omnipotens deus, ut quem enigmatice & sub
    aliena spetie cernimus . . .
    (Grant, we beseech Thee, Almight God, that Him whom we see
    darkly and under a different form . . .)

B[1] Efter þe measse cos hwen þe preost sacreð, þer er forȝeoteð al
    þe world . . .
    (After the kiss of peace in the Mass, when the priest communicates,
    forget the world . . .)

The inductive outer (formula) sections (*A*) prepare for the spiritual purging (*B*) and ultimately the dissolving of all physical things as Christ enters the bower (*B¹*). The assimilation of the Augustine passage into the prayers serves contextually to expose a soul unworthy of the gifts about to be bestowed and is in a strictly confessional sense a plea for forgiveness and future grace:

> But what place is there in me into which my God may come,
> and remain in me, God, who made heaven and earth? Is there,
> O Lord my God, that in me which may receive Thee? Wilt Thou
> come into my heart and inebriate it, and shall I embrace Thee,
> my only good? What art Thou to me? Pity me, that I may speak.
> The house of my soul is too narrow for Thee to enter. Let it be
> enlarged by Thee. It is in ruins. Repair it . . .

In the Rule the images reenact the religious mystery even to the point of the embrace of the *leofmon*.

The return to the Mass—'After the kiss of peace in the Mass, when the priest communicates'—involves the ritual act that initiates the high point of the ceremony and brings to an abrupt end the incantation of Latin prayers by a sudden shift to English. Cleansed and receptive, the communicant responds when the sacramental eating of the Body infuses the soul with spirit and sensual fervor, interpreted here in the literal sense as a physical lover entering the bower of the beloved. The objective correlative of the mystic's experience—intermingled divine light and human transcendence—conforms to the Rule's consistent reliance on concrete example and physical detail rather than abstraction:

> Efter þe measse cos hwen þe preost sacreð, þer forȝeoteð al þe
> world, þer beoð al ut of bodi, þer i sperclinde luue biclupped ower
> leofmon þe in to ower breostes bur is iliht of heouene, & halded
> him heteueste aþet he habbe iȝettet ow al þet ȝe eauer easkið.
>
> (21/18–23)

The brief but telling description of 'religious intimacies' *i sperclinde luue* concludes this segment of Part One. The segment has followed an orderly, intelligible course from beginning to end. The effect of the Mass passage relies heavily on a succession of images sensuous and sensual: the house of the soul, the house in ruins, sacramental feeding on the Body, the Mass kiss, the lover come into the breast's bower, the special favors asked of Him, and the like. The dominant object or vehicle is the *body* (with its analogical properties); but always the presence of light, actual or impending, promises to bring Grace. The phases of change in the penitent's condition (his worthiness to receive God) are delicately joined to the steps of the communion and to the advent of light. The lament of Augustine ('Set quis est locus in me . . . ') gives way to prayers and versicles intoned in heavy Latin accents in which the pleas are continued and ended finally by the appeal to Him 'whom we see darkly and under a different form,' that 'we may see Him face to face as He is.'

The response comes immediately upon the Mass-kiss when the Lover enters the bower 'i sperclinde luue,' a mystical union of the soul 'al ut of bodi' and Christ, the 'leofmon.' The movement inward is experienced mystically with the extraordinary entry of the Beloved into the bower, a symbolic place analogous with the *house* of the *Confessions*.

Thus far two movements have been at play, the first inward through external images (the Mass); the other outward in gestures, postures in adoration of the Cross. In the next segment, devotions to the Virgin, which has already been discussed, matter is finally spiritualized, on earth by sanctification, in heaven through beatitude. Flux, the interaction of matter and spirit, becomes apparent as the author carries Mary up from his cautious utterance of her immaculate nature to her coronation in heaven. The doubts and pleas of earlier segments are quieted and resolved by the Five Joys, even as the cumulating imagery within the Joys create a new ascending spiral in this most concentrated and detailed devotion.

In summary, Parts One and Eight of the Rule are said to deal with outer things, with externals, with regulations helpful in the ordering of the inner life. Yet no narrow limitations on themes and development can express fairly the dimensions of the author's skill or religious fervor, particularly in Part One, which begins and ends with devotions to the Trinity yet has as its core a meditation on Mary. She, the handmaiden of the Lord, is central in the mystery, and within the structural design of Part One she occupies the central place. Moreover, there is hardly a devotion in which Mary is not remembered, even if only in an incidental way (as in the prayers to the Cross where 'Devotions' begins). The space and time set aside to honor her far exceed whatever is given to the Trinity; her presence hovers over the offices and the Hours, but so delicately that the casual reader overlooks her.

The many minor items of 'Devotions' sometimes threaten to overwhelm the reader with their detail. Insofar as the chapter is packed with duties, prayers for numerous intentions, private devotions, hymns, collects, etc., all conforming to the daily observance expected of the anchoress whether an inner Rule is to follow or not, Part One *is* external—that is, largely instructional. Yet even within the mass of formulae, a substantial fluidity is achieved. Early in Part One the author takes up the Hours, returns to them at the end, and refers to them briefly in the intervals between concentrated prayer. He does the same with seasons (in summer, matins at dawn; in winter, at night), with holy days, divisions of the day, with duties to be performed in good health and in sickness. Symbolic numbers do not pass in orderly succession but mix freely from beginning to end, generating the many vocal repetitions which, though unremarkable in themselves, can lead the anchoress to the 'interior comfort' in which contemplation becomes possible. The importance of physical detail in minor matters and the ordinary bodily activity of the day is respected, though subordinated to service to the soul. And though the final passages are unabashedly instructional, the presence of physical realities keeps alive and moving the outer-inner structure.

In the accompanying diagram I have tried to suggest by means of concentric circles the arrangement of devotion *around the central Joys*. The offices and prayers at the left of the median line are indicated in the order of their occurrence up to the Joys; there is a steady movement away from physical matters as the Rule turns inward to the meditation on the Virgin. From that point prayers and duties convey us slowly outward and away from the spiritual core. The subjects to the right of the line show the Rule's progress away from the Joys toward greater activity until duties on retiring. The patterns of devotions on either side of the Joys are sufficiently alike to permit their being enclosed within corresponding segments of the circles.

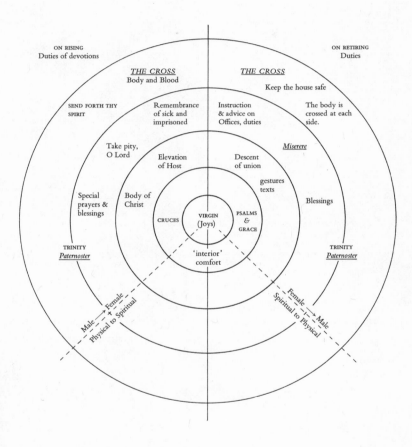

The second part of the Rule is concerned with the discipline of the senses, the regulation of the body and the outer life. In this section the author introduces the beginning of systematized analogy, exploiting from the first the possibilities of subtle relationships within the anchorhold as they involve the sins of the eye, the mouth, and the hand.

The five senses, irresponsible and desultory, guard the restless heart wherein lies the health of the soul. But conversely, they are avenues by which temptations may enter to corrupt the heart. Like a beast that leaps from its sanctuary toward a powerful but irresistible enemy, the heart rushes out of the reckless body through the window of the eye. 'Therefore,' warns the author, striking an analogy in his first appeal to the sisters, 'be as little fond of your windows as possible.'

The interaction and interdependence of inner and outer is established here by the relationship of *Anchoress: Anchorhold:: Eye: Window:: Heart: Body*—one physical reality enclosing another and, ultimately, a physical presence protecting a spiritual core. Here, perhaps more easily than elsewhere in the Rule, we can see evolving a technique of expanding images from a purely visual perception (a watchman, window, curtain, etc.) to a symbolic one where spiritual truth is discovered naturally. Thus it may be useful and morally productive to compare the anchorhold to a castle (as the author soon will do), but the anchorhold is not a castle except fancifully, and no spears and swords assail the walls. However, by the time the author gets to the development of this motif, the connotations that have accrued to the metaphor are so numerous and so familiar in terms of everyday experience that the allegory is convincing.

The author begins with a citation from Proverbs 4:23, *Omni custodia serva cor tuum quia ex ipso vita procedit*, and builds on this base his treatment of the five senses that have custody over the heart. The first segment expands the opening Latin line and introduces the motif of the *leap* in the example of David, one whose heart had fled against his will:

Ant hwer edbrec ha ut from dauið, þe hali king, godes prophete?
Hwer? Godd wat, ed his ehþurl; þurh a sihðe þet he seh, þurh a
bihaldunge, as ʒe schulen efter iheren.   (30/18–21)

*And where did it break away from the holy king David, God's
prophet? Where? God knows, at the window of his eye; through a
sight that he saw, through something at which he looked, as you shall
later hear.*

Sight, then is the first of the senses to be taken up. The imaginative transition from the window of the eye of David to the window of the
anchorhold seems abrupt at this point, for we have not as yet become
used to the author's habit of bridging experience as if all of life were
refractions of a central design. The accessibility of the eye as a passage
for the entry of sin (and the reciprocal leap of the heart out of the body)
finds a reasonable corollary in the window curtain of the anchorhold,
which shuts out the source of temptation and protects the chastity of the
anchoress within. The curtain, with its white cross on a black field pro-
claiming humility and chastity, divides the anchoress' world from the
world of the living; for the fact of enclosure signifies that these women
are dead to the world, and for the dead to dote on the living is unnatural
—a point hardly worth disputing.

The black cloth of the curtain has practical value, but even the commonplace of color and texture submit to the growth of symbolism:

Þe blake cla ð alswa teke þe bitacnunge, de ð leasse eil to þe ehnen
& is þiccre aʒein þe wind & wurse to seon þurh, ant halt his heow
betere for wind & for oðerhwet.   (30/9–12)

*The black cloth is not only symbolic, but also less harmful to the eyes
than other colours, and it is stouter against the wind and more difficult
to see through, and it keeps its colour better, against the wind and
other things.*

The black cloth preserves the health of the sight—shrouds the window;
thus neither can the soul issue from the dwelling (or body), nor can the
devil enter in from the outside. The danger, though it seems twofold as

presented (the anchoress struggling against the tendency of her heart—
what more than normal curiosity!—and the mischief outside waiting
for the chance to breach her defenses), is really an expansion of the
notion of the leap of the heart as a wild animal, the leap which
culminates in the series of three leaps, and the leap which will bring the
animal to the bottom of the pit where he rots.

The author's advice to 'see that the parlor window is fastened and well
locked on all sides' may allude to a popular sermon figure of the winds as
buffets of sin, kindling the hearts of men; he has already described the
black cloth a 'þiccre aʒein þe wind.' This fastening of windows antici-
pates an assault played out in Part Two against the romantic landscape of
castle siege when the lady's life will depend on how well protected she is,
how carefully she has arranged her defense against the enemy.

Armed with the intention to keep her eyes inside, the anchoress is
given further proofs of the dangers of peeping out; and it is in these
proofs borrowed from Scripture, and with images of pasture and fortress
that the full threat to her holy life is explored.

What begins as an innocent diversion (a harmless look out of the window) ends in nothing less than the Fall of Man. Similarly, the author's
approach to the matter begins with simple precepts and enlarges to
include extravagant (but contextually convincing) metaphors. Whatever
misery was, is now, and ever shall be—all comes from looking. Biblical
evidence begins with Lucifer's leap into pride and continues into the
three leaps of Eve from eye to apple, from the apple in Paradise down to
the earth, and from earth to hell 'þer ha lei i prisun fowr þusent ʒer &
mare.'[1] The leaps are related to the animal imagery of the opening segment, where the heart is described as an animal that lightly leaps out:

Þe heorte is a ful wilde beast & makeð moni liht lupe . . . Na þing
ne etflid mon sonre þen his ahne heorte.   (29/9–11)

The signification of the leaps of the heart out of the body and the body
into hell is ingeniously construed to prove that it was a peeping out—a

1. For a discussion of the three leaps of Eve as they relate to Christ's leaps over the
hills and mountains of Part Seven, see R. E. Kaske, 'The Three Leaps of Eve,' *Medium
Aevum*, 29 (1960), 22–24.

little light glance—that started it all: 'Biginnunge & rote of al þis ilke reoðe was aliht sihðe.' The sudden return in this line to the instructional tone of the initial warnings serves to reestablish the didactic purpose of the segment and provides a caveat that could be tacked on to any one of the examples.

The leaps of Eve belong to the series begun historically in Lucifer's leap into pride, continued in Eve's, and, unhappily, in the leaps of the daughters of Eve (here, the anchoress) who protest with predictable over-confidence that they are unassailable:

Me wenest tu, seið sum, þet ich wulle leapen on him þah ich loki on him? Godd wat, leoue suster, mare wunder ilomp.   (32/3–5)

'But do you think,' someone will say, 'that I shall leap upon him because I look at him?' God knows, my dear sister, more surprising things have happened.

The leaps of Eve which concern the author at this point are actual con-sequences of 'harmless' peeping—but enlarged so mightily beyond the narrow confines of the anchorhold that a new dimension, more grave and far-reaching, is created, one that is not lost upon these 'daughters of Eve.' In this way Eve's leaps complete a spiral of gradually cumulating images that began with the image of heart as animal: 'Þe heorte is a ful wilde beast & makeð moni liht lupe.'

Just as parts of the Rule are linked together structurally, so too are the sins. The evil that comes of looking out engenders lust, as the biblical examples bear out in the case first of the wanton eye of Eve; then by the curiosity of Dinah, who allowed herself to be looked upon (reciproca-tion) and was led into harlotry (here we have backward-forward move-ment of eye and heart); finally, the shamelessness of Bathsheba, who bathed naked before the eyes of David.[2] The disrobing of Bathsheba and the figurative disrobing of the anchoress when she allows herself to be

---

2. David here is more sinned against than sinning, though the reader is tempted to ask where his eyes were. Presumably, they were not offended by the body they looked upon. That, of course, is the author's point—temptation is the first assault of sin. Owst in *Literature and Pulpit* (New York, 1966) gives examples of typical attitudes toward women in sermon literature (pp. 118–120).

seen by a male visitor are connected by the word 'fall' to the biblical
law of restitution in the example of the open pit of Exodus 21:33, 34:

> ... vor alle þeo þroe sunnen þet ich spec of last ... ne com nout
> for þui þet te wummen lokede cangliche o weopmen, auh dude
> þuruh þet heo unwrien ham ine monne eih sihðe, & duden hwar
> þuruh heo muhten uallen into sunnen .... Uor þi was i hoten a
> godes half iþen olde lawe þet put were euer iwrien, & ȝif eni unwrie
> put were & best feolle þer inne, he hit schulde ȝelden þet þene
> put un-wreih.   (Nero 25/2–10)

> *... for all those three sins which I have just spoken of ... all happened,*
> *not because the women looked lustfully upon the men, but because they*
> *unclothed themselves before the eyes of men, thus being the occasion of*
> *sin in them. ... For this reason it was commanded in God's name in the*
> *Old Law that a pit should always be covered; and if an animal fell*
> *into an uncovered pit, the man who had uncovered the pit had to pay*
> *the penalty.*

Logically, if not apparently, the figure of the pit is the point of convergence of the imagery of heart as animal which lightly leaps out and of
the leaps of Lucifer into pride (the pit of hell) and Eve into death (the
grave). So the leaps end in physical and spiritual death. The animal falls
and dies, and the heart—the wild animal that often leaps lightly out—
lands in the pit and perishes.

Implicit in the author's development of the theme, and common to all
the examples, is the guilt of the female in exposing herself and others to
temptation by looking out, in bringing down entire kingdoms, as Eve
had brought all mankind to ruin. What begins lightly may well end in
disaster. Forewarned, the wise anchoress will not peep out!

A few comments on the interpretation of the pit by the author are
appropriate, since he is explicit in defining the pit as a woman's fair face,
neck, etc.; and, quoting the law, insists that the pit be covered (as the
black cloth would shut out the world at the window):

> Þe put is hire veire neb & hire hwite sweore & hire liht eie ...
> Þes put he hat þet beo euer i lided & i wrien leste eni best ualle
> þerinne & druncnie ine sunne. Best is þe bestliche mon.
>   (Nero 25/13–20)

*The pit is her fair face, and her white neck, and her light eye ... He
commands that this pit should always be covered with a lid, lest any
animal should fall into it and perish in sin. 'Animal' here means the
animal man.*

We can understand how the outsider, in this context tempted by the
anchoress, might fall, but the analogy seems unworkable when it reverts
to the anchoress. This difficulty is settled by the line 'animal here means
the animal man.' But the machinery of his creative mind has been antici-
pating the paradoxical function of the pit, which, if it is also seen to be
beauty and vanity (or pride) arising from physical beauty and over-
confidence, becomes as much a fatal trap for the anchoress as for a man.
Eve, we recall, was foolishly deceived by what she saw; Lucifer saw his
own beauty and leaped into pride; and the author, speaking for the
anchoress, by his very insistence on the mischief of the eye, seems to have
some reason to doubt her strength—at least at this early stage of the Rule.

Thus far the dangers to the anchoress and the health of the soul have
been examined through the figure of the leaping animal (man or beast),
beginning with the leap of the heart and ending with the fall into the
pit. The proofs are plentiful, and the author need go no further than
scriptural history to verify the threat to the heart when the watchman,
sight, relaxes his vigil. But he is not satisfied with biblical witness alone
and continues his development of the eye-heart motif against the allegorical backdrop of siege warfare. The senses as watchmen ('wardeins')
of the heart are now applied to the epic landscape of castle under assault,
where they do indeed guard the lady's castle against the devil's attacks
with arrows, spears, and swords.

The castle here is only indirectly a metaphor of the anchorhold that
guards the anchoress. In the present context the castle is the senses that
guard the heart against the vanguard of the devil's assault, lust.[3] The

3. Probably the least applicable is the metaphor that comes first to the reader's mind,
that of body and soul. The figure comprehends the soul, but the author defers an
elaborate allegorical treatment to Part Seven. The lady must pass through the stages of
purification and growth implicit in the graduated progress of the Rule before the
allegory takes on the mystical dimension in which the Christ-knight comes to release
the lady, the soul, from bondage. The homiletic origins of the castle allegory are discussed by Owst in *Literature and Pulpit*, pp. 77–85. There is no predictable handling of

implements, 'scute, spere, sweord,' are eminently suited to the sin as they are to the actual battle,[4] since the devil's offensive is initiated partly by the lady's own recklessness in exposing herself at the window:

Þe kerneaus of þe castle beoð hire huses þurles. Ne aboutie heo nout vt et ham leste heo þes deofles quarreaus habbe amid-den þen eien er heo leste wene.   (Nero 26/36–27/3)

The battlements of the castle are the windows of her house. Let her not lean out from them lest the devil's bolts strike her between the eyes when she least expects it.

The 'devil's bolts' penetrate her defenses, striking her between the eyes (a variation of the 'eyes of the heart'); the heart is blinded by the arrows of the eye—the first weapon in lust's attack being sight, peeping out:

Ablinde þe heorte, heo is ed ouercumen & i brouht sone mid sunne to grunde.   (Nero 27/5–6)

Blind the heart, and it is easily overcome, and soon brought low with sin.

Thus sin is reciprocal in a very real sense in this colorful passage, and the darts of wanton looks strike the heart itself. It were best the anchoress keep her eyes at home!

Speech as a guardian of the heart is the second sense to be considered, for it belongs properly to the mouth and to the ear. The author has prepared in advance for this subject by comparing speech to a pit into which man, like the animal of the Old Law, can fall: '& al ȝet beoð hire word put buten heo beon þe bet biset' (Nero 25/15). So, we again have the familiar figure of the pit as deep sin and hell pain. The pit as metaphor of the mouth is visually acceptable; of a woman's face grotesque but imaginatively adaptable to the moral argument under way. The pit (of death) is the upshot of Eve's vain defense of her innocence when she is

---

such figures in the Rule, as the author alters his sense to conform to his needs at the moment and the spiritual progress of the anchoress. The author's source here may be the Lambeth Homilies, in which the Castle of Mansoul is defended by the five senses against the devil's attacks. The influence of 'Mansoul' has been discussed by Hope Emily Allen in 'On the Author of the *AR*,' *PMLA*, 44 (1929), 679–680.

4. The sexual suggestions are repeated in Part Seven. There, the impalement and erotic symbols of fire and heat are transformed into spiritual *affectus*.

reproved for looking on the apple:

Hwerof chalengest to me? Þe eappel þet ich loki on is forbode me
to eotene & nawt to bihalden. Þus walde eue inohreaðe habben
iondsweret. . . . As eue haueð monie dehtren þe folhið hare moder
þe ondswerieð o þisse wise.   (32/27–3)

*'Of what are you accusing me? I am forbidden to eat the apple at
which I am looking; I am not forbidden to look at it.' Thus Eve would
have answered readily enough . . . and she has many daughters, who
following their mother, answer in the same way.*

We have not wandered far from Paradise after all, for Eve looked upon
the apple and fell; but first she gave away her secrets through babbling
in conversation with the serpent, so that when he learned her weakness,
he knew how to destroy her. In this way, sins of speech lead to sins of
sight:

Eue heold i parais long tale wið þe neddre, talde him al þe lesceun
þet godd hefde ired hire & Adam of þe eappel, & swa þe feond
þurh hire word understod ananriht hire wacnesse, & ifond wei
toward hire of hire forlorenesse.   (35/9–13)

*In Paradise Eve talked a great deal to the serpent and told him all that
God had taught her and Adam about the apple, and so the devil soon
learned her weakness through her own words, and found out how to
destroy her.*

The reappearance of Eve as an example of the frightful results of
reckless speech carries into this section the earlier warnings against peeping out as expressed by Eve's leaps and the assaults on the castle. Counsels
against foolish speech are supported by the Scripture, particularly the
proverbs of Solomon that initiate a series of important images, beginning
with that of an unwalled city exposed to the darts of the enemy:

Hwa se ne wiðhalt his wordes, seið Salomon þe wise, he is as þe
burh wið ute wal þet ferde mei in ouer al. Þe feond of helle mid
his ferd wend þurh ut te tutel þe is eauer open in to þe heorte.
                                                              (40/10–14)

*'Whosoever does not control his speech,' says the wise Solomon, 'is like
a city without a wall into which an army can enter from all sides.' The
devil enters with his army by the chattering mouth which is always
open, into the heart.*

The lady exposes her vulnerable position and is brought low; her castle
is taken and her people slain. The connection of the passage with the
besieged castle and the penetration of lust through the arrows of the eye
is clear. The devil enters the heart through the eyes, but also 'þurh ut te
tutel þe is eauer open.' This is typical of the author's habit of developing
a theme, putting it aside temporarily, then reviving it in a slightly
different context. The effect of this technique is a sense of movement and
continuity, in which themes and motifs remain individualized even
while they accrete to new arguments.

The section on speech takes the same curious turns as did its predecessor, sight—beginning with the innocuous and customary regulations on
restraint at the parlor window and winding inward from the anchorhold
to the heart until the careless diversions of conversation are revealed to
be the most dangerous weapon in the devil's arsenal: 'Ma sleað word þen
sweord.'

There is, moreover, a reciprocal loss to the soul when the mouth is
open. The image of the escaping heart (the animal that lightly leaps out),
released through the enfeebling of the senses, is conveyed as the flight of
hope from the heart in the loss of sweetly spiced breath. When the mouth
is closed, hope and sweetness strengthen the soul; but the chattering
mouth scatters the good breath and hope is carried off.

All in all, the author's emphasis thus far has been the expansion of the
first line, 'Wið alles cunnes warde, dohter, seið Salomon, wite wel þin
heorte, for sawle lif is in hire ȝef ha is wel iloket.' But there are dangers
also from outside pollutants, particularly the evil speech of others.
Venomous, idle slander makes vicious assaults on the ears of the good
anchoress, nourishing the devil and encouraging corruption. Among
the most damaging assailants is the backbiter, for he spews forth venom
like the adder and tears apart frail flesh like a bird of hell. An earlier reference to birds as 'cackling hens' had drawn an unflattering sketch of
the chattering mother hen who loses her eggs (good works) to the clever
chough:

Kimeð þe kaue ananriht & reaueð hire hire eairen & fret of þet
schulde forð bringe cwike briddes. Al riht alswa þe caue deouel
bereð awei from cakelinde ancres & forswolheð al þe god þet ha
istreonet habbeð þet schulde as briddes beoren ham up towart
heouene, ȝef hit nere icakelet.   (36/20–25)

*The chough comes at once, and takes her eggs away from her, and eats
the eggs which should have brought forth living birds. In just the same
way the chough, that is the devil, steals from cackling anchoresses, and
devours all the good which they have brought forth, and which should,
like birds, have carried them up to heaven if it had not been cackled away.*

The backbiter, who 'cheoweð ofte monnes flesch i fridei,' is presented in
more violent and vigorous imagery;[5] and the figure of the torn flesh
serves as a reminder of the pit into which the 'animal' had fallen and the
responsibility in opening that pit, for which loss the anchoress must pay
out of her own purse at the Last Judgment. Similarly, the devil's bird is
related to the snares with which the devil captures the heart of the unwary
anchoress. The snare is laid where it is least expected.

Backbiter and flatterer converge at the pit, the privy-hole, where they
alternately open and close the cover of the world's filth (the mouth
again). The powerful, repugnant stench they release at the hole and in the
'breað of hare stinkinde þrote' evokes by contrast the sweet smell of
spice in the mouth of the good anchoress, which feeds the heart and
nurtures the soul. Such vicious speech, moreover, is not even human, not
the speech of men, but the blasts of the devil's own voice—and here we
should recall the window curtain of the anchorhold, which is 'stouter
against the wind.'

Within the last segments on sins of the mouth and ear the Rule has
enumerated the tactics of backbiters and flatterers and, to prove its case,
invoked the authority of the Bible, the Church fathers, and the knowledge that comes of experience. Generally, such is the formal arrangement
of argument in the work.

The author's handling of imagery here has taken several discernible
directions. The major pattern rises from the initial warnings to the

5. The sources of the backbiter passage is St. Bernard's *Sermons on the Canticles*, *PL*
183, col. 896.

anchoress that the heart is easily betrayed by its own wilfullness. The senses, sight and speech, must keep relentless vigil over their charge and must themselves be severely disciplined. The animal within leaps out of its refuge and, drawn toward a temptation that has passed through lax defenses, meets its death in the pit. The death of the animal is analogous to the death of hope in the heart; the idea is expanded on minor levels by the imagery of the mother hen who loses her eggs to the chough and the chattering woman who grinds chaff in the clappers of her mouth and loses the wheat. The pit tended by venomous tongues of flatterers and backbiters is a corollary of the open pit into which the unsuspecting animal falls.

An offshoot of the major symbolism is the motif of the leaps of Satan and especially of Eve, who pulled mankind to death with her fall, not only because she was curious—'looked out'—but because she exposed her weaknesses through unguarded speech. Satan's pit is hell; that of Eve and her descendants is death, the pit of the grave. Pulling these various threads together is the assurance that the woman (a daughter of Eve), like the man who in Scripture opened the pit, must make restitution for the slain animal—the other sinner, yes, but most significantly, her own soul, the heart 'that lightly leaps out.' *Mea culpa!* the anchoress must cry at the settling of accounts

But what of remedies, rewards, what of the hope the anchoress has been admonished to keep locked in her heart like sweet breath behind a closed mouth? At this midpoint of Chapter Two, while *AW* is still immersed in an extensive lesson on disciplining the senses, a remarkable shift of theme is under way. As the author returns to a collective discussion of the senses as custodians of the heart, integrating motifs he has developed to this point, he begins to redefine the nature of these watchmen. No longer are they watchmen who are themselves vulnerable, but guardians who are so scrupulously attentive that they become identified with the attributes of the Bridegroom, jealously attendant on the spouse in the rich Bernardine sense:

Ich am, he seið bi him seolf, þe geluse godd. . . . Wite þe nu ful wel. His eare is eauer toward te & he hereð al. His ehe aa behalt te, ȝef þu makest ei semblant, eani luue lates toward unþeawes.

(48/6–13)

*I am a jealous God, He says of Himself. . . . Now understand this well:
His ear is always inclined towards you and He hears everything; if you
make any show of love towards what is not virtuous, His eye always
sees you.*

The senses now serve Him, and the outer-inner movement of the
heart shifts from the physical reality of anchoress and the world outside
(soul and sense) to move inward to the delicate relation of God and the
soul: 'Bihald inward þer ich am, & ne sech þu me nawt wið ute þin
heorte'—she must look inward if she would find Him, and not seek
Him outside her own heart. He is reflected in the mirror of her face, not
in the face turned to the window. The senses with which she must
perceive and enjoy Him must remain inward, turned toward her own
heart where He is engraved and from which He is reflected in her
eye:

Eauer se recluse toteð mare utward, se ha haueð leasse leome of ure
lauerd inward.   (49/1–3)

*The more a recluse looks outward the less inward light will she have
from Our Lord.*

Inner sight is gained at the expense of the outer: 'For þi, mine leoue
sustren, beoð wið ute blinde' (49/11–12). The rewards of this blindness
are twofold: to 'seon & cnawen [godd]' (49/14) and to 'seon alle þe
deofles wiheles (49/15–16).

The devil's presence and his continuing threat remind her of the risks
of letting the eyes stray out. The Rule has referred to a blinding before, in
the castle allegory where the battlements are the lady's windows:

Holde hire eien inne, vor beo heo erest ablend, heo is eð fallen.
Ablinde þe heorte, heo is eð ouercumen & i brouht sone mid
sunne to grunde.   (Nero 27/3–6)

*Let her keep her eyes at home, for, once blinded, she is easily overthrown.
Blind the heart, and it is easily overcome, and soon brought low with sin.*

The opposite of the blinding of the heart is the delectation that will come when, with eyes turned inward, the anchoress will see reflected in the mirror of her heart the joys of heaven. *All* the senses will then be gratified, for the wedding gifts in the spiritual nuptials that are being prepared now in this earthly anchorhold will be swiftness and bright sight:

Swiftnes aʒeines þet ha beoð na swa bipinnet; leome of briht sihðe aʒeines þet ha her þeostrið nu ham seoluen, ne nulleð nowðer iseo mon, ne of mon beon isehene.   (50/18–22)

Swiftness in recompense for their being here so narrowly enclosed, and the light of clear sight in recompense for their living here in voluntary obscurity, wishing neither to see nor to be seen by man.

The cultivation of inner sight, though primarily a means to see through the false world and the snares laid by men (agents of the devil), has as its true goal the glimpse of the Bridegroom and the study of His love. Thus closing her eyes to the world outside the anchorhold will open them to Christ who dwells within—whether anchorhold or heart or soul. It is her relation to Him that comes as the precise opposite of the destructive attachment to the world. To Him she freely shows her face, to Him she speaks fair words and becomes beloved:

Ich ihere mi leof speoken. He cleopeð me. Ich mot gan. Ant ʒe gan ananriht to ower deore leofman, & meaneð ow to his earen þe luueliche cleopeð ow to him wið þes wordes . . . Aris up, hihe þe heonewart, & cum to me, mi leofman, mi culure, mi feire, & mi schene spuse. . . . Schaw to me þi leoue neb, & ti lufsume leor. Went te from oþre.   (52/19–28)

'I hear my beloved speaking. He calls me and I must go.' And go to your dear Lover, and make your complaint to Him who with love calls you to Him with these words . . . 'Arise up, hasten towards heaven and come to Me, my beloved, my dove, my fair, my beautiful spouse. Show me thy face, thy fair countenance. Turn away from others.'

The devil's voice may be persuasive as the anchoress harkens to his speech, but Christ too has a response to the worldly anchoress who meddles and listens to scandal and gossip. The author includes this in his development of the senses' reaction to Christ as Bridegroom, but the language and imagery of Christ's active interest in the conduct of the anchoress are connected to the developing intimacies of Bridegroom and soul.

To this worldly anchoress, Christ's accents are harsh and scornful (as the devil's are soft and comforting). 'Go forth,' He says, 'and follow the goats.' The end of this fall is her exile to the land of 'stinking goats' and 'foul bucks,' reminders of evil smells and animal imagery. The bird who in a milder vein cackles away her unhatched young (the loss is less severe when her eggs are stolen), is at the later point the victim who throws away her life when she 'puts out her beak like an untamed bird in a cage.' This is a variation on the figure of anchoress showing herself on the battlements of the castle. Her end is more violent, for the cat of hell catches the 'head of the heart' and drags out the body with the claws of sharp temptations. Such swift and merciless death seems inevitable when, tracing their rise and fall through the chapter, the Rule shows us senses that have become so inured to temptation that Christ Himself turns aside from them. 'Go forth and follow the goats.'

It is to Christ, the Bridegroom, that the anchoress is to turn her face and her ear:

Swucche cheoseð iesu crist to leofmon & to spuse. ʒef þu wilt swuch beon, ne schaw þu na mon þi wlite, ne ne leote bliðeliche here þi speche. Ah turn ham ba to iesu crist.   (53/6–9)

Jesus Christ chooses such as these for His beloved and His bride. If you would be thus, show your face to no man and do not let your voice be lightly heard, but turn them both to Jesus Christ.

As the Rule moves toward the conclusion of Part Two, it becomes more deeply involved with the Bridegroom. The custody of the senses, which had begun with defenses against the spiritual and physical corruption arising from doting on the world outside, ends with a promise of the attainment of Christ. Antithesis and paradox are carefully managed in the analogous situations of Eve and Mary, juxtaposed as symbols of a world lost and a world regained, recklessness and restraint, pride and humility. Eve leaped into pride (like Satan) and to her death after babbling her secrets until the serpent knew how to destroy her; Mary spoke but little and then only what was required, in full modesty, though through her Son all Eve's mischief would be undone.

The possibility of good grows more pronounced as the senses undergo discipline. The figures of animals rotting in traps, of ravens tearing the flesh—of goats and bucks wallowing in dirt—begin to fade, giving way to original sweetness, the innocence of the sweet-smelling kid, and the kiss of the Bridegroom in the 'bower of the heart': 'Cusse me mi leof-man wið þe coss of his muð, muðene swetest' (55/14–15).

Here is a new source of temptation—Christ, the Bridegroom, beckon-ing the anchoress to join Him in the bower, to share the sweetness of His favor in a retired place.

Sweetness implies smell and taste, and smell is a sense also susceptible to the devil's devices. It, too, stands as watchman over the heart and is careful not to be deceived by sweet odors which the anchoress may interpret as consolation. In so doing, she leaps into pride. The experience of smell is made meaningful by thrusting Christ in its midst on Calvary where 'decaying bodies often lay unburied in great stench,' a lesson to the anchoress to accept patiently unpleasant, even noisome smells, and an allusion to the animals rotting in the pit into which they have fallen.

With the sense of smell out of the way, the author gathers together at this time the memorable fragments of imagery of eye and mouth and transfers them to the body and sorrow of Christ crucified; and by example shows in bold strokes how He forbore the abuse of His senses, abuse that is repeated and prolonged by the 'chattering mouth' or 'grumbling tongue' of the anchoress who complains after having entered willingly 'in to godes prisun' (57/14).[6] Images of the lady in the castle,

---

6. Except for brief comments on Christ's fare of 'bitter gall' on Calvary, the Rule has little more to say on the subject of taste as a sense. Fastidiousness in diet is one of the sins of the mouth. The Rule has more to say on the subject in Part Six, 'Penance.'

the lady in her grave ('for hwet is ancre hus bute hire burinesse?'), the stormy sea that ever threatens the living, and the hunt for treasure that lies within the heart—all converge in the plea to forswear the sins of the mouth. Christ drank bitter gall; Christ was struck on the mouth—such are signs to the anchoress to suffer with Him some little pain.

Christ has emerged as the dominant figure—the hero of 'Custody of the Senses.' His presence is not only pervasive, but His sense experiences actually enclose those of the anchoress structurally: within the descriptions of His suffering in each of the senses come precepts on the handling of her senses by the anchoress. On Calvary, He smelled the stench of rotting bodies; saw the suffering of His mother and St. John and saw His disciples flee from Him; tasted the gall and suffered His mouth to be struck. Out of these, instructions on the discipline of the senses roll with highly emotional coloring, for what better place to put the small sacrifice of the anchoress than against the suffering and humiliation of Christ?

Touch, the fifth sense, is treated as an integral part of Christ's suffering in the touch of the nails and spear; by contrast, touch offers direct access of sin into the heart. The segment is especially intense in describing the physical and mental agonies of Christ, who suffered three sharp strokes to the heart. The threefold piercing, actual and symbolic, and the relation to touching had made their first appearance as the arrow-spear-sword assaults on the lady in the castle (where they betokened the thrusts of lust). Besides initiating an ingenious denouement, the description of Christ's sensitivity to touch, spiritual and physical, makes especially monstrous the acts of the anchoress who allows luxuria to touch her heart and thus wastes His sacrifice. The enormity of her sin is conveyed in the comparison of the nailed hands of Christ with the delicate, soft hands of the anchoress who lightly reaches out through her window to touch a man:

Godes honden weren ineilet o rode. Þurh þe ilke neiles ich halsi
ow ancres . . . haldeð ower honden inwið ower þurles.   (62/6–9)

*God's hands were nailed to the cross. By those nails I adjure you
anchoresses . . . keep your hands inside your windows.*

Or sits idly about admiring the whiteness of her hands:

> Hire seolf bihalden hire ahne hwite honden deð hearm moni ancre
> þe haueð ham to feire as þeo þe beoð foridlet. (62/21–23)

Looking at her own white hands does harm to many an anchoress whose hands are too beautiful because they are idle.

The Rule reaches a peak in the lengthy, emotional description of Christ's Passion. The crucifixion intensifies the seriousness of the playful heart that leaps lightly out when the senses, as guardians of the heart, have proven idle or reckless. Christ's sacrifice is made for her, the anchoress; indeed, to expiate the sins of the five senses, five holes were driven into Christ's flesh—a bloodletting to purge mankind of disease. But when blood is let, it is the healthy part that is opened in order to draw out the corruption:

> Ah in al þe world þe wes o þe feure, nes bimong al moncun an hal
> dale ifunden þe mahte beon ilete blod bute godes bodi ane, þe
> lette him blod o rode. (61/25–27)

But in all the fevered world there was not found any healthy part, among all mankind, which might be let blood, except only the body of God, which was let blood on the cross.

Herein is introduced one of the major motifs of *AW*, the festering sores of the sick, which stands mong the first of the themes to be developed in Part Three.

But for now the author, satisfied that he has made a good beginning, returns the Rule to the language and metaphor of the opening segment on the senses as watchmen of the heart 'þet sawle lif is inne' (as Solomon said), thus establishing a formal circularity.

Part Two has dealt with the senses, as the author had promised, but with such life and image-rich detail that the reader who comes to it unprepared to share in the action of imagery ever changing, ever generating new forms, finds himself exhausted or mystified. It is easy to become overwhelmed by the turns in the argument, by the overlapping of one sense upon another, the interweaving of fine motifs growing denser as the network of argumentation grows—and it will proliferate as the Rule proceeds. The devolving motifs move quickly, very quickly one into the other until a total pattern emerges. The reader finds himself surrounded on all sides by boldly animated canvasses working out their story independently but always harmonizing into a single major theme.

Thus, in Part Two, the images blend into motifs, as, for example, the escape of the animal, the leap into the pit, the rotting of the carcass; the motifs develop into allegories: the lady in the castle attacked by an army of devils, the hurling of weapons against the stronghold, the overthrow of the lady; the allegories prepare the way for anagogue—the inward turnings of the Rule that parallel the turning inward of the heart. The mystical presence of the Bridegroom comforting the spouse and delighting her senses is the fulfilment of the promise the anchoress secures from Christ when she denies her senses pleasure in this world— when, in other words, the senses become true guardians of the heart. The approach of the *leofmon* (the Bridegroom of Canticles) signals the turn in the chapter and in the spirituality of the anchoress, for hers is an increasing awareness that in her denial of the senses she joins Christ in suffering.

THREE 'REGULATION OF

THE INWARD FEELINGS'

'Custody' and 'Regulation' act as complementary exercises in the process of preparing or disciplining the heart. Their order in the text is determined by the difficulty of attainment as well as continuing progress into the inner Rule. Thus the senses, mediating between the two worlds, can be controlled by means of mechanical gestures—drawing the curtain or shutting the window. In 'Custody' the details of the Passion had emphasized Christ's suffering in His senses. The anchoress is made to feel the blows, the pain, the humiliation of Christ and, in so doing, has learned to control her own senses when temptations appear. It is reasonable that the inner Rule move from the senses and their immediate relation to the outside world to the inward feelings and their special relation to the heart. Inward feelings stand between the senses and the vital 'nesting' place of good works; they are more difficult to control because they must be purged from within, not simply shut out. But it is easier to dam up a river than to purify its waters (I am borrowing a metaphor from Part Two), and the poisons here—anger, pride, envy—threaten to kill the soul.

Anger dominates the chapter because it is inimical to love and thus destroys the possibility of good. Its terrible power is made impressive through the figure of the pelican killing its young; and even when, later, in the passages on sparrow and dove, anger has succumbed to patience and humility the very justification of these birds as symbols of victory over spiritual sin is the existence of sin, in the anchorhold as in the heart.

The essential metaphor of Part Three is set immediately in the nature of the pelican:

Pellican is a fuhel se weamed & se wreaðful þet hit sleað ofte o grome his ahne briddes hwen ha doð him teone. Ant þenne sone þrefter hit wurð swiðe sari, & makeð swiðe muche man, & smit him seolf wið his bile þet he sloh ear his briddes wið, & draheð blod of his breoste, & wið þet blod acwikeð eft his briddes isleine.

(63/21–26)

The pelican is a bird which is so prone to anger that it often kills its own
young when they have provoked it; and then soon afterwards it becomes
very repentant, and makes great lamentation, and strikes itself with its
bill, with which it has slain its young, and draws blood from its own
breast, and with that blood it brings to life again the young which have
been killed.

This useful bit of natural history serves several purposes. It illustrates
rather dramatically the destructiveness of the anchoress who strikes
out in anger, killing her good works as the pelican kills its young. It
suggests the traditional symbolism of Christ as explicated in medieval
bestiaries,[1] an aspect of the allegory the author does not develop. And it
continues and expands the bird–animal imagery introduced in Part Two,
branching off into a discussion of blood with which Part Two ended,
thus securing the pelican-Christ joint. In Part Two, also, Christ's suffering was presented as an example of forbearance and sacrifice; the threefold piercing of His body and the healing property of Christ's blood
purged mankind of the disease of sin, as in a blood-letting. A motif of
blood-letting takes its source in comments on the effluence of sweat
and blood:

For se ful of angosse wes þet ilke ned swat þet lihte of his licome
aȝein þe angoisuse deað þet he schulde þolien þet hit þuhte read
blod. . . . On oðer half swa largeliche & swa swiðe fleaw þet ilke
blodi swat of his blisfule bodi, þet te streames urnen dun to þer
eorðe.   (60/6–12)

For so full of anguish was that violent sweat which poured from His
body at the thought of the agonizing death He was to die, that it seemed

1. The pelican and phoenix are types of atonement, as are, occasionally, the eagle and
vulture. In his commentary on Psalm CII, St. Augustine names Christ as the pelican and
writes: 'These birds are said to slay their young with blows of their beaks, and for three
days to mourn them when slain by themselves in the nest: after which they say the
mother wounds herself deeply, and pours forth her blood over her young, bathed in
which they recover life.' *On the Psalms*, Library of Christian Fathers (Oxford, 1863),
pp. 9–10.

like red blood. . . . And then, that bloody sweat flowed so freely and in such quantity from His blessed body that it ran in streams to the ground.

The effect is powerful in the context of disciplining the senses, which until this direct appeal to the emotions has been based largely on historical–allegorical arguments.

Now, the feelings must be purged, the diseased heart cleansed from within. The purgative then is the blood–letting which restores the health of the soul, and revives the pelican's young.

Anger, the first irritant of the inward feelings to be overcome, is connected by the violence of the pelican's act to blood running out of its pierced breast. Anger makes both pelican and its progeny victims, for it ruins whatever it touches and then turns upon itself. The restorative power of blood-letting is transferred here to the pelican's contrite act and simultaneously to the repentant anchoress, who is urged to do as the pelican does:

Ofþunche hit swiðe sone, & wið hire ahne bile beaki hire breoste, þet is, wið schrift of hire muð þet ha sunegede wið, & sloh hire gode werkes, drahe þet blod of sunne ut of hire breoste, þet is, of þe heorte þet sawle lif is inne; ant swa schulen eft acwikien hire isleine briddes, þet beoð hire gode werkes. (63/1–64/6)

Let her be sorry for it at once, and with her own bill strike her breast, that is, through confession by her mouth, with which she has sinned, and so killed her good works, let her draw the blood of sin out of her breast, that is, out of the heart, in which is the life of the soul, and thus her slain young will come alive again, that is, her good works.

The pelican is one species of bird in a chapter pervaded by birds and their movements. We may say that getting the bird aloft and soaring (as the anchoress rises spiritually out of the flesh, her earth) is the direction the imagery takes in the very real sense of animated motion; and we must wait until the next 'distinction' on temptations to find how very successful this elevation of spirit has been.

The singular power of the bird lies in its wings. The vehicle that carries it upward is the wind, puffs of air that, once mastered, enable the bird to fly. Wind—the link between the purging of the inner feeling of anger and the eventual upward movement—is introduced first as an initiator of anger. What is a word but wind? the author asks—the puff of wind that can cast the anchoress into sin (she has already been advised in Part Two that her curtain guards her against the buffets of wind), or, conversely, lift her up to heaven:

> Þe ilke puf of his muð, ȝef þu hit wurpe under þe, hit schulde
> beore þe uppart toward te blisse of heouene.   (65/6–8)
>
> *And that same puff of breath, if you cast it beneath you, shall lift you*
> *up towards the happiness of heaven.*

To this interesting play on aerodynamics are added the examples of the saints whose cruel deaths carried them upward in body as well as in soul:

> Seint Andrew mahte þolien þet te hearde rode heue him toward
> heouene, & luueliche biclupte hire. Sein lorenz alswa þolede þet te
> gridil heue him uppardes wið bearninde gleden.   (65/10–13)
>
> *St. Andrew was able to endure that the cruel cross should lift him up*
> *towards heaven, and he embraced it with love; in the same way St.*
> *Lawrence allowed the gridiron with its burning coals to lift him upwards.*

The violent deaths of the martyrs Andrew, Lawrence, and, a bit later, Stephen bring historical proofs to the author's argument.[2] But the plea that the Rule makes is not for restraint in the face of injury alone, but for an act of charity, forgiving, that impels the heart to love the hand that smites. The evil man thus unwittingly serves the good. That evil hand will 'plait your crown for you' in the double sense of suffering and joy: the crown of thorns and the coronation in heaven.

Who then would resist the hand that raises him up to heaven, or the mouth that helps to shape the crown? Within these images lies the double sense of wind as the test of strength; first as it nudges the bird upward,

---

2. 'Seinte stefne þet te stanes þet me sende him & underueng ham gleadliche, & bed for ham þe ham senden him wið hommen ifalden' (65/13–15). The joy of Andrew in martyrdom is described by Peter of Blois in 'Sermo in Festo S. Andreae': 'Andreas clamat: Salve crux speciosa! securus et gaudens ad te venio, suscipe Discipulum ejus qui pependit in te magister meus Christus.' *Opera*, ed. I. A. Giles (London, 1847), V, 21.

next as it cools with 'puffs of air' the newly forged crown that is even now being prepared for the anchoress. The paltry sting of a wind-borne wound pales before the suffering of the saints who embraced the instruments that lifted them up bodily and in spirit. And with this convoluted assessment of a mortal fault, the author reduces angry indignation to the ridiculous, to a puff of wind, mere air that can neither wound the flesh nor stain the soul 'unless you yourself make it so.'

The series of exempla and precepts that has served to present and amplify this aspect of the sin of anger ends with a characteristically reversed function of wind, for now the wind stirs up the fire of an already inflamed heart, kindled by God's love: 'for þear as much fur is, hit waxeð wið winde' (66/14–15). The fire and wind have begun to transform the metal of which a crown will be fashioned.

In this section, so pervaded by the presence and habits of birds, animals of the four-legged variety make frequent appearances. The wolf, lion, and unicorn are creatures the anchoress is said to imitate when she flies into a rage. So powerful is anger, an instrument of the devil, that it 'blinds the heart,' robs a man of understanding and makes a beast of him. Typical of the author's treatment of vices is his balancing of an exemplary virtue against the sin, as when the she-wolf is compared with Christ, the gentle lamb led to slaughter: 'ah namare þen a schep, as þe hali writ seið, cwich ne cweð he neauer' (65/27–28).

The fox gets special attention in the Rule, as in much medieval literature, and is identified here with greed or acquisitiveness. His opposite is Judith, the model anchoress, the modest widow whose fasts and vigils must teach the anchoress how to conduct her own religious life. Judith is a favorite figure of conduct striving for excellence. She appears here and elsewhere in Part Two wherever exemplary restraint is needed to oppose fleshly indulgence, particularly greed and gluttony. The alternative to a life of abstinence, as represented by Judith, is gluttonous excess, represented by the swine who is fattened up for the stroke of the axe.[3] The fat calf grown weak and indolent, which must be rehabili-

---

3. 'Swin ipund isti to feattin & to greatin aȝein þe cul of þe axe' (67/2–68/3). The author reserves a discussion of gluttony for Part Four ('Temptations'). The detailed treatment of the subject is actually anticipated here.

tated; the indulgent flesh 'kicking out like a fat and idle mare' that must be tamed—against these symbolic sins of the flesh stands Judith, the good anchoress, armed with fasts, vigils, and hard work. With these weapons she slew the devil:

> On ebreische ledene oloferne is þe feond þe makeð feble &
> unstrong feat kealf & to wilde, þet is, þet flesch þe awildgeð sone
> se hit eauer featteð þurh eise & þurh este. . . . Sone se flesch haueð
> his wil, hit regibeð anan ase feat meare & idel. Þis featte kealf
> haueð þe feond strengðe to unstrengen & buhen toward sunne,
> for swa muche seið þis nome oloferne. Ah ancre schal beo Iudith
> þurh heard lif & þurh soð schrift, & slean as dude iudith þes uuel
> oloferne.   (72/10–20)

> *In the Hebrew language, Holofernes is the devil who weakens the fat
> calf, which has grown too wild, that is, the flesh, which grows wild as
> soon as ever it grows fat with ease and indulgence. . . . As soon as the
> flesh has what it wants, it kicks out like a fat and idle mare. The devil has
> the power to make this fat calf weak, and to incline it to sin; so much the
> name of Holofernes tells us; but an anchoress must be a Judith, of hard
> life and true confession, and must slay, as Judith did, the evil Holofernes.*

The author carries the images of flesh into a rancid, maggot-ridden carcass while urging at the same time wise restraint in controlling the flesh. Decay afflicts the flesh not only through sin and indulgence, but by excessive mortification, which is offensive to God: 'Ah þulli sacrefise stinkeð ure lauerd' (73/5). There is a wisdom in handling the body that applies as easily to wounding by sin as healing by penance.

The fox, however, is both gluttonous and voracious—like the false anchoress when she has lapsed into sin. First gluttony, then greed—as though the infection of one sin breeds the spores of another; greed the worse of the two because of the damage it does to others. These damages presumably will be paid out of the hide of whoever 'opens the pit' that traps the unsuspecting animal:

> Fox ec is a frech beast & freotewil mid alle, & te false ancre draheð
> in to hire hole & fret ase fox deð baðe ges & hennen.   (68/12–14)

The fox is also a gluttonous and voracious animal, and the false anchoress digs into her hole and devours both geese and hens, as the fox does.

The fox serves also as the symbol of hateful hypocrisy.[4] The anchoress who befouls her enclosure with greed and lies is truly a fox when she should be a bird of heaven, a distinction borrowed from Matthew 8:20 and Luke 9:58: 'Foxes habbeð hare holen, & briddes of heouene habbeð hare nestes' (68/6–7).

The background of these lively images is Scripture; the comparisons of animals with scriptural characters are consonant with the homely, uncluttered settings of the Rule. The overall moral intent of the animal *exempla* may be a *reductio ad absurdum* of human faults in the sense that the sinner descends to the level of animals when he imitates habits natural to them. So, into the hole flees the crafty fox, just as the unfaithful anchoress flees into her anchorhold and the enraged Saul of Scripture fled into the cave, all to devour their catch. In Saul's case, persecution of the innocent David (the good anchorite) makes of him a devil with sharp claws (the fox) who has fled into the cave in order to defile it with the blood of an innocent. All are as foxes in their fury and swine in their appetites. There is hardly an animal in the Rule who does not typify weakness of some kind or mortal sin. Only the birds, and very special types such as eagle and sparrow, escape equation with sin. Earthbound creatures are very much more vulnerable, as, for instance, the chattering hen whose eggs are stolen by the chough and the ostrich, who makes a great show of beating the air but never can leave the ground.

Up to now the author has been moving exclusively from the initiative 'foxes have their holes.' But what of the rest of the verse, 'and the birds of heaven their nests'? The round of imagery is completed in Judith, the perfect anchoress, a bird who nests above the earth. Judith, by choosing to fast, rejects the life of the swine and the fox. She is like the pelican:

---

4. The fox in monk's habit or as false priest beguiling an unsuspecting flock might be included as a matter left undiscussed by the author of the Rule, but insinuated by the many cautions against friendships with religious men in Part Two and elsewhere. A full discussion of attributes and symbolism of foxes appears in E. P. Evans' *Animal Symbolism in Ecclesiastical Architecture* (London, 1896), pp. 205–245.

Ich am pellican ilich þe wuneð bi him ane. Ant ancre ah þus to seggen,
& beon ilich pellican onond þet hit is leane.   (67/23–25)

'I am like a pelican, which lives alone.' This is what the anchoress should
say, and, too, she should be like the pelican in its leanness.

The pelican middles between sin and good, at least initially. That the
anchoress is advised to be like the pelican suggests it offers a nature
worthy to be emulated. But what of the pelican's slaying of its young?
If we follow the author's reading of the young as good works and the
killing as an expression of anger, then we ought to interpret the pelican's
nature as vicious. The solution lies in Judith, specifically in the etymological reading of the name:

Þenne is ha iudith þe sloh oloferne, for iudith on ebreisch is schrift
on englisch, þet sleað gasteliche þen deouel of helle. Iudith:
confessio.   (72/2–5)

Then she will be Judith, who slew Holofernes, for the Hebrew 'Judith'
is in English 'Penance', and it slays spiritually the devil of hell. Judith
means Confession.

Though the young have been slain, they may be revived. By an act of
penance the sin is redeemed: in the pelican, a blood-letting that washes
away death; in the anchoress, confession that purges her of sinful anger
(Judith slaying Holofernes, the power of the devil). Judith, we remember,
is the good anchoress.

Allusions to flight, direct or oblique, have been carefully distributed
throughout Part Three, from the earliest description of the pelican to the
saints lifted upward by the instrument of martyrdom to the nesting of
birds in heaven. The definition of the true anchoress as the bird who
leaves the earth and flies upward towards heaven—'leaueð þe eorðe, þet
is, þe luue of alle worltliche þinges, & þurh ʒirnunge of heorte to heouenliche þinges fleoð uppart toward heouene' (69/22–44)—comes not
merely as a figurative play on the desirable idealism, but as a multi-
dimensional summary of past analogies.

The scrupulously close interaction of a handful of images can be
measured by the gradual ascent of the bird from earth, conveyed upward

by blasts of wind. The movement from earth to sky is traced here in a set of excerpts:

THE PUFF OF WIND FROM THE
MOUTH OF THE DETRACTOR

ȝef me misseið þe, þench þet tu art eorðe. Ne totret me eorðe? Ne bispit me eorðe? (65/18–19)

If people speak ill of you, remember that you are made of earth. Is not earth trodden and spat upon?

—the example is Christ's humiliation—

THROWS HER TO EARTH

To wac ha is istrengðet þet a windes puf, a word, mei afellen & warpen in to sunne. (65/1–3)

She is very weakly fortified whom a puff of wind can cast down and throw into sin.

—the anchoress is compared to dust and unstable matter—

BUT WITH SELF-CONTROL AND
HUMILITY

Þe ilke puf of his muð, ȝef þu hit wurpe under þe, hit schulde beore þe uppart toward te blisse of heouene. (65/6–8)

And that same puff of breath, if you cast it beneath you, shall lift you up towards the happiness of heaven.

—the martyrdom and elevation of Sts. Andrew and Lawrence are cited—

SHE LIFTS HERSELF UP FROM
EARTH

Treowe ancres beoð briddes icleopede, for ha leaueð þe eorðe. (69/22–23)

True anchoresses are called birds because they leave the earth.

—fondness for the world falls away as she lifts herself up—

HER ARMS OUTSPREAD IN THE
FORM OF A CROSS

Ha spreadeð hare wengen & makieð
creoiz of ham seolf as brid deð
hwen hit flið, þet is, i þoht of
heorte & i bitternesse of flesch
beoreð godes rode.   (69/8–10)

*They spread their wings and make
themselves into the form of a cross as
the bird does while it is in flight, that
is, in the intention of their heart and
and in the suffering of their bodies,
they carry God's cross.*

The movement of theme and image is not strictly vertical; instead, it
follows a line that rises, retreats, and rises again, leveling off finally at a
point that corresponds to the anchoress' spiritual progress. The segments
form a pattern which, in its irregular line, suggests the halting advances
of the anchoress.

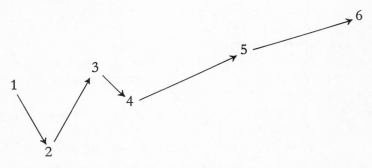

The pelican's leanness, its second characteristic, is now joined to its
power of flight as a new spiral of imagery becomes activated: 'Þeo
briddes fleoð wel þe habbeð lutel flesch, as þe pellican haueð, & feole
fiðeren' (70/11–12). Flesh (identified with the sensual anchoress) keeps
the bird earthbound like the ostrich, which cannot fly despite her many
feathers and must make her nest on the ground (where she is vulnerable
to attack by predators). These are not the 'briddes of heouen' dear to God,
who seeks only those who fly up or nest high above the ground. The
good anchoress remains aloft except when she must attend to physical

needs which bring her to earth, like the bird that descends 'forte sechen his mete for þe flesches neode' (70/4–5). But once down, the bird must beware the devil's snares, the traps set for her 'þe hwil ha sit se lahe.' The idea and figure are 'second-stage' developments of the tricks of the wily fox of lines 68/11–22, who beguiles his prey, the geese and hens—fat and earthbound birds—only to devour them soon after.

The destructive nature of sin is to be understood not merely as tainting the frail or gullible anchoress, but as a corrupting and *killing* force that arises from within the heart and kills it. The shifting allegorizations tend to obscure the single source of this mischief, the anger, greed, or gluttony of the anchoress herself, which must throw her down. Because of her body, continues the Rule, she is vulnerable no matter how high she flies, no matter what level of perfection she may achieve: 'Alswa þe gode ancre ne fleo ha neauer se hehe, ha mot lihten oðerhwiles dun to þer eorðe of hire bodi' (70/7–8).

The nests of these birds that fly toward heaven, thorny on the outside but soft and yielding within, is another subject drawn from nature. The relation of the thorns to the crown of thorns is a possible inference when we consider the author's slow building of the motif of the heavenly crown plaited out of the lengths of earthly pain and discomfort. The image is a good example of how a single object may have multiple referents, all capable of moving inward to anagogue from a purely expository beginning.

In the earlier segment on the crown, the Rule had spoken of the shaping of the crown: 'Let him, & þet gleadliche, breide þi crune' (66/21); '"Iblescet beo þi muð," sei, "for þu makest lome þrof to timbri mi crune"' (66/28–1). The point was to encourage forbearance of injury by word or deed. The bird's nest of thorns that prick is enlarged to include the unusual hardships of enclosed life, which inwardly must be 'soft and yielding' like the heart, but outwardly dressed with thorns— that is, toughened by discipline of the flesh. The anchoress who hurts herself physically, mortifying the flesh beyond reasonable limits, embitters her heart and reverses the natural order—her nest is soft on the outside and thorny within, the sense of this being the softening or collapse of the body because of prolonged disciplines. The outer fabric becomes flaccid in the bitter anchoress. Such recluses cannot bring forth their young from these nests; their good works are stillborn, or they perish in the nest. This loss has been anticipated in the statement of the pelican's first characteristic: 'Hire briddes beoð hire gode werkes þet ha sleað ofte wið bile of scharp wreððe' (63/27–28). In every way, it is the sinner who suffers. The care of the heart has always been the first concern of the Rule, whether envisioned as an animal 'lightly leaping out' of its den or as a nest of the soul sheltering good works.

Having treated the allegorical and moral significance of the bird's nest (and coincidentally the outer-inner physical structure of the nest and heart), the author turns his attention to the eagle, who tends the nest to protect his young birds; and to the agate, a gem noted for its power to neutralize the venom of serpents and scorpions.[5] Implanting Christ in the nest (the heart) reinforces the moral instruction to keep a soft and tender haven within:

> Do him i þi nest, þet is, i þin heorte. Þench hwuch pine he þolede on his flesch wiðuten, hu swote he wes iheortet, hu softe wiðinnen; & swa þu schalt driuen ut euch atter of þin heorte, & bitternesse of þi bodi.   (71/13–16)

> *Place Him in your nest, that is, in your heart; think what pain He suffered in His outer flesh, and how sweet was His heart, how tender within, and so you will drive all poison out of your heart, and bitterness from your body.*

In this way, the anchoress' young, her good works, will be safe from the poison of the adder of hell. We may add also that the idea contains a strong recollection of the pelican's striking out in anger against its young; the angry recluse in so doing becomes an instrument of the devil when this poison has entered her heart.

5. Some connections in the Rule are too tenuous to admit analysis, but the author's fondness of anticipating himself seems to be at work here. The agate, a semiprecious stone said to ward off serpents (and here identified as Christ) is occasionally the token of John the Baptist, whom the author deals with in ll. 82/2 ff. An account of the agate's typifying John the Baptist is found in Evans, *Animal Symbolism*, p. 47: 'It is said of the pearl-fishers, that they attach an agate to a cord and let it down into the sea, where it is drawn towards the pearls by a mysterious attraction.' The 'pearl of great price' here is Christ.

The eagle and the pelican are parallel creatures in the Rule. Each guards its offspring in relation to the spiritual maturity of the anchoress. Thus in the earliest stages of regulation of the inward feelings, the pelican strikes down its young birds and then tears at itself in order to undo the murder. Anger is purged by blood-letting, and diseased or dying parts are restored to life. The emergence of the eagle in a role of parent or protector of the nest is indicative of the growth of restraint and wisdom. The function of these birds is antithetical in direction. The eagle is briefly and significantly turned inward and treated as a mystical symbol of the guardian of the heart or nest where good is nurtured. But this *good* must be understood to be Christ Himself, just as the nest is a womb and the anchoress another Mary. Moreover, the presence of the symbolic agate drawing off poison (analogies: a blood-letting, a crucifixion), strengthens the claims for sacrifice through which good is created and preserved.

We might imagine the pelican and eagle living as far apart symbolically as they do in nature, and their acts representing different stages of the anchoress' ability to regulate her feelings. The pelican strikes out wildly and then turns upon itself. The eagle shrewdly wards off anger with the mystical agate—for the anchoress, Christ, or a token of His power, the crucifix:

Eagle: the young are good works protected in the nest by the agate

> Christ the agate draws off venom (anger) through His suffering. (the crucifix)
>
> "Do him i þi nest, þet is, i þin heorte. . . . & swa þu schalt driuen ut euch atter of þin heorte, & bitterness of þi bodi.' (71/13–16)

Christ in the crucifix (*memoria Christi*) drives out anger and keeps good works secure.

The implanting of Christ in the heart is a slowly executed process that for some anchoresses must begin with a bold reminder of Christ's suffering. Such is the *memoria Christi*, that hangs in the 'nest' of the anchorhold.

In that place where she studies the crucifix, there she may find the agate that wards off evil and keeps the heart free from anger and bitterness. Christ's perpetual posture of suffering is the reminder that anger is deflected to Him in the triple sense: He took God's anger upon Himself; He offers Himself to be crucified again when the anchoress falls into the sin of anger; He promises in the atonement a refuge for those who show patience and forgive offenses.[6] The outward movement of the Rule from symbols to physical reality of the crucifix is especially clear at this point in the refracted experience of Christ.

It was the *memoria Christi* on the wall of the 'outer nest' that initiated the progression outward from the capabilities of the heart and the analogy of the eagle's nest. Moving into the contrast and union of body and soul, which, following Augustine's comment on the subject, the author views with amazement and awe,[7] the direction of the Rule now pivots inward.

The Rule has many times referred to the body as earth and dust, but in each use the figure has served only casually to develop the immediate theme. We can trace the references in these excerpts:

Ʒef me misseið þe, þench þet tu art　　　　(earth trod and spat upon)
eorðe. Ne totret me eorðe? Ne bispit
me eorðe? (65/18–19)

On oðer half ʒetten, ne schaweð ha þet　　(dust blown about by
ha is dust & unstable þing, þe wið a lute　　　　wind of a word)
wordes wind is anan toblawen? (65/4–6)

Treowe ancres beoð briddes icleopede, for　(ascent from the earth
ha leaueð þe eorðe, þet is, þe luue of alle　　which is love of the
worltliche þinges. (69/22–23)　　　　　　　　　　　　　world)

6. 'For what can be so efficacious for curing wounds of the conscience and for purifying the eye of the soul as assiduous meditation on the Wounds of the Redeemer?' St. Bernard in Sermon LXII, *Sermons on the Canticles*, trans. by a priest of Mount Melleray (Dublin, 1920), II, 214.

7. 'Augustinus: Natura mentis humane que ad ymaginem dei creata est, & sine peccato est, solus deus maior est. Ant tis is an of þe measte wundres on eorðe, þet te heste þing under godd, þet is, monnes sawle, as seint Austin witneð, schal beo se feste ifeiet to flesch, þet nis but fen & a ful eorðe' (73/11–16).

Þeos ne beoð nawt ilich þe leane fuhel
pellican; ne ne fleoð nawt on heh, ah
beoð eorð briddes & nisteð on eorðe.
(70/21–23)

(earth birds that make
their nest on the
ground)

A clod of earth, man's body, despite its essentially unstable nature now becomes the weight designed by God to hold the soul down so that it will not leap 'i prude' and fall, as Lucifer fell. But conveyed later after death by the lightness of the soul (like the flight of the bird borne upward by the power of its wings in air), the body rises up against its own nature, counter to natural law:

Þe ilke puf of his muð ȝef þu hit wurpe under þe, hit schulde beore þe uppart toward te blisse of heouene. (65/6–8)

Ah þurh þe hehschipe of hire, hit schal wurðe ful liht, lihtre þen þe wind is & brihtre þen þe sunne. (74/4–6)

(*And that same puff of breath, if you cast it beneath you, shall lift you up towards the happiness of heaven.*

But because of the soul's high nature, the body shall later become very light, lighter than the wind and brighter than the sun.)

This recalls the promise of Part One that the anchoress shall be repaid in heaven with swiftness and bright sight.

Still to be overcome is the flesh of this life, which in a sympathetic environment of earth is often the master, clinging to the ground, imprisoning the soul by sheer weight. The segment, dominated by animal imagery, ends with an allusion to the bird's leanness, which by now has taken on considerable allegorical and anagogic meanings; the former dominated by the exemplary Judith, the latter by the soul's capacity for flight.

Our attention is drawn here by the author's deliberate repeating of earlier lines where the attributes of 'lutel flesch' and 'feole fiðeren' in the recluse would have been puzzling without development. In lines 70/11–12 the second characteristic of the pelican (leanness) was launched with 'Þeo briddes fleoð wel þe habbeð lutel flesch as þe pellican haueð & feole fiðeren.' The recurrence of image and language in lines 74/15–17 perfects the circularity of the spiral:

> Ah ancre, as ich habbe iseid, ah to beon al gastelich ʒef ha wule
> wel fleon as brid þet haueð lutel flesch & feole fiðeren.

But the author adds a new idea to a familiar image—it is the duty of her holy life that the anchoress give strength to others by her prayers and conduct. The terminal thus serves as transition to the next subject, another gathering of images centered around the pelican or, more exactly, the 'nightbird in the house.'

'Similis factus sum pellicano solitudinis; factus sum sicut nicticorax in domicilio.'[8] The nightbird *in domicilio* is the anchoress in her house, which is affixed to the church, supporting it with strength and constancy. The figure of the Church as a ship in a storm, blown about by the puffing of the devil and stabilized by the anchor—that is, the anchoress—is accommodated easily into the signification of the supports of the church (anchorhold) which buttress the walls while they are being battered. She is to support others by her example and her prayers; such was the author's instruction in summing up the pelican's leanness. As the nightbird gathers its food in the dark, so does the anchoress keep vigils (to gather food of the soul). The enumeration of reasons for keeping vigils ends in a call for humility, to do good deeds quietly, and to gather food in darkness, as the nightbird does.

This is not the first appeal for humility in the performance of good works,[9] but at this point the handling of the subject in relation to earthly and heavenly reward becomes necessary and central (morally and structurally), whereas in earlier instances it had seemed incidental.

True humility, like the motions of the nightbird, lies in secrecy, in restraint of words that would proclaim good deeds to the world for worldly praise. This 'wind's puff of praise' is quite as damaging to the

---

8. 'I am like a pelican of the wilderness: I am like an owl of the desert. I watch, and am as a sparrow alone upon the house top,' Psalm 102:6, 7 (A.V.). In the Vulgate, 101:7, 8 (. . . Vigilavi, et factus sum sicut passer solitarius in tecto.).

9. 'Treowe ancres . . . fleon hehe wið heh lif & hali. Haldeð þah þe heaued lah þurh milde eadmodnesse, as brid fleonninde buheð þet heaued' (69/22–27); 'Hwen ʒe al habbeð wel idon, he seið ure lauerd, seggeð þet ʒe beoð unnete þrealles. Fleoð hehe & haldeð þah þet heaued eauer lahe' (69/2–4).

anchoress as the puff of wind from the detractor's mouth by which the weak anchoress, 'dust and unstable matter,' is blown about and cast down —in the first demonstration by anger and here by boasting and vainglory:

> For þi, ʒef ei deð eani god, ne drahe ha hit nawt utward ne ʒelpe nawiht þrof, for wið a lutel puf, wið a wordes wind, hit mei beon al toweauet. (78/9–11)

Therefore, if anyone does anything that is good, let her not bring it into sight or boast about it at all, for with a little puff, with the breath of a word, it may be carried quite away.

The good, like the sweet spice in the mouth (in Part Two), vanishes in 'thin air.'

The Rule's intention to examine and purge the inner feelings through distension of a basic image (here, the nest-heart) becomes apparent in the recurring act of opening the breast and so exposing the treasure within to danger. The terms and figures naturally have been modified since the initial statements when the pelican, having slain its young, revived them with its blood; and the anchoress' progress has been substantially quickened toward a spiritually perfect life. This is the direction of the modulated rhetoric, advancing by small leaps of differing lengths into the heart. The death of the pelican's young (63/21 ff.) should be compared to the death of hope when the bosom is opened to the world's sight (i.e., earthly glory). When the treasure house is opened, hope flies out, stirred by the breath of a word.[10] The measure of reward denied by the loss of hope is heavier to bear than the sacrifice of the pelican; first, because pride is more dangerous to the soul than anger, and secondly, because the pelican gives its body to save its young (good works) while the vain anchoress gives away her young for the comfort and acclaim of the body.

The image of the fig tree, stripped of its bark, bare of fruit and leaves, and fit for the fire only, is another metaphor of the barren reward of pride, well suited to the figurative bird-anchoress. Elsewhere, true

---

10. These inner places are reserved for the Bridegroom. Compare 49/18–21 of 'Custody': 'Bihald inward; þer ich am, & ne sech þu me nawt wið ute þin heorte. Ich am wohere scheomeful. Ne nule ich nohwer bicluppe mi leofmon bute i stude dearne.'

anchoresses had been described as birds 'sitting and singing in happiness on the green boughs, that is, lifting up their minds to the happiness of heaven, which never fades but is always green.'[11] By seeking the world's praise, the anchoress ruins the efficacy of good deeds. The bark of the tree is pulled back, the tender core is exposed, and the fruit on which God feeds is killed.[12]

In the character of the sparrow, the last of the birds, the author completes the range of major image: *Pellicanus solitudinis, nicticorax in domicilio, passer solitarius in tecto*, the sparrow that sits alone upon the housetop.

'I have watched and am become as a sparrow' continues the prayer from Psalms. The verse had appeared earlier to introduce Vigils. Here its purpose is ambiguous, for as a bird notorious for its 'twittering' and 'chatter', its example is to be avoided by the anchoress. She has already been warned of the dangers of speech and of peeping out in Chapter Two. There the cat waited in readiness to snatch her away. But David expressly speaks in the psalm of the sparrow that sits alone, and so comparison of anchoress and sparrow is justified.

We now find ourselves at a juncture similar to the one that occurred in Part Two. The plan of this chapter follows generally that of the preceding part, so that at a point where the author has developed major patterns of imagery and moral argument, he launches into a parallel exposition, pitched to anagogic level. The earthly pelican of the first half is transformed into the sparrow that flies toward heaven in the last; the winds that bear the sparrow ever higher are those 'puffs of air' that stirred up anger and remorse in the foolish pelican.

The key to this ideal state is solitude; the object, love; the *leofmon*, Christ. Scriptural truths from the Old and New Law testify to the sanctity and special privilege of seclusion, where God reveals 'hidden things', such mysteries as the Rule had dwelt upon in Christ's coming to the bower in Part Two. The anchoress 'raised up towards heaven

11. Salu, p. 59; in *AW*, 70/26–1, within the segment on the leanness of the pelican: 'Treowe ancres beoð ariht briddes of heouene þe fleoð on heh & sitteð singinde murie o þe grene bohes, þet is, þencheð uppart of þe blisse of heouene þe neauer ne faleweð, ah is aa grene.'

12. The fig tree was regarded from antiquity as sacred. The author may be thinking of Christ's wish to eat figs after lodging in Bethany (Matthew 21:19).

above her own nature'—echoes of birds in flight, martyred saints, soul struggling out of its clay—may find in the life of John the Baptist model conduct and spiritual comfort. John supplants Judith, the Old Testament gives way to the New, the outer to the inner, the patriarchs and prophets to Christ Himself.

The enviable solitary life! John chose the wilderness over 'þe feolah-schipe of fule men' (83/25); Mary, whom the angel found in a place of solitude, dwelt indoors; Christ went alone into the hills to pray and fast. It is the author's sudden 'discovery' of Christ as the perfect example of the solitary life that brings the point home:

> Hwet seche ich oþer? Of godd ane were inoh forbisne to alle, þe
> wende him self in to anli stude & feaste, þeras he wes ane i
> wildernesse forte schawin þerbi þet bimong monne þrung ne mei
> nan makien riht penitence.   (84/20–23)

But why do I look for other examples, when that of God's own solitude
would be sufficient example for all? He Himself went into a place of
solitude, and while He was alone in the wilderness He fasted, to show that
true penance cannot be done in a throng of people.

From Christ, who not only endured a hard life and lonely fast but was sorely tempted by the devil, the Rule turns to the anchoress and eight reasons why she must flee from the world. Before, the author had offered the same number for standing fast.[13] More than mere doctrine, the eight reasons intensify the promise of Christ's love and hurl the anchoress into a distinguished company (Is she not one with the martyrs in kind, if not degree?).

Basically, the eight reasons (safety, chastity, the promise of heaven, nobility, liberality, spiritual nuptials, swiftness and clear sight, honor) stand as a self-sustaining unit, organized into a graduated raising of the soul from the time it seeks refuge from the raging lion of hell (first reason) to the seventh reason (or step) when the soul finds refuge in heaven. Oddly, the author does not carry the spiritual progress into the eighth reason, but shows by means of extended exegesis and etymology

13. The eight reasons for keeping Vigils, 75/3–76/20, beginning 'Eahte þinges nome-liche leaðieð us to wakien eauer.'

how good may be turned back upon the world by the anchoress who is true. Her 'good works'—the young the pelican saves in the sacrifice of its blood—is analogous with the saving by Esther of her people who had been condemned to die.

The gradations of spiritual worthiness implied in these eight reasons have a material base in the circumstances of the anchoress' life. The imagery is drawn from established tenors, but most striking is the recurrence of the motif of wealth, riches, explicit or implied, which the anchoress may expect as a consolation for a hard life.

A degree of her progress is suggested by the ascent of the images upward. She begins by fleeing to the anchorhold to escape the raging lion. She defends her chastity—a frail vessel as fragile as glass (here are strong echoes of Augustine's pleas of Part One). She wins heaven in the third reason, which sees a culmination of images of flight. Within the scope of this 'reason', she casts the inconstant moon under her feet. A similar image appeared in Part Two in the discussion of a lapse into sin by the anchoress ('Cang dohter iwurð as mone i wonunge; þriueð as þe cangun se lengre se wurse,' 58/14–16). Casting the world under her feet like the saints who made this world their footstool to reach heaven suggests the bird imagery wherein a breath of anger lifts the bird in his climb.

The fourth and fifth reasons seem to be appeals to the social standing and financial condition of the anchoress. However, whatever their place in life before becoming anchoresses, they are now God's chosen and are ennobled. The fourth reason also eschews the carrying of packs and purses in the style of the beggar-woman or burgher's wife.[14]

The sixth reason gives way to the Bridegroom, who leads the anchoress to 'a place of solitude,' with all the promises she must recall from the spiritual nuptials described in 'Custody.' The language of the sixth and seventh reasons (the uppermost steps connoting significantly the imminence of reward) is especially reminiscent of the section on withdrawal and solitude in Part Two. In 'Custody' the author had summarized the special pleasures reserved for the anchoress, borrowing the symbolism of

14. Carrying purses or treasure in a conspicuous manner, however these are interpreted, invites trouble, as, for instance in 79/21–24: 'Þis world nis bute a wei to heouene oðer to helle & is al biset of hellene mucheres, þe robbið alle þe golthordes þet ha mahen underʒeoten, þet mon oðer wummon iþis wei openeð.'

Bridegroom and spouse from Canticles to show the need for quiet: 'I am not a bold lover. I will embrace my beloved only in a retired place.'[15] And the anchoress will be comforted in heaven for her narrow dwelling in this life with two wedding gifts, swiftness and the light of clear sight:

> . . . swiftnes aȝeines þet ha beoð nu swa bipinnet; leome of briht sihðe aȝeines þet ha her þeostrið nu ham seoluen. . . . Alle þeo in heouene schule beon ase swifte as is nu monnes þoht, as is þe sunne gleam þe smit from est in to west, as þe ehe openeð. (50/18–51/24)

> . . . *swiftness in recompense for their being here so narrowly enclosed, and the light of clear sight in recompense for their living here in voluntary obscurity. . . . All, in heaven, shall be as swift as human thought is now, or as a shaft of the sun striking from east to west, in the twinkling of an eye.*

Juxtaposition of these metaphors recurs here in Part Three in the promise of the Lord to speak only in a retired place (the sixth reason to flee from the world) and in the comparison of the anchoress' enclosure to confinement as in a sepulchre:

> Þe Seoueðe reisun is forte beo þe brihtre & brihtluker seon in heouene godes brihte nebscheft for ȝe beoð iflohe þe world & hudeð ow for hire her. Ȝet ter teken þet ȝe beon swifte as þe sunne gleam for ȝe beoð wið iesu crist bitund as i sepulcre, bibarret, as he wes o þe deore rode, as is iseid þruppe. (88/18–23)

> *The seventh reason is that you may shine the more clearly, and see the bright countenance of God the more clearly in heaven because of having fled the world and hidden yourselves from it here on earth; and further, that you may there move as swiftly as a sunbeam because of having been enclosed with Jesus Christ as in a sepulchre, confined, as He was on the precious cross, as I have said before.*

The relation of the seclusion to the advent of Christ as *leofmon* and the fruit of this union (nurtured in the nest of the heart) begins to yield to a newly rising theme, which took its beginnings in the willing entry of the

---

15. 'Ich am wohere scheomeful. Ne nule ich nohwer bicluppe mi leofman bute i stude dearne' (49/19–21).

anchoress into God's prison, the anchorhold, where she has died to the world. The new theme, the emerging out of a tomblike place in a rebirth or resurrection, must await elaboration in Part Six, 'Penance,' and by then we are much better equipped to grasp the broader meanings that will have accreted to the idea.

All of the reasons enumerated by the author summarize in anagogic terms the special rewards that have been prepared for the anchoress, but in the eighth reason the author sums up through etymology the value of the true anchoress to God and to the world, and repeats the warning that she must keep herself 'hidden,' turned inward towards the heart. The moral lessons of the eighth reason are derived from an exegesis of the stories of Esther and Mordecai, Semei and Solomon. Compared to what has come before in this series, the eighth reason is long, explicit in recounting the biblical stories, and ingenious in its restatement of moral precepts. The familiar escape of the heart is refashioned as the flight of Semei's servants from his house; the blessedness of seclusion is compared to the intimacy of Esther and Assuerus. The king grants Esther's petitions on behalf of her people; God bends His ear to the prayers of the anchoress who, like Esther, is hidden. 'Be Esther the hidden,' advises the author, just as earlier he had advised her to be the pelican and the sparrow. And the reward of obedience and humility will be a raising up into the happiness of heaven, not only in imitation of Esther who was 'raised up among the people,' but, by inference, of Mary, 'raised up from a poor maiden to a queen.'[16]

With these references to Part Two strongly engrained, the effect of continuity of 'Custody' and 'Regulation' is reinforced. Both parts have dealt with the life of the anchoress and her mastery of self-control, first with the outer life and the senses as guardians; next with the inner life, with anger, greed, pride—sins that belong to the inner feelings whose seat is the heart. The outer-to-inner movement of the 'pair' of parts duplicates the experience of the anchoress and is itself an analogue of her spiritual progress and her withdrawal inward.

---

16. *AW* 90/24–1. Mary is not named, but she is typified by Esther. The many references to solitude and, finally, the reward of coronation in heaven, apply most aptly to the Virgin.

The concluding statements provide explicit instructions on the safe-
guards of enclosure, proving by inversion of a rather early account of
Christ's humiliating death on a gibbet how uselessly the foolish anchoress
sacrifices herself when like a simple animal she falls into the claws of the
deceitful man or lets her heart be caught outside and killed.[17] If we
summon up the opening lines of Part Two, 'Custody of the Senses,'—
'the heart is a very wild animal and often lightly leaps out'—the circularity of the two sections becomes apparent.

The pelican's solitary life and finally the sparrow's 'falling sickness'
(*fallinde uuel*)—the adjunct to her solitude whereby she may be humbled
in pride—combine to form a paradox of rise and fall in flight. The sickness, an affliction that heals, saves the recluse from a leap into pride:

Godd hit wule for þi þet ha beo eauer eadmod, &, wið lah haldung
of hire seoluen, falle to þer eorðe leste ha falle i prude.   (91/10–12)

*God therefore wishes that she should always be humble, and, keeping and
considering herself low, fall to the earth lest she fall into pride.*

In a series of related images that grow continually, the Rule has traced
the approach of the anchoress to holiness and the 'inner heart.' In every
way she has been prepared for the next stage of the ascent, 'Temptations,'
a trial in the desert through which she must pass unshaken, if not un-
scathed.[18]

17. In 65/24–28, the anchoress is asked to remember Christ's mildness as a remedy
for anger, for 'He was led out the next morning to be hung upon a felon's gibbet.'
In 90/10–14, the heart 'þer þe sawle lif is' will be led forth to the gallows, 'þe wearitreo
of helle.'

18. It is possible to see in *AW* the reenactment of the Mass ritual from the awakening
of the conscience to sin to the act of communion. Each chapter of the inner Rule brings
the celebrant closer to grace, with 'Temptations' acting as the testing ground of
readiness. So—

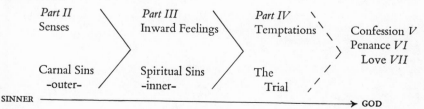

Part II	Part III	Part IV	
Senses	Inward Feelings	Temptations	Confession *V*
			Penance *VI*
			Love *VII*
Carnal Sins	Spiritual Sins	The	
–outer–	–inner–	Trial	

SINNER ⟶ GOD

FOUR 'TEMPTATIONS'

'Temptations' brings the Rule to midpoint, a good place to consider where we have been and what new turn, if any, the author will give to the spiritual dangers and faults that formed the substance of 'Custody of the Senses' and 'Regulation of the Inward Feelings.' The author is determined to let us know what progress has been made, for in this transitional section we find the anchoress 'high,' so high 'on the hill of holy, exalted life' that the dangers are multiplied: 'for se þe hul is herre, se þe wind is mare þron.'[1]

1. In Bernard's 'Fourteenth Sermon on Psalm XC,' there is sounded a warning of the dangers to those eminently placed on the 'pinnacle of the temple' after the struggle in the wilderness has been undergone: 'But I think such a one will be convinced of what I say if he recalls the testimony of holy Job, "The life of man upon earth is warfare." For bearing this in mind, he will understand that the temptations to intemperance in the desert, to vainglory on the pinnacle, and to ambition on the mountain-top, were not the only ones endured by Christ.' *Sermons for the Seasons and Principal Festivals*, trans. by a priest of Mount Melleray (Westminster, Md., 1950), I, 272. Most of Chapter Four takes place in the wilderness, where the battle of anchoress and the Sins takes place. She is found on a hill in the beginning, on a mountain (symbolically) at the end, signs of her further spiritualization.

Richard of St. Victor in the *Benjamin Major* devotes many chapters to the ascent to the summit and the difficulties of habitation; but his work is addressed to contemplatives, and the various heights of the hill are compared to levels of contemplation, as in 'For what is this climbing up into the mount but a rising up into the high place of the heart, according to the prophet's saying.' (*Selected Writings on Contemplation*, trans. Clare Kirchberger (London, 1957), p. 176). The author of the Rule avoids the intellectual approach in favor of the dramatic confrontation, though the end result will be the same, a mystical flight to the summit. Richard makes the point in the *Benjamin Minor*: 'It is very rare to ascend this mountain but much rarer to stand upon the top and there rest... Many have failed in this ascent because of the exceeding labor of climbing, many have come down too soon from the difficult summit because of the effort of standing still. ... Learn to live there and make your abode, and if distracted by any wanderings of the mind, return up there again.' *Selected Writings*, pp. 114–115.

For the recluse who has mastered the preliminary stages of perfection by enduring and overcoming first the many assaults of the enemies of the senses and then the inner, insidious faults of anger and vainglory, there awaits greater trial, inner and outer temptations that afflict the body and assail the soul. The continuing struggle with unworthiness is translated in this chapter into confrontation in the solitary wilderness with beasts and vipers—the Seven Deadly Sins, emissaries of the devil[2]—and finally between the arch-fiend and Christ, the champion, in a hand-to-hand 'wrestling match.'

The animals are the more frightening and loathsome and the attacks more overt because the anchoress is now a more precious prize, having scaled by degrees of self-examination and discipline the ascent (hill) to God. Her very progress is in itself the occasion of a trial, for the wind-swept hill threatens a fall into pride or a strong battering by the elements. In this exalted station, she stands in danger of both. Thus the Rule's immediate concern is to warn the anchoress to beware the extremes of confidence and despair. The warning is continued into the illustration of both the wounds of the diseased man who dies for lack of leech-craft and the man too greatly beset with pain to endure a cure.

The wind imagery and its connotations link together the peripheries, or end segments, of 'Custody,' 'Regulation,' and 'Temptations.' And while the first of these, 'Custody of the Senses,' introduced the image of a moving, rushing wind rather obliquely during the description of the window curtains of the anchorhold, it was in the middle section, 'Regulation,' that the figure was most fully developed and explored as a blast of wind, a puff of breath and air. In 'Temptations' there is a tapering off of the literal image (the activity of wind remains understood) in deference to a newly emerging 'control' image, the most important of motifs thus far constructed in the Rule, the festering wound.

2. St. Bernard's thirteenth and fourteenth sermons on Psalm XC, 'On the Four Vices of Obstinacy, Envy, Anger and Pusillanimity,' deal with four animals (real and legendary) which the soul encounters on her journey. The temptations of the four sins are mollified by consolations and the cardinal virtues. The distinctions are not as sharp as they are in the Rule. *Sermons*, I, 259 ff. Bernard also speaks of the demons who 'live at large in this hanging mass of windy, wandering air.' The notion is of the sublunary habitation of the devil and evil spirits.

Structurally, the ground has been prepared for the 'wound' imagery. First, we have the alternating prominence and diminution of wind-wound motifs in the past chapters; so, early in 'Custody' minor references to wind give way to major concentration on Christ's wounds; 'Regulation' opens with the wound of the pelican and continues into the development of wind as puffs of air. Here in 'Temptations' the anchoress is faced briefly with the winds of the high hill and will be afflicted with wounds of battle, and will take refuge in the clefts of Christ's wounds later.[3] Next, there are several references to magical and medical science in 'Regulation,' particularly 61/23–24 on blood-letting and 64/14–18 on the cooling of blood and the transforming of man into beast. But the major link to the wound motif is the pierced breast of the pelican and the blood-letting that is required to restore the young:

> Do as deð þe pellican . . . Drahe þet blod of sunne ut of hire breoste,
> þet is, of þe heorte þet sawle lif is inne. (63/1–5)

Having borrowed the imagery of Parts Two and Three to convey the anchoress to this height, the Rule prepares to reexamine the threats to her spiritual life, such threats and snares as have indeed been exposed in those two parts, but almost as preliminary exercises to prepare her for an energetic defense against attack by the Seven Deadly Sins.

3. While wind and wound provide peripheral joints to the chapters, they are integral parts of the whole. Christ's wounds in the Passion give way to the pelican's breast wound, then to the wounds of the anchoress and of Christ again (in the latter instance, symbolically in the imagery of Canticles). Wind imagery and attendant matters (birds in flight, at rest, nesting, etc.) dominate Part Three but end there, giving way entirely to the wound or sores of disease. The pattern of recurrence thus far may be expressed as follows:

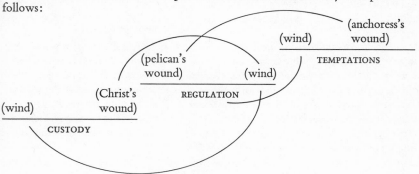

The two kinds of temptation are exterior and interior. Temptations include those trials that have appeared before, such as pain from illness, discomfort, dishonor, misfortune, and every form of bodily suffering that afflicts the flesh; and pain from within: sickness of heart, anger and wrath. These dangerous interior temptations 'from the devil, from the world, sometimes from our flesh'[4] correspond in seriousness to the part of the man they attack. Thus there are bodily assaults by gluttony, lechery, and sloth; and there are assaults on the spirit by pride, envy, anger, and covetousness. The Seven Deadly Sins burrow like worms into host tissue, eating away, weakening, destroying the life of the soul. That the author regards the sins of the flesh as less destructive than those of the spirit is conveyed by the comparison of a wound in the foot with one in the breast. 'Bodily temptations seem greater because they are easily felt,' but the breast wound in its proximity to the heart is more dangerous because it festers painlessly '& draheð to eche deað ear me least wene.' This comment is a further expansion of the introductory example of the man who does not seek a cure for his disease and so dies, and the man whose wounds are so sensitive that he refuses salves that would heal:[5]

Sec mon haueð estaz swiðe dredfule; þet an is hwen he ne feleð
nawt his ahne secnesse, & for þi ne secheð nawt leche ne lechecreft,
ne easkeð namon read, & asteoureð ferliche ear me least wene.

(92/3–6)

4. 'Þeos inre fondunge kimeð of þe feond, of þe world, of ure flesch oðerhwile' (94/17–18). St. Bernard speaks of these forces as *winds*: 'But so long as we live here below, we are exposed to the three winds of the greatest power and malignity, namely: the world, the flesh and the devil, which endeavor to extinguish the light of our conscience by blowing in upon our heart's evil desires and illicit notions.' *Sermons*, I, 334–335.

5. Spiritual wounds and the healing powers of Christ as Divine Physician are common figures in patristic literature from the time of Origen. The Rule seems indebted, however, to St. Bernard for the idea of the harshness of the cure: 'Thou perhaps, O my brother, desirest to be restored to health, yet fearest the sharpness of the remedy, conscious of the desperate nature of thy disease and of the tenderness of thy flesh . . . . Thy gladness increases on discovering that He is not a harsh Physician and uses no bitter remedies, for otherwise the short-lived pain of the cure might appear to thee more intolerable than the continuance of the malady.' *Sermons*, I, 366–367.

Þet oþer dredfule estat þet te seke haueð is al frommard þis, þet is hwen he feleð se muchel angoise þet he ne mei þolien þet me hondli his sar ne þet me him heale. (92/11–93/13)

How to minister to these wounds once they have been recognized as temptations besetting the outer senses and inward feelings is the subject of the segments that follow; and though we may return to the images of wounds and disease from time to time, the Rule develops the argument as a series of recognitions, of confrontations and battles, and finally of recovery.[6] We understand that symbolically the disease is there, painful and potentially killing; the fight against death is waged; the body begins to rally when medicines are tendered; the battle is won with the help of the Divine Physician. (The point has already been made of the restorative power of Christ's blood.)[7] Allegorically, the anchoress is beset on all sides by the animal-sins as she passes through the wilderness. She must overcome their attacks or die. There is no other way. Waiting for her at a particular place in the desert is a Champion who will take up her cause if only she can reach Him.

Of the many disguises the devil assumes in order to deceive men and women in holy orders, that of the physician is especially to be feared:

He haueð se monie buistes ful of his letuaires, þe luðere leche of helle, þe forsakeð an, he beot an oðer forð ananriht, þe þridde, þe feorðe. (116/1–117/4)

6. The struggle dramatized in 'Temptations' follows closely the Rule's advice that the anchoress imitate the bird's 'falling sickness' and *not* fall into pride. God sometimes reveals the emptiness of human vanity through the severity of trials, 'for as a physician uses not only an ointment but also fire and knife to cut out and burn all superfluous matter . . . so God the Physician of souls afflicts with temptations, inflicts tribulations on such a soul, which is so cast down and humbled by them that its joy turns to grief.' *Steps of Humility*, p. 195.

7. In 'Custody,' 61/23–2: 'A mon for uuel þet he haueð, ne let him nawt blod o þe seke halue, ah deð o þe hale to heale þe seke. Ah in al þe world þe wes o þe feure, nes bimong al moncun an hal dale ifunden þe mahte beon ilete blod bute godes bodi ane, þe lette him blod o rode; nawt o þe earm ane, ah dude o fif halue, forte healen moncun of þe secnesse þet te fif wittes hefden awakenet. Þus lo þe hale half & te cwike dale droh þet uuele blod ut frommard te unhale, & healde swa þe seke.'

He has so many cases full of his medicines, the evil physician of hell, that if anyone refuses one, he at once offers him another, a third, a fourth.

And another still, until he finds one that is suitable. Appropriately, the motif of the medicinal salves and powders offered by the false physician of hell and the recurrence of the ever-assailing winds close the first half of 'Temptations,' but in reversed order from the opening passages in which the windswept hill of holy life had been followed by the illustration of the wounds:

> For se þe hul is herre, se þe wind is mare þron. Se þe hul is herre of hali lif & of heh, se þe feondes puffes, þe windes of fondunges, beoð strengre þron & mare. . . . Sec mon haueð estaz swiðe dred-fule; þet an is hwen he ne feleð nawt his ahne secnesse . . .
>
> (92/24 ff.)

Now that she has withstood attack and at least temporarily overcome the enemy, she stands on the hill again:

> Siker beo of fondunge hwa se eauer stont in heh lif. Ant þis is þe earste froure, for eauer se herre tur, se haueð mare windes.
>
> (117/9–11)

Anyone who leads a holy life is sure to be tempted, and this is the first comfort, for the higher the tower the stronger the winds.

By reversing the order, the author is able to strike out on a new set of counteractions and images—the palliatives of the wound, *comforts*. Once again, the Rule has come full circle, generating a new spiral out of familiar currents.

Comforts are followed by *remedies*, cures that will restore the health of the soul. Remedies are intended to heal the wound—that which the anchoress has been warned to attend to from the start of the chapter—the kind that is so minor at first that it goes unheeded, and the other kind of wound that is too painful to stand a cure. The metaphor has been elaborated on the tropological level both as the anchoress who feels herself so severely persecuted by sin and temptation that she despairs, and, conversely, she who leaps into pride by underestimating the subtleties of the devil.

The wound has been inflicted (tropologically, in Christ's crucifixion; allegorically, in the pelican's slaying of its young and the opening of its breast). Trials exacerbate the wound, comforts allay, and remedies heal. Remedies come as prescriptions, strong medicine to 'burn out' disease— the scalding waters of tears and prayers—and close up wounds. Once they have been detailed, and the anchoress presumably recovered sufficiently to count this a victory over world, flesh, and devil, the Rule begins to reconsider the subject in light of the reopening of old wounds (a device of the devil to stir up memories of past temptations). This relapse represents overconfidence (we should recall the 'falling sickness' of the sparrow, which illustrated the need for humility). The image now is of a wound healed and scarred over, but festering underneath because of the delight experienced in recalling past sins. The carnal sins (wounds of the foot) had been described as inflicting lesser wounds than those of the spirit, but they prove to be equally dangerous, for the venom is carried up through the body and inflames the heart. The sins of the spirit are so destructive that unless they are quickly excised, they must deal a death blow to the heart '& ȝeoueð deaðes dunt anan buten ha beon isaluet' (142/24–25).

The resurgence of idiom drawn from medical diagnosis and 'leech-craft' in the last parts of 'Temptations' connects this sequence to the opening images of disease and the stricken sinner (anchoress). But the crisis has come and passed, and the antidotes in the form of comforts and remedies have been made available to her. She cannot now plead ignorance or despair of a cure.

The author uses the frame of injury and disease to recapitulate the sins and remedies of 'sawles hearm and heale':

Prude salue is eadmodnesse; ondes, feolahlich luue; wreaððes, þolemodnesse; accidies, redunge, misliche werkes, gastelich froure...

(142/27 ff.)

The remedy for Pride is humility, for Envy brotherly love, for Wrath patience, for Sloth, reading, various kinds of work, and spiritual comfort...

And so on until his route takes him into the body once more and an

examination of the seat of disease, of a perusal of the human anatomy and
the inherent corruption of flesh:

> I þe licome is fulðe & unstrengðe. Ne kimeð of þet vetles swuch
> þing as þer is in? Of þi flesches fetles kimeð þer smeal of aromaz
> oðer of swote basme? Deale drue spritlen beoreð win berien;
> breres, rose blostmen. Þi flesch, hwet frut bereð hit in alle his
> openunges? Amid te menske of þi neb, þet is þe fehereste deal,
> bitweonen muðes smech & neases smeal, ne berest tu as twa priue
> þurles? Nart tu icumen of ful slim? Nart tu fulðe fette? Ne bist tu
> wurme fode?   (142/7–143/14)

> *In the body there is uncleanness and weakness. Does there not come out of*
> *a vessel such stuff as is in it? And from the vessel of your flesh, does there*
> *come the odour of spices or of sweet balsam? Precious few dry twigs bear*
> *grapes, or thorns roses. Your flesh, what fruit does it bear at all its*
> *apertures? In the middle of your face, which is a noble part of you and the*
> *fairest, between the mouth with its taste and the nose with its faculty of*
> *smelling, have you not as it were two privy holes? Have you not come*
> *from foul slime? Are you not a vessel of filth? Are you not destined to be*
> *food for worms?*

By understanding this as the nature and destiny of her body, the anchoress
accepts humility (the 'falling sickness') as the best defense against sin.
With humility on her side her resistance grows, she reverses the attacks,
beats off affliction (cudgels the devil who comes in the form of a dog
sniffing at the carcass), and seeks refuge in a place where her full strength
will be restored. This refuge is in the pits of Christ's wounds:

> Creop in ham wið þi þoht. Ne beoð ha al opene? & wið his
> deorewurðe blod biblodde þin heorte.   (151/12–14)

> *Creep into them, in thought. Are they not wide open? And with His*
> *precious blood cover your heart.*

She is received there after the siege, a sign of victory and health. Yet the
very fact that Christ's pits provide sanctuary suggests that her salvation
lies in His body, that His blood-letting brings her to life, that He assumes

the wounds of the flesh and the disease that should have killed her. Here as everywhere, Christ dies for her.

The source and progress of the wound (and it is a little history evolving that will not have run its course until the end of Chapter Six, 'Penance') is the major image motif of 'Temptations.' But there are minor shoots from this trunk—minor only in the sense that there is less systematic development of the idea through imagery. The issue raised and allegorized with less focus on detail is the *why* of it all, that is, the morality of the trials and the attendant miseries. Admitting that sin itself is sufficient cause does not satisfy the mere mortal who finds himself besieged on all sides; nor does it completely exonerate God, who seems to have withdrawn Himself when He is most needed, leaving the anchoress to fend for herself.

The two lesser motifs derive from the uses of gold in the crafting of an artifact and the human love of parent and child. Although there is separate development of the motifs, they do touch at one point at least—touch in the literal sense of interlocking and dependence—and both attempt to justify means and end of temptations through familiar experience.

The first of these, the image of gold purified in fire, begins to emerge in a twofold design that will eventually form the crown that had been promised to the anchoress in Part Three. Like the metaphoric inflicting of the wound in the pelican's breast, the root of this image may be found in 'Regulation of the Inward Feelings' in the martyrdom that raised up the saints, in the stings and slurs the good anchoress abides in expectation of a heavenly crown that the slanderer plaits for her on earth. The illustration in Part Three of the bag of ransom thrown against the heart of the prisoner should be recalled in this connection:

> . . . nalde he cunne god þonc a mon þe duste uppon him of
> peonehes a bigurdel forte reimin him wið & lesen him of pinc,
> þah he wurpe hit ful hearde aʒeines his heorte?   (66/19–1)

> . . . *would he not be very grateful to anyone who threw a bag of money at*
> *him, with which he could settle the debt and set himself free from suffering,*
> *even if it were thrown violently against his heart?*

Forbearance alters the course of the bag of ransom, so that it lands in the treasure chest out of which God is to be paid on Doomsday (67/25–15).

These exempla promised future reward for the slights of men who 'plait her crown.' But the real assaying of the anchoress, like a purifying of gold, entails a trial by fire. 'He has chosen thee for his wife, but he will not crown thee unless thou be tried first,' said Aelred of Rievaulx,[8] thinking somewhat more narrowly of the fire of lechery than our author, to whom these fires are all manner of trials. Physical suffering is such a trial—sickness that enlarges a man's understanding, pain that makes him aware of his feebleness and mortality, hard trials that make him equal with the martyrs.

Illness sent by God is but one kind of exterior temptation; the worldly counterpart is the malicious injury done by man, also to be patiently endured. What is sickness but a goldsmith:

> Secnesse is þi goldsmið þe iþe blisse of heouene ouerguldeð þi crune. Se þe secnesse is mare, se þe goldsmið is bisgre; & se hit lengre least, se he brihteð hire swiðere. (95/14–16)

> *Illness is your goldsmith who in the happiness of heaven is gilding your crown. The greater the illness, the busier the goldsmith, and the longer it lasts, the more he burnishes the crown.*

Compared to these labors in eternity, physical suffering in this life must be patiently, even greedily borne. But there seems to be less of a choice remaining to the anchoress, for the author's language is stronger and the threats more harrowing. The alternative of a buffet in the world is a spear

---

8. In a passage on temptations to commit lechery, Aelred uses the figure of the testing of gold, continuing: 'He that is not tempted is not tried. Now maidenhood is gold, thy cell a furnace, the blower to melt a vessel of earth wherein gold is put to be assayed; wherefore, if this vessel bursts through great fire of temptation, the gold is spilled out, and never again will this vessel be made what it was no matter how crafty the work-man.' *Informacio ad sororem suam inclusam*, trans. Thomas N., ed. C. Horstmann, *Englische Studien*, 7 (1884), 305. This version of the *Regula* begins at Caput XXI in Migne's *PL* 32. The source may be Eccles. 27:6: 'The furnace proves the potter's vessel; and trial and tribulation prove righteous men.' See *AW* 85/7–86/5 (the second reason to flee the world) for the Rule's comparison of virginity to the balm in a frail vessel, brittle as glass, which once broken can never be restored.

wound in eternity; of the prick of a needle, the edge of the axe; of a beating, a hanging forever on the gallows of hell:

> Nalde me tellen him alre monne dusegest þe forseke a buffet for a speres wunde? a nelde pricchunge for an bihefdunge? a beatunge for an hongunge on helle wearitreo aa, on ecnesse? (95/19–22)

In 'Temptations' the rewards prepared for the patient, gentle anchoress as well as the slanderer begin to materialize into the image of the artisan's tool that files way corruption and makes metal smooth and bright, as in the polishing of the crown, already plaited by her enemies:

> Let him & þet gleadliche breide þi crune. ('Regulation,' 66/21–22)

> Hwa se eauer misseið þe oðer misdeð þe, nim ȝeme & understond þet he is þi vile þe lorimers habbeð, & fileð al þi rust awei & ti ruhe of sunne. For he fret him seoluen, weilawei, as þe file deð, ah he makeð smeðe & brihteð þi sawle. (95/2–6)

> *If anyone speaks evil of you or does you some wrong, consider and understand that for you he is a file, such as metal-workers use, and he is filing away all your rust and the roughness of sin, for he consumes himself, alas, as a file does, but he makes your soul smooth and bright.*

The file is the tormentor that spends himself in the process of creating a better artifact,[9] one which is not only a bright and shiny soul, but a crown that the anchoress will wear in heaven.

The file yields yet to another use, though the ultimate aim is the same, when in an abrupt shift of place and tone, the file is transformed into a rod which the angry but loving parent applies to his children. Like the file that wears itself out smoothing away abrasions in the precious metal,

---

9. The tools used to refurbish precious metals are metaphors of trial and penance to St. Peter Damian in the *Book of 'The Lord Be with You'*: 'You are the kiln in which the vessels of the Eternal King are shaped; where they are beaten to an everlasting brightness by the hammer of penance and polished with the file of wholesome chastisement; where the rust of the worn-out soul is destroyed and the rough dross of sin is cast aside.' *Selected Writings*, trans. Patricia McNulty (London, 1959), p. 75.

the rod is an instrument of declining usefulness that is cast finally into the fire:

> For as þe feader hwen he haueð inoh ibeaten his child & haueð hit
> ituht wel warpeð þe ȝerde i þe fur, for ha nis noht namare, alswa
> þe feder of heouene hwen he haueð ibeaten wið an unwreast mon
> oþer an unwrest wummon his leoue child for his god, he warpeð
> þe ȝerde, þet is, þe unwreste, in to þe fur of helle.   (96/13–18)

> *For just as a father, when he has chastised his child enough, and brought it*
> *up well, throws his rod into the fire because he no longer has any use for it,*
> *so the Father of heaven, when He has chastised His dear child for its own*
> *good, with an evil man or an evil woman, throws the rod, that is, the evil*
> *person, into the fire of hell.*

The series of cumulating images of the fashioning of the crown from crude, untried metals which prove themselves in the fire follows the growth of the anchoress' resistance to temptations. The image reappears later when the anchoress is emerging from the bitter conflicts with the Sins, provided at that advanced stage as part of comforts. The 'comfort' offered is the example of the saints, 'true champions' who won for themselves the 'victor's crown,' fashioned by God in the fire of temptation as the goldsmith purifies gold in fire:

> Sein Beneit, Seint Antonie & te oþre, wel ȝe witen hu ha weren
> itemptet, & þurh þe temptatiuns ipruuede to treowe champiuns, &
> swa wið rihte ofserueden kempene crune. Ant þis is þe eahtuðe
> elne, þet alswa as þe goltsmið cleanseð þet gold iþe fur, alswa deð
> godd te sawle i fur of fondunge.   (121/27–4)

Finally, the ninth comfort casts the detractors, slanderers—all who would lead her into sin—into the person of the devil, who plaits not one crown but as many as there are temptations withstood:

> Þe þridde fret his heorte of sar grome & of teone þet he, unþonc
> hise teð, i þe temptatiun þet tu stondest aȝein, muchleð þi mede,
> ant for pine þet he wende forte drahe þe toward, breideð þe crune
> of blisse, & nawt ane an ne twa, ah ase feole siðen as þu ouer-
> kimest him, ase feole crunen.   (121/10–15)

On account of the third, his heart is eaten up with great anger and vexation that he, in spite of himself, is increasing your reward while he is tempting you and you are resisting, and that instead of drawing you into torment as he meant to do, he is plaiting for you a crown of happiness, and not only one, or two, but as many crowns as there are occasions of defeating him.

Her progress has been substantial, not only because the multiple crown suggests sustained resistance to temptations, but because her victory is threefold: 'Ne schal nan beon icrunet, seið seint pawel, bute hwa se strongliche & treoweliche fehteð aʒein þe world, aʒein him seolf, aʒein þe feond of helle' (122/10–12).

In the last image of the series, the author settles the question of justifying these severe trials as purges to separate forever gold from dross. God forges His *elect* out of this pure metal after much fire and much hammering:

Al þis world is godes smið to smeoðien his icorene. Wult tu þet godd nabbe na fur in his smiðð e, ne bealies, ne homeres? Fur is scheome & pine; þine bealies beoð þe þe misseggeð; þine homeres, þe þe hearmið.

(147/23–27)

The whole of this world is God's smith who is to forge His elect. Would you have God without fire in His smithy, or bellows, or hammers? Shame and pain are the fire; those who speak evil of you are your bellows; those who do you injury your hammers.

Who these elect are and what special relationship they have with God are still to be discussed, and will be in 'Penance,' where there are few crowns but very many labors. We see, however, that through the terminal image the author has at least implied that a place among God's *icorene* belongs to the anchoress. We have yet to judge for ourselves how deserving she is of this privilege.

An interesting side issue raised by the conclusion of these figures is the role of God in forcing these trials as a condition of attaining heaven. Beyond the temptations of world, flesh, and devil is God's providence, which has set the lesser, certainly malign forces into motion against the anchoress in order to perfect and prepare her. The destructive powers of the world as independent forces are illusory insofar as they work out God's will, damning themselves as they raise her up (as the author has often pointed out). Thus, 'al þis world is godes smið to smeoðien his icorene.'

But the ordeal remains severe, the test so harsh that the loving, benevolent God might at times seem to disappear into the cruel taskmaster. Thus the second of the lesser motifs, the action of a parent toward his child, seeks to understand and justify suffering. The manner is familiar— the moral argument will accompany the exegesis of a colorful drama, which has analogies elsewhere in the Rule. In this case the relation of parent and child is analogous to that of pelican and its young and God and His martyrs.

The bookish example of the pelican striking its fledglings, the sad (but remote) acts of the saints make convincing history, natural and biblical, within a contextual premise that presumes upon the anchoress' faith in traditional authority. But there is special appeal in bringing the issue into the home, in deriving exempla from human behavior that is suddenly thrown into a new light.

Here it is the angry parent who applies the disciplining stick to the children because he loves them.[10] He saves them at the expense of the rod, the instrument of discipline, which, like the file, is worn down and thrown away:

> . . . alswa þe feder of heouene, hwen he haueð ibeaten wið an
> unwreast mon oþer an unwrest wummon his leoue child for his
> god, he warpeð þe ȝerde, þet is, þe unwreste, in to þe fur of helle.
>
> (96/15–18)

The symbolic thrashing of the child leads the author to a second experience of childhood that emphasizes the filial relation of God and

10. The source of the passage on disciplining the child is Proverbs 22:13, 14: 'Withhold not correction from the child; for if thou beatest him with the rod, he shall not die. Thou shalt beat him with the rod, and shalt deliver his soul from hell.'

anchoress. And again the sensitive handling of a familiar (and so, neglected) nostrum deepens her awareness of God's love:

Þet child ʒef hit spurneð o sum þing oðer hurteð, me beat þet hit
hurte on, & þet child is wel ipaiet, forʒeteð al his hurt & stilleð hise
teares . . . Godd schal o domesdei don as þah he seide: Dohter,
hurte þes þe? Dude he þe spurnen i wreaððe oðer in heorte sar, i
scheome oðer in eani teone? Loke, dohter, loke, he seið, hu he hit
schal abuggen.
(97/17–24)

*If a child bumps into something or stumbles against something, we strike
with our hand the thing it has run into, and the child is very pleased,
forgets all its hurt and stops crying. On the day of judgement God will act
as though He were saying: 'Daughter, did this man injure you? Did he
make you stumble into anger or grief of heart, into shame or any
vexation? Look, daughter, see how he shall pay for it.'*

Without dwelling on the torments promised the damned, the author has
no doubt made a deep impression with such simple figures as these. He
has also kept alive and uncluttered the rewards of the suffering martyrs,
the wronged and slandered.

The understanding of children's ways is movingly displayed throughout the chapter, particularly later when in describing the sixth comfort
for temptations, the author again evokes the child-parent relation and we
are made aware of the author's insight into the affinities of human and
religious experience. God's 'game' with the soul, which has left the
anchoress despondent and almost without hope, is compared to a
mother's teasing of her child:

Ure lauerd, hwen he þoleð þet we beon itemptet, he pleieð wið us
as þe moder wið hire ʒunge deorling. Flið from him & hut hire, &
let him sitten ane & lokin ʒeorne abuten, cleopien 'Dame! Dame!'
& wepen ane hwile; & þenne wið spredde earmes leapeð lahhinde
forð, cluppeð, & cusseð, & wipeð his ehnen.
(118/6–119/12)

*Our Lord, when He allows us to be tempted, is playing with us as a
mother with her darling child. She runs away from him and hides, and
leaves him on his own, and he looks around for her, calling 'Mama!*

Mama!' and crying a little, and then she runs out to him quickly, her arms outspread, and she puts them around him, and kisses him, and wipes his eyes.

The mother who playfully hides from her child; the cries of 'Dame! Dame!'; the embrace of love and consolation following the ordeal, are made analogous with God's apparent withdrawal of His grace, 'þet we ne findeð swetnesse i na þing þet we wel doð, ne sauur of heorte.'

The little allegory of the game, disarmingly simple, serves an essentially didactic purpose. Even so, it is possible to detect a significant advance in the anchoress' progress, for the situation has changed from one of salutary disciplining to a warm embrace and a show of love. The effect is heightened when in the sixth comfort the author suddenly adopts the language of Canticles to teach her (as if she were the child newly transformed by the anguish of the game), how to use her strength when God, who seemed to be hiding from her, returns:

> . . . þet tu þrefter þe wisluker wite him, hwen þu hauest icaht him
> & festluker halde, & segge wið his leofmon: Tenui eum nec
> dimittam.   (120/25–27)

> . . . *you should then be so much wiser about keeping Him with you, and
> holding Him fast, when you have caught Him, and that you should say,
> with His beloved,* I held him, and I will not let him go.

The anchoress does indeed assume this bold, aggressive posture later in 'Temptations' when she *demands* that Christ come to her aid. And He will.

The many references and examples involving child and parent in the Rule show a fine sensitivity on the author's part; surely the appeal to the anchoress, as a woman, was strong. The high articulation of homely illustration and moral lesson keeps sentimentality at a distance; indeed, the colorful exempla judiciously played out are relentlessly functional for all their charm. And though we might wish this chapter were less definitive in lists, enumerations, and definitions, these human touches make Part Four vital and engaging. Most important, they bring the rationale of temptations into sharper focus, justifying as it were the ways of God to man.

She will 'play in the pastures of heaven' because she was confined on earth.[11] The outpouring of love, parental in the human sphere, and divine in the final judgments of God the Father brings forward the action of the pelican, the death wound it imparts and the reviving to life of its young. The young birds, the saints, and the child are connected analogously in suffering and the promise of renewal to Christ Himself in the crucifixion and resurrection. When set against this *memoria Christi*, the slights and rebuffs of ordinary men are pale, bloodless.

Such gradually developing motifs show a life of their own, though their purpose seems to be to level a casual force against the main action, which, of course, is the battle of anchoress and the Seven Deadly Sins. We return then to the beginning, which finds the anchoress alone on the symbolic hill in the wilderness where the threefold temptations of the world, the flesh, and the devil are strongest.

The figure of the hill recalls the progress of the anchoress through the preliminary stages of her religious journey, represented by Parts Two and Three; and the special dangers that await her on the hill of 'holy and exalted life': 'Se þe hul is herre of hali lif & of heh, se þe feondes puffes þe windes of fondunges beoð strengre þron & mare.' The bitter trials come in the form of predators of the wilderness. By repeating the images of hill and wilderness, the author reconstructs the metaphoric landscape for the battle with the Sins in their allegorical animal dress:

Hul þet is heh lif, þer þe deofles asawz ofte beoð strengest.
Wildernesse is anlich lif of ancre wununge.   (101/9–11)

The hill is a life of holiness, in which the assaults of the devil are often strongest. The wilderness is the life of solitude, the way of life of an anchoress.

The flight into the wilderness and the struggle against temptations are an inevitable and desirable crisis, as the Rule has implied many times with

11. In 'Custody of the Senses' the marriage gifts of the Bridegroom are swiftness and bright sight; the images evoked are of a child delighting in play: 'Ah ancres, bisperret her, schulen beo þer, ȝef ei mei, lihtre ba & swiftre, & i se wide schakeles as me seið pleien in heouene large lesewen, þet te bodi schal beon hwer se eauer þe gast wule, in an hondhwile' (51/24–28).

respect to the martyrdom of the saints and, more directly, to the exemplary experience of John the Baptist and Christ Himself, both having wrestled with temptations.[12] The Seven Deadly Sins, beasts of the desert and their offspring, initiate inner temptations; the battlefield is the lonely place in the midst of the wilderness where the struggle of Part Four takes place. Exterior temptations, physical suffering, have presumably been overcome by the time the Sins are ready to advance against the anchoress.

The author sets forth the long and elaborate panoply of the Seven Deadly Sins, scrupulously detailed to include as many specific vices as can evolve from the generic sin. For convenience, the animal-sins are summarized by their numerous distinctions (whelps, cubs, etc.) in the Gregorian order followed by the author.[13] Next to each Sin appears the 'weapon of true faith' drawn from an event in Christ's life which the anchoress will use to counter the attacks and neutralize the poisons:

| LION OF PRIDE (101/26–103/9) | vainglory disdain hypocrisy presumption disobedience loquacity blasphemy impatience contumacy contention [unnamed, possibly affectation] | *Against Pride:* How little He made Himself ('hu lutel þe muchele lauerd makede him in wið a poure meidenes breoste') (127/22–24) |
| SERPENT OF ENVY (103/10–104/13) | ingratitude rancor pleasure in another's grief | *Against Envy:* How He suffered for others ('iesu, godd, nawt for his god, ah for oþres god, |

12. In 'Regulation,' John the Baptist seeks solitude in the wilderness (83/12–13); and Christ's temptations occur in the wilderness: 'Þer he þolede þet te feond fondede him feoleweis . . . " (84/22–1). Her turn has now come.

13. In 99/7–8, the author enumerated the carnal-spiritual order. On the classification of sins in the Rule, see Morton W. Bloomfield, *The Seven Deadly Sins* (Ann Arbor, 1952), pp. 148–150.

	faultfinding backbiting mockery suspicion enmity malevolent silence	dude & seide & þolede al þet he þolede') (127/25–26)
UNICORN OF WRATH (104/14–105/28)	contention rage vilification cursing striking wishing harm evil mischief	*Against Wrath:* How He was a peace-maker ('godd lihte on eorðe to makien þrofald sahte bitweone mon & mon, bitweone godd & mon, bitweone mon & engel') (127/5–7)
BEAR OF SLOTH (105/28–15)	torpor pusillanimity heaviness of heart idleness grudging heart deathly grief negligence despair	*Against Sloth:* How active He was on earth ('swiðe bisi ure lauerd wes on eorðe . . . hu he i þe euen of his lif swong o þe hearde rode') (132/1–4)
FOX OF COVETOUSNESS (105/16–106/9)	treachery, deceit theft rapine extortion false witness simony excessive taxation usury meanness stinginess murder	*Against Covetousness:* How narrow was His birthplace ('þa he wes iboren earst, þe þet wrahte þe eorðe, ne fond nawt on eorðe swa muche place as his lutle licome mahte beon ileid up on') (133/16–19)
SOW OF GLUTTONY (106/10–14)	too early too delicately	*Against Gluttony:* How poor was His pittance

	too voraciously too much too often	('his poure pitance þet he hefde o rode') (134/18–19)
SCORPION OF LECHERY (106/15–108/18)	fornication adultery loss of maidenhood incest	*Against Lechery:* How He was born of a maiden ('his iborenesse of þet cleane meiden & al his cleane lif þet he leadde on eorðe') (134/19–20)

The progeny of these beasts perpetuate the vice of the parent, each offspring personifying a subdivision of the mother Sin. The Sins are presented with extraordinary consistency (considering that herein is the first appearance of the animal-sins in English literature). Each of the young is perfectly adapted to the characteristic of the mother. The author's special touch in recognizing human faults, especially little imperfections in the female, often enlivens his lengthy catalogue, as in the pampering of the eleventh cub of Pride, fed with worrying too much about the veil, clothing, colors, and pleating:

. . . gurdles ant gurdunge o dameiseles wise; scleaterunge mid smirles fule fluðrunges; heowin her, litien leor; pinchin bruhen oðer bencin ham uppart wið wete fingres.   (103/23–26)

. . . girdles and girdling the waist like a girl living in the world; daubing unguents on pimples; colouring the hair or the cheeks, plucking the eyebrows or pushing them up with moistened fingers.

Of the sin of 'suspicion,' the eighth offspring of the Serpent of Envy, the author makes this observation, nailing a rather common paranoia in the woman who thinks other women talk about her:

Ʒe, ne luueð ha me nawt. Herof ha wreide me. Lo nu ha speokeð of me, þe twa . . . þe sitteð togederes. Swuch ha is & swuch, & for uuel ha hit dude.   (104/28–3)

Yes, she doesn't like me. She has accused me of such and such. Look now how they are talking about me, the two of them . . . sitting there together. She is this, and that, and she did it with evil intent.'

The persecution described as a delusion of Envy may well have been one of the most disruptive forces in the religious community.[14] The point, of course, is not whether there is real substance to the charge, but how successfully the anchoress can keep herself untainted by the poison spewed forth by suspicion. Envy prepares the victim; the Unicorn of Wrath, the next animal-sin (retributive anger?), kills him off with thrusts of its horn.[15]

The Bear of Sloth and its sluggish cubs cover a wide range of sins from 'torpor' to 'despair.' The seriousness of Sloth is indicated by its position among the spiritual sins, and by the author's assertion that the last of the Bear's cubs is most offensive to God. 'Þe eahtuðe is unhope'—eighth and last by reason of its sluggishness; 'grimmest of alle' because it swallows up God's mercy, His immeasurable grace. This cub is despair.[16]

With the exception of the Scorpion of Lechery, where the grotesqueness of the creature's body and female face is made the correlative of the author's disgust for the sin, the allegorized animals are quickly and soundly dealt with. The young of the Fox of Covetousness personify many of the traits of avarice discussed earlier in 'Regulation.' For the offspring of the Sow of Gluttony, the Rule reserves labels that characterize excess in eating and drinking. All of these Sins assume real identities as creatures of the desert, though the struggle must be understood as being essentially inward, the beasts and demons arising from within the heart itself—the nest where the young cubs are whelped—and so are far more insidious than the outright confrontations of ordinary life.

The four offspring of the Scorpion of Lechery (fornication, adultery,

14. In the *De amicitia christiana* of Peter of Blois, there is a similar passage on the fears of the suspicious person, who is rejected as totally incapable of the qualities necessary for peace of heart: 'If he sees his friend do a good turn for another or being pleasant, he thinks he is being scorned; he interprets his friend's criticism as hatred and a smile as derision. He colors everything with his own perversity.' *PL* 207, col. 884.

15. Such a classification is made by Peter of Blois in *De amicitia christiana*, col. 882: 'From the sin of anger come five other vices, like the five heads of the Hydra, each able to kill friendship. These are insult, false accusation, arrogance, betraying a confidence, cunning snares to trap others.' The hydra and the dragon are described as creatures of anger more often than is the unicorn, which is identified with pride.

16. The changing ascription of the sin of sloth probably accounts for its place here among the spiritual sins. Previously the author had listed sloth as a sin of the body.

loss of maidenhood, incest) cover all subtle as well as overt enticements to lust that must be zealously avoided by whoever 'i þe muchele fulðe nule fenniliche fallen' (106/2). The unnatural offspring of this poison-tailed scorpion of the devil is nourished with her lechery, 'with or without a companion.' The Rule shows uncharacteristic caution in handling the subject, probably because of the delicate 'phantoms' that might be accidentally urged to the surface by an evocative comment.[17] There are matters of sexuality he hesitates to speak of, though he makes the protection of chastity the duty of conscious processes (the 'guardians' of the heart). The anchoress must ever be at it:

> Ah þenche on hire ahne aweariede fundles in hire galnesse, for hu se
> hit eauer is icwenct, wakinde & willes, wið flesches licunge, bute
> ane i wedlac, hit geað to deadlich sunne.   (107/12–15)

> *But let her take thought about her own accursed inventions in lechery, for
> in whatever way this is slaked, in a waking state and voluntarily, to the
> pleasure of the flesh, except only in marriage, it is a mortal sin.*

Those affected by guilt are advised to vomit out the poison in confession; those nourishing the scorpion's offspring in the heart must shake it out in confession and 'kill it with penance.' The metaphoric quality of the language is not impaired even if we are slightly amused by the figure of an alarmed woman swooping down with her besom broom on some confused insect.

The anatomy of the scorpion and the sin of lechery join together organically in the interpretive turn given its face and tail. It puts up a fair front with a face much like a woman's, then stings from behind. Yet this

---

17. Aelred also deals with the problem, which arises because of the chatter of the gossip at the window. The recluse's ears are filled with rumor and scandal. 'Her heart dwells upon these stories: and as she thinks upon these things raised in conversation the images grow more violent and kindle her desire. She falters as if drunk in her psalms, she loses heart in her reading, hesitates in her prayers. . . . For already it becomes clear that she is not being inflamed by the sermon but rather by filling herself with sensual delights, where and when and with whom she can realize her day-dreams.' *Regula*, Cap. IV, col. 1452.

is as far as the 'tail' goes as an instrument of lechery, for it is diverted into the 'venom of sharp compunction and penance' which stings here on earth. Thus she who finds such a tail should consider herself fortunate, for the alternative of the painful sting on earth is the everlasting pain of hell.

Now that the Seven Deadly Sins have been ferreted out and exposed, the Rule turns to a discussion of those who perish in the mouth of the Lion of Pride or on the horn of the Unicorn of Wrath. Not only are these sinners dead to God, but they serve the devil at court as retainers. The structural function of the segment describing the ministers of hell (109/3 ff.) is twofold. First, the devil's court parallels the kingdom of heaven toward which the anchoress is traveling in the wilderness ('wið godes folc toward ierusalemes lond, þet is, þe riche of heouene'). Second, the references to courts and kingdoms suggest castle allegory and related motifs—imagery that becomes increasingly important as the Rule moves forward.

In the devil's entourage are those who have succumbed to sin. They serve their lord best by indulging themselves, though they are unwittingly preparing their own deaths. The proud, who are the devil's trumpeters, are related to boastful men who crave earthly reward, drawing in worldly praise, blowing out noisy blasts. The court jester, another subject in the devil's service, amuses the master with wild contortions of face, twisted lip and sneer of envy (graphically chiseled in ecclesiastical stone of the age and no doubt in the flawed expression of a bad anchoress). These are foreshadowings of the ugly grimaces of the devil himself in his battle for primacy later in the chapter.

The juggler of wrath is the third member of the court, throwing his knives and balancing swords upon his tongue. But the knives and swords of spiteful speech are a small taste of the sharp hooks on which devils will toss and juggle the sinner about 'like a piece of old fur' (110/11). The slothful man can be found, as one might expect, sleeping soundly in the devil's bosom 'as his deore deorling.' Sloth here is a child, lazy and heedless, coddled by the devil as his own. In hell he will be made to keep a sorry vigil, roused from torpor by the inescapable summons: *Surgite, aiunt mortui. Surgite & venite ad iudicium saluatoris* (110/21–22).

The covetous man is the devil's cinder-jack who sweeps together dead ashes,[18] blows upon them, draws figures in the dust, reckoning up his piles of gold and silver—mere ashes. His portion in hell will be worms and toads.

. The glutton is the devil's manciple; he keeps busy in the cellar or in the kitchen, his nose in the pots:

> His heorte is i þe dissches; his þoht al i þe neppes; his lif i þe tunne; his sawle i þe crohhe.   (111/11–13)

> *His heart is in the dishes, his thought all on the cups, his life in the casks, his soul in the pitcher.*

In hell, devils will force open his reluctant jaws to receive a draught of boiling brass.

Finally, there are the lechers, the courtesans of the devil's court who give pleasure to their lord with the foul stench of body and breath. They defile themselves indiscriminately; and though the devil delights in their rank smell, they stink before God. In the Rule, vile smells are usually associated with lust; so, the anecdote from the Lives of the Fathers, which the author cites now, emphasizes the likeness of the smell to that of a rotting corpse. This throws into striking relief the repugnance of the sin to Christ, who delights in sweetness.

This lively entourage projects the activity into the future of punishment-befitted-to-crimes without any loss of immediacy. The devil's court entices now; the congregation of sins and sinners (a kind of perverse, infernal aristocracy) stands ready to open its ranks to a willing initiate. But the devil's court does not offer endless indulgence, just endless glutting, as the author's examples point up; and these manage to make even the sins of the world wholly distasteful.

The ploys of the devil are extremely subtle, and evil is often clothed in apparent good, as when, for example, the devil, failing to lure the anchoress into gluttony, urges her on to an excessive abstinence that weakens and kills the soul. Immoderate abstinence 'þet te sawle asteorue' in the double sense may hurt her as much as gluttony or fastidious eating

---

18. Miss Salu translates *eskibah* (110/23) as 'cinder-jack.' Nero gives *askebaðie*, a bather or wallower in ashes.

habits, for this (as she has already been warned) toughens the heart which ought to be kept soft and yielding. The devil fits the bait to the nature of the prey. If he fails to trap her through gluttony or abstinence, he may win her through liberality. He studies her compassion for the poor, then leads her on to taking collections, first for the needy, then for her friends, until she comes to love possessions and neglect God. She prepares feasts and clamors for worldly reputation, thereby leaping into pride. And when she has become so important, she has taken on the devil as her loyal counsellor. Thus the devil's court meets in the anchorhold, and the service of anchoress and devil is reciprocal. The assembly is a counter-court of the anagogic house of the Bridegroom and allegorical castle of the Christ-knight.

The danger of temptations, the violence and malice of the animal-sins, and the inevitable judgment of those who serve in the devil's court have been treated as if they were immanent threats to the anchoress from the moment she entered the religious life. Often, the author reminds her, the recluse passes her first few years in ease, free of temptation; then with the onslaught of trials, she thinks God has become displeased with her, she grows frightened and desperate (112/24 ff.). The homily which the author uses to illustrate this point marks the beginning of *comforts*. The actual enumeration of comforts *per se* as a list of particulars to allay temptations will follow this transitional introduction, but we must look here at the 'gentle tolerance' of a husband toward his bride for the first sign of recovery. The idea of the homily restates the earlier defense of the father's chastising of his child and the comfort of once again being loved:

Makeð him swiðe sturne, & went te grimme toð to forte fondin ჳetten ჳef he mahte hire luue toward him unfestnin. Alest hwen he understont þet ha is al wel ituht, ne for þing þet he deð hire ne luueð him þe leasse, ah mare & mare, ჳef ha mei, from deie to deie, þenne schaweð he hire þet he hire luueð sweteliche . . . Þenne is al þet wa iwurðe to wunne. (113/10–17)

He pretends to be very stern, and puts on a fierce expression in order to try whether he might still remove her love from him. Finally, when he sees that she has been well disciplined and that she loves him no less for anything that he does to her, but more and more, if that is possible, then he shows her that he loves her dearly . . . Then all that sorrow is turned to joy.

Fast upon this follows the scriptural example of the Hebrews brought to bodily comfort in 'a land flowing with milk and honey' after their release from bondage in Egypt and the crossing of the desert wilderness. This is the second instance of historical significance being given the anchoress' allegorical journey, for the similarity of her experience to that of the Hebrews was noted in the introduction to the beasts of the wilderness. There she was counted among God's people wending their way to Jerusalem, the kingdom of heaven.

God treats the anchoress with the same subtlety that he reserved for His people, whom He 'deceived' into thinking that their liberty could be won easily. So, God waits until the anchoress is 'tough' and ready to suffer before He allows her to be tempted; she must be not only sturdy enough to withstand hardships, but clever enough to distinguish kinds of temptations, especially interior temptations, which are most to be feared:

Moni þet ne weneð nawt bret in hire breoste sum liunes hwelp,
sum neddre cundel þe forfret þe sawle.   (115/15–17)

Many a woman who does not at all suspect it is nourishing in her bosom some lion-cub or some young serpent which is eating away her soul.

The union of the beasts of the wilderness and the heart of the anchoress indicates that, on the tropological level at least, the Rule has never really left the heart, the 'life of the soul'. The emphatic note of vigilance echoes the dangers to the soul which persist even while comforts are being delivered.

The nine comforts against temptations help to counterbalance the imposing weight of the Seven Deadly Sins, and together with the *remedies* ('salue') enable the anchoress to withstand the assaults of the Sins and overcome the disabling wounds of spiritual disease. The incidental 'battle of lists and numbers' threatens at times to make the long chapter unmanageable, but by casting the catalogues into allegorical dress, the author gives life and color to an otherwise endless series of precepts, fine distinctions, and theological qualifications. The body of doctrinal

material in Part Four is of first importance, but the manner of arrangement and presentation must have been a major problem to the author.
The solution lay in a simple division about midpoint (116/24–117/8),
followed by the orderly enumeration of comforts ('froure') and
remedies ('salue') within the allegorical construct of injuries suffered in
battle.

The comforts sketch the history of the anchoress' confrontation with
the devil and temptations from the beginning of battle to the end,
envisioned as a victory for her. They constitute a separate unit within the
Rule, though the ideas and imagery are closely related to those already
introduced. Within the total development of comforts, the substance and
action of 'Temptations' is reenacted, as this summary suggests:

First comfort: The anchoress is compared to a tower held
together by love.

Second comfort: She must expect attack by the devil as a sign
that she is not yet in his power.

Third comfort: She will be able to resist temptations as long as
her heart and reason do not consent to them.

Fourth comfort: If she fights well, God will help her. God allows
the devil to tempt so far, and no farther.[19]

Fifth comfort: The devil can do nothing without God's
permission. God allows him to tempt His
children for their own good.

Sixth comfort: She must not fear those times when God seems
to have withdrawn His grace and comfort. He
does this to prove His love. There are six
reasons for God's 'game.'

Seventh comfort: She should think of the saints and martyrs who
overcame the devil, proved themselves true
champions and won the victor's crown.

19. Of the limits set by God, *AW* says: 'Tempte hire swa feor, ah ne schalt tu gan
na forðre. Ant swa feor he ȝeueð hire strengðe to wið stonden, þe feond ne mei nawt
forðre gan a pricke' (118/11–14). However, consent of the will alters the balance. In this,
the human will must make a choice.

Eighth comfort: God purifies the soul in the fire of temptation just as the goldsmith purifies gold in a forge.

Ninth comfort: The anchoress will wear as many crowns in heaven as equal the number of trials she has borne on earth. The devil plaits her crown.

The comforts begin in an allegorical tower. The figure replaces the hills temporarily as the devil's 'military' objective and suggests the setting of the castle siege and enemy assaults to which the Christ-knight will soon respond:

Ant þis is þe earste froure, for eauer se herre tur, se haueð mare windes. Ʒe beoð tur ow seoluen, mine leoue sustren.   (117/10–12)

And this is the first comfort, for the higher the tower the stronger the winds. You yourselves are a tower, my dear sisters.

The second comfort develops the image further with a glancing allusion to the tower or castle as the individual soul:

Þe tur nis nawt asailet, ne castel ne cite, hwen ha beoð iwunnen. Alswa þe helle weorrur ne asaileð nan wið fondunge þe he haueð in his hond.   (117/21–24)

A tower is not attacked (or a castle, or a city) after they are won. And so the warrior of hell does not attack with temptations anyone who is already in his power.

So, though fears of unworthiness occasioned by hard temptations are inevitable in holy life, the very persistence of temptations is evidence that the prize has not been won. The tower image has been useful to 'place' the reader in the physical field. It is important, too, in assessing the achievement of the anchoress, for though the author abandons the image for a time in order to develop comforts, this 'refuge' above yet in the midst of the wilderness is in itself a comfort. Indeed, it is from the tower that later, in remedies, she will pour down scalding water upon the enemy, the 'hot tears' of prayer and remorse. The nine comforts that begin in the allegorical tower end in a symbolic victory over temptations and the devil, her adversary.

Against the background of warfare, other important motifs are developing, which have been discussed earlier in these pages. One is the company of God's elect, the saints and martyrs, whom the anchoress joins by loving her enemies. Another is the proving of the metal of which her crown will be made. The third, and most important, is the relation of God and man, expressed as the love of parent for child, though he disciplines. The sense of spiritual isolation from God, the fear that He has withdrawn Himself forever, like the game played by the mother, is a part of the struggle leading ultimately to the comfort of consolation.

After comforts come the remedies—remedies against multiple ills arising from spiritual wounds, from bodily wounds suffered in battle with the Sins, from future bouts with temptation. Of the remedies, interior meditations ('halie meditatiuns inwarde') are presented first as a series of rhymed injunctions, *think*:

> þench ofte wið sar of þine sunnen
>   (think often with sorrow of your sins)
> þench of helle wa, of heoueriches wunnen
>   (think of hell's pain, of heaven's joy)
> þench of þine ahne deað, of godes deað o rode
>   (think of your own death, of God's death on the cross)
> þe grimme dom of domesdei munneð ofte,
>   (remember the terrible judgment of Judgment Day)
>
> (123/19–22)

The alternating sets (indicated by linking curves) act to connect organically the three realms of experience, earth, heaven, and hell. These objects of meditation, the reality of corruption and death and the terrors of Judgment Day, fuse together into a reminder of the futility of worldly things:

> Þench hu fals is þe worlt   Þench hwet tu ahest godd
> hwucche beoð hire meden.   for his goddeden.

The rewards of the false world are not only shadows, but death. By a curious inversion of word order the antithetical statement of the good deeds bestowed by God imposes an immediate obligation of gratitude (in response to 'godes deað o rode,' 123/20–21), and sets the anchoress in the role of potential gift-giver. The world offers as its reward the pains of hell, whereas God's good deeds may bring her ultimately to the joys of heaven. Pain and joy in this life are but shadows of what God has in store,[20] paintings of the Real world:

Wa & wunne i þis world al nis bute peintunge, al nis bute schadewe.
(124/8–9)

Besides these meditations, there is some relief to be found from continuing temptations in four kinds of thoughts: 'dredfule, wunderfule, gleadfule, & sorhfule, willes wið ute neod arearet iþe heorte' (thoughts inspiring fear, thoughts inspiring wonder, thoughts inspiring joy, and thoughts inspiring sorrow, feelings stirred up in the heart without any actual occasion). The elaboration of the four thoughts depends heavily on conditional 'if' clauses. This emphasizes the difference between reality and shadow:

Þenchen hwet tu waldest don
    Ӡef þe sehe openliche stonde biuore þe & Ӡeoniende wide up o þe þen deouel of helle,

    Ӡef me Ӡeide fur, fur, þet te chirche bearnde,

    Ӡef þe herdest burgurs breoke þine wahes,

    Ӡef þu sehe iesu crist & herdest him easki þe hwet te were leouest efter þi saluatiun,

    Ӡef þu sehe al witerliche heouene ware & helle ware,

    Ӡef me come & talde þe þet mon þet te is leouest . . . were icoren to pape,

    Ӡef þu herdest seggen þet mon þet te is leouest were ferliche adrenct

(124/16 ff.)

---

20. On the author's knowledge of Hugh of St. Victor's use of the Neoplatonic terms *schadewe* and *peintunge*, see G. V. Smithers, "Two Typological Terms in the Ancrene Riwle," *Medium Aevum*, 34 (1965), 126–128. Other references to the shadow occur in 98/14–99/22 and 100/5–7.

These lines are drawn from descriptions of the four 'þohtes' with which temptations can be fought off in the event holy meditations fail, but indirectly they reinforce the idea of insubstantiality of temptations—a system initiated by the dominant figure of the shadow. Earthly joy and pain are mere shadows of heaven and hell; so the anchoress must preserve herself against 'shadows' (temptations) which could destroy her were they to materialize into deeds.

From meditations (the first of the medicines that heal the wounds of temptations), one progresses to prayers 'sincere, unceasing and stead-fast,' by which the 'carnal temptations from carnal minds' are uprooted. The power of prayer to beat down the devil is treated in rising and falling images. Prayer rising up to heaven 'draheð adun sucurs' against the devil, as in the example of the holy man Publius:

Publius, an hali mon, wes in his bonen, & com þe feond fleonninde
bi þe lufte . . . & warð ibunden heteueste wið þe hali monne bonen
þe oftoken him as ha fluhen uppard toward heouene.   (125/12–17)

A holy man called Publius was occupied in prayer when the devil came
flying through the air above him . . . The devil was overtaken and
transfixed by the holy man's prayers as they rose towards heaven.

The salving properties of prayer 'bind and burn' as good medicines should, but these also singe the devil; hell's torments are turned against the disease.

But the best of all prayers are those graced with tears, for these 'take God by storm':[21]

Beoden smirieð him wið softe olhnunge, ah teares prikieð him ne ne
ȝeoueð him neauer þes ear þen he ȝetti ham al þet ha easkið.

(125/26–28)

Prayers as it were anoint Him with sweet words, but tears pierce Him
and give Him no peace until He has granted what they ask for.

21. Salu, p. 108. The idiom expresses the spirit of the original line: 'eadi bone softeð
& paieð ure lauerd, ah teares doð him strengðe' (125/25–26).

The reversal of the wounds of the Passion ('teares prikieð him') also re-vives the memory of child–parent relationship (in that the tears of the child break down the resistance), though with the subtle interchange of players so that here the anchoress has the mastery over Christ, as if over a lover. Such is the power of Love's sovereignty in Part Seven. 'She may do with Him as she likes.'

But the tears that wrest concessions from Christ and the prayers that bind and burn the devil carry forward the imagery of the castle under attack and the enemy's rout. The language suggests the passage on Greek fire in Part Seven:

> Hwen me asaleð burhes oðer castel, þeo wið innen healdeð
> scaldinde weater ut & werieð swa þe walles. Ant ȝe don alswa; as
> ofte as þe feond asaileð ower castel & te sawle burh, wið inwarde
> bonen warpeð ut up on him scaldinde teares.   (125/1–5)

> *When cities or castles are attacked, those who are inside them pour out*
> *from them scalding water by way of defending the walls. Do the same.*
> *Whenever the devil attacks your castle, the city of your soul, dash scalding*
> *tears out on him as you make your heart-felt prayers.*

In this transitional chapter, prayers like spears transfix the enemy and hot tears thrown down upon him scald and drive him off. In Part Seven, the scalding tears will be transformed into Greek fire, at once destructive and redemptive, inflaming those it touches with love.

The castle under attack is doubly fortified when the surrounding moat of humility ('deop eadmodnesse') is filled with the water of tears ('wete teares þerto'). And the tears have other uses, for a great wind is laid with a little rain, the soft rain of tears and a few words:

> Alswa a muche temptatiun, þet is, þe feondes bleas, afealleð wið a
> softe rein of ane lut wordes teares.   (126/16–18)

The segment ends with the reminder that prayers have been the subject and that the effect of prayers pierces the clouds. The flight of prayer is upward to the very seat of God. The suggestive movements of prayers as birds; the blasts of wind against the hill; the increasingly firm hold of the anchoress on hill or castle or tower are basic but unvoiced assurances of her 'recovery' from disease, from temptations.

With strong and robust faith ('hardi bileaue') the devil is very quickly put to flight. The new segment now takes up the next remedy after holy meditations and prayers, a weapon that contextually continues the retreat of the devil already begun in his fear of scalding waters of tearful prayers. The measure of the anchoress's progress can be inferred from the confidence the Rule shows in her self-control:

> Beoð hardi of godes help, & witeð hu he is wac, þe na strengðe naueð on us bute of us seoluen. (126/10–11)

> *Be confident of God's help, and remember how weak the devil is, who has no power over us except with our permission.*

During comforts, it was pointed out that such power was God's prerogative. Now the reins seem to be passing into the anchoress' hands. A further indication of her growing resistance to temptations comes in her contemptuous rebuke of the 'old ape', whom she repulses by scornful laughter:

> Scarnið him, lahheð þe alde eape lude to bismere þurh treowe bileaue, & he halt him ischent & deð him o fluht swiðe. (126/13–16)

The spiritual recovery of the anchoress assured, she is aggressively ready to put to flight the Seven Deadly Sins 'through the power of true faith,' aided by Christ's strategy:

> I sahtnesse is godes stude, ant hwer se sahte is & luue þear he bringeð to nawt al þes deofles strengðe. Þer, he brekeð his bohe, hit seið, þet beoð dearne fondunges þet he scheot of feor, & his sweord baðe, þet beoð temptatiuns keoruinde of neh & kene. (128/28–4)

> *God's place is in peace, and wherever there is concord and love He confounds the power of the devil. There, it says, He breaks his bows, which are secret temptations that he shoots from afar, and his swords too, sharp temptations, weapons of close, fierce combat.*

The anchoress' weapons are the Virtues, but not the rarified abstractions of psychomachia. The Rule deals with the problem where it exists —in the anchorhold—and to the extent that temptation to sin would disrupt a life ideally in imitation of Christ within the anchorhold. Thus the heavy concentration of exhortation to keep peace and harmony where strife would be ruinous is underscored by examples from Christ's life.

The entire segment is directed inward, beginning and ending in love— human love by example of divine love, both interacting in conformity to the Divine Will. The remedy against wrath was given by Christ Himself not only as part of His ministry on earth, but in His parting words to His friends 'of swote luue & of sahtnesse': *Pacem relinquo vobis*. The union of peace and love enjoined upon His disciples by Christ at the time of His ascension recurs in Part Seven when Christ is about to leave His friends, withdrawing His body so that the spirit might descend upon them. At this point in Part Four, however, the object is to dispel contention from the anchorhold. Peace is the weapon and the key:

> Bi þet ȝe schulen icnawen, qð he, þet ȝe beoð mine deciples, ȝef
> swete luue & sahtnesse is eauer ow bitweonen.   (128/21–23)

> *If there is always harmonious love and peace among you, by that you*
> *shall know,' He said, 'that you are my disciples.'*

Love counters wrath, kills it before it burrows into the heart: 'for iesu is al luue, & i luue he resteð him & haueð his wonunge' (128/25–26). The nest of the heart is preserved intact when, through love, Christ dissipates the devil's power: 'He brekeð his bohe.'

Still involved in the machinery and idiom of warfare, the Rule proves the need for constancy and amity in a series of attacks, the first against a solidly united army, and then against a herd of dumb animals who cling together instinctively to save themselves from the wolf.

The opposing forces of devil and animal-sins and Christ and anchoress link together the two basic subjects of the chapter, temptations and cures. Christ and Satan, love and war, conceived of as instantly and eternally in conflict, meet in the experience of the anchoress. Within the frame of remedies, she shows herself ready to deal resolutely with the enemy whether he comes as an army of devils or animals, or less dramatically in wind and sea currents.[22]

The ubiquitous 'little puff of wind' that scattered about earth and dust and finally, thrust under the bird in 'Regulation,' lifted it up toward heaven, has now changed into a destructive force. The theme is still amity and concord; the metaphor is different:

> Dust & greot, as ʒe seoð, for hit is isundret & nan ne halt to oþer,
> a lutel windes puf to driueð hit al to nawt. Þear hit is in a clot
> ilimet to gederes, hit lið al stille. (129/9–12)
>
> *Dust and grit, as you can see, when broken up into particles, and not*
> *cohering together, can be completely blown away by a little puff of wind,*
> *but when it sticks together in a heap, it lies quite still.*

In the same way, a handful of rods is hard to break, but each stick is itself easily broken. A tree, too, that is about to fall can be made to stand fast when propped up by another. The proximity of wind and tree suggests strongly that they are more than convenient images to bring home the point, and that the tree is related to the imagery of 'Regulation' in which the fig tree, stripped of its bark, soon dies.

As a final example of the dangers of discord and singularity, the author turns to Judges 15:4 and the foxes, each with its face turned away from the other yet tied together by their tails with burning brands. The terms and exegesis, though explicitly applicable to the fox, are reminiscent of the nature of the scorpion, which the author had identified earlier with the sin of lust. The foxes tied and 'burning' signify in this context the temptations that threaten whoever turns away from the group, isolation inviting danger in the form of lust. Conversely, the anchoress must keep her face turned toward her sisters with loving and cheerful looks.

The unusual length of remedies against wrath and, in particular, the emphasis on the need for fellowship suggest that things did not always run smoothly in religious communities. The passage, characteristic of the

22. 'To wel we witen hu þe wei of þis world is slubbri, hu þe wind & te stream of fondunge aren stronge' (129/1–3). On the fierceness of the world's stream, see 'Custody' 58/17–23. Also, in 124/3–7, the anchoress is said to be on a bridge of heaven, overlooking the sea of the world, and she is warned not to shy like a frightened horse at its own shadow and fall into the stream.

revision for an enlarged community (*AW* speaks of twenty now, or more, living together) indicates that such narrow quarters may have led to quarreling and pettiness. These side issues draw the Rule outward and away from allegory and anagogue; yet they put forth images to connect with a summing up of the dangers of disunity and wrath in a coda of word-play:

Ӡe beoð as þe moderhus þet heo beoð of istreonet
  You are as it were the mother house from which they have sprung

Ӡe beoð ase wealle
  You are the spring, as it were

Ӡef þe wealle woreð, þe strunden worið alswa
  If the spring dries up, the streams too grow dry

A weila, Ӡef Ӡe worið, ne bide ich hit neauer
  Ah, if you were to grow dry, I could not bear it

(130/28–2)

The remedy for sloth includes details of the endurance and tireless ascent on the cross of Christ, and ends with an interesting lesson to the late riser:

ToӠeines slawe & sleperes is swiðe openliche his earliche ariste from deaðe to liue.   (132/13–14)

His rising from death to life in the early morning is a very clear reproach to those who are slothful and too fond of sleep.

Against the sin of covetousness, the next wound of temptation awaiting cure, is posed Christ's lifelong poverty: His cramped crib; His hunger on Palm Sunday; the one foot of earth He owned where the cross was set; His surfeit of pain. The remedy for gluttony is the memory of Christ's 'poure pitance' on the cross, a sponge of gall—meager fare for one who has just 'let blood' (134/21). Christ's bitter sop is to be imitated in principle rather than degree, the author warns (mindful of the dangers to the overzealous recluse who might starve herself), lest in rejecting what God has sent her in His goodness, she incur His wrath and He withdraw His hand '& prefter wið to muche wøne abeate ure prude' (134/13–14).

And to counteract the wounds of lechery there are the examples of the

Virgin, Christ's own maidenhood and His clean life on earth. Think, think, urges the author quoting St. Paul, how Christ resisted His flesh:

Þencheð, þencheð, seið seinte pawel, hwen ჳe wergið i feht aჳeines þe deouel, hu ure lauerd seolf wiðseide his fleschliche wil, & wiðseggeð ower. (135/1–3)

'Think, think,' says St. Paul, 'when you grow weary in your fight against the devil, how Our Lord Himself denied the will of His flesh, and then deny your own.'

Lest the anchoress feel alone and outmatched in the battle, Christ's material presence on the wall in the crucifix and His substantial presence in the bread of the Mass are with her always to comfort her during the trials of denial. The figure fixed to the wall or communicated in bread can be only partially realized, however, for in His own form 'ure ehnen ne mahten nawt þe brihte sihðe þolien' (135/10).

As the remedies are being prescribed on the one hand and, on the other, the war continues, the images and lessons have been preponderantly given over to Christ, as if signaling His approach. So, He appears mystically in the Mass or figuratively on the wall. But He is more than this; He is a spiritual force capable of action on her behalf:

Ah swa he schaweð him ow, as þah he seide: Lowr, ich her. Hwet wulle ჳe? Seggeð me hwet were ow leof. Hwerto neodeð ow? Meaneð ower neode. (135/10–13)

But He shows Himself to you in this way, as though He were saying: 'See, I am here. What do you desire? Tell me what you would like. Of what are you in want? Complain to me of your need.'

The consolations offered by Christ here become an active force in Part Seven when the Christ-knight appears tendering service and life. The anticipatory development of the Christ-knight allegory becomes evident in the reappearance of the devil's forces making renewed assaults:

Ჳef þe feondes ferd, þet beoð his temptatiuns, asailið ow swiðe, ondswerieð him & seggeð . . . We beoð iloget her bi þe þet art stan of help, tur of treowe sucurs, castel of strengðe, & te deofles ferd is woddre up on us þen up on eani oþre. (135/13–18)

And if the forces of the devil, his temptations, are making strong assault upon you, answer and say . . . We are lodged here near You who are the Stone of Help, the Tower of True Succour, the Castle of Strength, and the devil's army is more enraged against us than against any others.

The juxtaposition of Christ's real presence and the devil's encampment outside the symbolic castle marks the first solid indication of the direction toward which symbols and metaphors are drifting. The biblical citations and etymologies that follow upon the suggestion of battle between the two forces give historical validity and a sense of timelessness to the conflict, inspiring confidence among the members of God's party.[23]

In response to Christ's question, 'Hwet wulle ȝe? Seggeð me hwet were ow leof,' we have the anchoress's pleas in the midst of battle:

Hwen godd kimeð biuoren ow & freineð hwet ȝe wulleð, & in euch time hwen ȝe neode habbeð, schawið hit swa sweteliche to his swote earen. Ȝef he sone ne hereð ow, ȝeieð luddre & meadlesluker, & þreatið þet ȝe wulleð ȝelden up þe castel bute he sende ow sonre help, & hihi þe swiðere.   (136/14–137/19)

When God comes before you and asks what you want, tell it thus softly in His gracious ear. If He does not at once hear you, cry out more loudly and more violently, and threaten to give up the castle if He does not send help to you more speedily, and make more haste.

These soft pleas in His ear give way to clamorous cries for help in the heat of battle.[24] To these cries for 'reinforcements,' He responds at once:

Ne beo ȝe nawt offearede. Ne drede ȝe ham nawiht þah ha beon stronge & monie. Þe feht is min, nawt ower.   (137/21–23)

---

23. *AW* 135/13 ff.

24. St. Bernard's 'Sermons on Psalm XC' provide many images to the Rule, particularly in Part Seven. Here, too, the author seems indebted to Bernard's advice on handling severe temptations: 'Whenever, therefore, we feel in our minds the violent impulse of temptation, let us immediately have recourse to Him, and beg His assistance. But if sometimes the enemy surprises us . . . then, my brethren, we ought to beseech Him earnestly to support us with His hand.' *Sermons,* I, 142–143. Also from this collection: 'As often as thou feelest the pressure of violent temptation, as often as bitter

'Do not be afraid. Do not be at all afraid of them though they are many and strong. The battle is mine, not yours.'

Christ's assurance that He will enter the fray for the anchoress if she will stand firm against the enemy is evidence of her progress in the religious life. The pledge in response to her need may be compared with the passage in 'Custody of the Senses' in which God draws away from her voice because it has been bent on worldly chatter:

Hwa se wule þenne þet godes eare beo neh hire tunge, firsi hire from þe world, elles ha mei longe ȝeiȝen ear godd hire ihere.

(41/24–26)

If anyone, then, wants the ears of God to be turned towards her voice, let her set herself far from the world, or else she may cry out for a long time before God will listen to her.

These, then, have been the remedies of strong and robust faith that will give the anchoress the strength to stand up straight, so that unbowed by the pressures of temptation, she cannot be mounted and ridden by the devil. The devil mounts her when she bows down for lack of robust faith, and deceives her into believing that she may shake him off with the power of confession (137/10–11). Too soon they become fast companions like horse and rider, and she is toppled into the pit of hell because of the heavy load. Although a sexual 'mounting' is implied in these figures, it is the anchoress' total compromise with the devil that will kill her soul. The pit stands open to receive both, an echo perhaps of the pit into which the animal falls in 'Custody.' No matter how far the anchoress has progressed or how well she has borne trials, the dangers of lapse into sin persist. The Rule, therefore, may speak approvingly at one moment of the spiritual growth of the anchoress, and soon after remind her of her vulnerability (as, for example, in the devil's mount).

---

tribulation threatens to engulf thee: invoke thy guardian, call upon thy guide, cry to thy "helper in due times of tribulation." Call out to him and say, "Lord, save me, I perish." "He neither slumbereth nor sleepeth that keepeth" thee (although he sometimes hides himself from thee for a space) lest perchance thou, not knowing that he is supporting thee, should to thy great peril throw thyself out of his arms.' *Sermons*, I, 256–257.

The remedy of strong and robust faith by which the Seven Deadly Sins have been 'scotched' through Christ draws to a close in the efficacy of the Mass and the descent into the body of the anchoress of 'þe meidene bearn iesu, godd, godes sune,' who makes His abode (*herbearhe*) within her.

The vitality of the sacrament has been building up ever since the fact of Christ's maidenhood was offered as a remedy against lechery. The materialization of her Champion through the power of the Mass began with the assertion that Christ comes daily in the form of bread and wine. He promises His help as she battles the Sins; and when a relapse threatens the anchoress, He is there in the eucharist, entering her body to save her through the miracle of grace and her 'robust faith':

> Hardiliche ileueð þet al þe deofles strengðe mealteð þurh þe grace of þet hali sacrement hest ouer oþre, þet ʒe seoð as ofte as þe preost measseð, þe meidene bearn iesu, godd, godes sune, þe licomliche lihteð oðerhwiles to ower in, & inwið ow eadmodliche nimeð his herbearhe.   (138/21–25)

> *Believe firmly that all the strength of the devil will melt away through the grace of the holy Sacrament which is above all the rest, and which you see as often as the priest says Mass, the Child of the Maiden, Jesus, God, the Son of God, who descends in bodily manner to your hostelry and humbly takes up His abode within you.*

The sequence of images leading to the Mass is perfectly adapted to the needs of the allegorical method, but viewed as a unit, the Mass passages seem a subtle precursor of the next chapter on confession, the natural successor of temptations.

The melting away of the devil's strength in 138/21 hints at the references to fire and the forging of the triumphal crown in heaven; the devil is the fuel. It also fulfils the promise made at the start of the section on strong, robust faith: 'Hardi bileaue bringeð þe deouel o fluht ananrihtes' (126/5). Significant too is the manner of the devil's dissolution—a melting away initiated by the scalding waters of tearful prayers in the very fires with which he would have aroused the flesh. The passage is interesting also in the vaguely sensual inferences of the physical descent of Christ into the anchoress (the opposite of the devil's mounting); in His alighting upon her as on an orchard or flower-bed—as God's grace dropped dew on Mary; and finally in its strong similarity to the passage in Part One in which Christ as a lover passes into the lady's bower where she holds Him fast until He grants her all she asks.

The anchoress' advances have been so substantial that, confident in the power communicated to her in the sacrament, she now has the mastery of the situation. This creates a new danger:

> . . . nulle ӡe bute lahhen him lude to bismere þet he is se muchel ald cang þe kimeð his pine to echen & breiden ow crune.   (139/4–6)

> *. . . you will merely laugh him loudly to scorn because he is such an old fool that he goes about to increase his own torments while plaiting a crown for you.*

The danger, of course, is overconfidence. The author assails the carelessness of weakened defenses in a long exegesis of 2 Kings 4:5, 6, supplemented by passages from St. Gregory's *Morals* on the reopening of old wounds. Scoring the human body as a well of corruption,[25] he offers humility as the only reasonable alternative—and a practical one. Humility, the mother of all virtues, will bring forth the weapons the anchoress must have to beat off the devil.

Now, energized by a series of cumulating images borrowed from earlier passages, the Rule moves to a major stage—that in which the anchoress, armed with the strength of humility, turns the devil's traps against him and wins the day. She learns the art of combat from Christ. One 'fights fire with fire,' as Christ proved when He beheld by what stratagems the devil brought low the proud or lecherous man, swinging him up and tossing him down into hell. Christ's ploy in this wrestling match is the 'falling trick':

> Ich schal do þe a turn þet tu ne cuðest neauer, ne ne maht neauer cunnen, þe turn of eadmodnesse, þet is, þe fallinde turn; & feol from heouene to eorðe, & strahte him swa bi þe eorðe, þet te

25. The subject of wounds as a theme in the Rule is discussed on pp. 82–89.

feond wende þet he were al eorðlich & wes bilurd wið þet turn, & is зet euche dei of eadmode men & wummen þe hine wel cunnen.   (144/12–145/17)

I shall play you a trick which you have never known and which you never could know, the trick of humility, that is, the 'falling stratagem'; and He fell, down from heaven to earth, and lay stretched out upon the earth in such a way that the devil thought that He was completely of the earth, and was deceived by this stratagem, and is still deceived every day by humble men and women who know it well.

The 'falling trick' recalls the 'falling sickness' of 'Regulation,' in which the sparrow is said to fly high with her head bowed low, a sign of humility. The paradox of strength in humility is vigorously explored as the recognition of one's own weaknesses; no one may stand up unless he falls in this way. The false elevation of pride, held on high by a flimsy bag of wind, is easily deflated by the prick of a pin. A wound made by a small prick or slight stitch soon brings low the proud man (145/8–10).[26]

The anchoress has passed the point where she must passively abide the injuries of evil men (though their strokes will prove profitable to her later in heaven); now she is prepared to activate her own power to love, and with this weapon—grieving with another in his pain and sharing in his joy—she kills the serpent envy. Love is not only the remedy for envy, it is the instrument by which whatever is coveted is made one's own. It makes another's good our good too. Yet this will to love is so powerful an undertaking that the anchoress may not be prepared to handle it. For the anchoress whose heart is not yet softened sufficiently, the Rule advises pressing demands on Christ with repentant sighs day and night, giving Him no peace until He turns His grace toward her. Christ once again becomes the Beloved who must finally yield to pleas, and the tie between the lady and the *leofmon* is stronger now than in earlier segments

26. One of many references to the pricks of pins, needles, thorns, etc., that deflate pride, inflict suffering, teach patience; but also related to the practice of bloodletting or similar medical techniques. So, in 95/19–21: 'Nalde me tellen him alre monne dusegest þe forseke a buffet for a speres wunde? a nelde pricchunge for an bihefdunge?' Also, 45/5–7: 'Þe fikelere blent mon & put him preon i þe ehe he wið fikeleð . . . Clauum in oculo figit.'

when she was advised to study the crucifix if she had not set the agate in the nest of the heart.

The crucifix becomes a formidable weapon in the hands of the anchoress, her only weapon in the last of the battles of 'Temptations.' The physical character of the adversary has changed. The devil leaps at her, not as a rider upon the mount, but as a dog ready to seize its prey and rend it to pieces. The change in attitude, in ferocity, of the devil is a sign of his continuing frustration and the anchoress' strengthened resistance. Thus attacked by the dog of hell, she fights back, crucifix in hand, smiting the foul cur with 'stronge bac duntes' (149/8–150/12).

The feverish recital of prayers that follows this encounter dramatizes the frenzy of the allegorical fight; crucifix and incantation beat back the dog of hell as if by exorcism; the heavily accented and alliterated English phrases that introduce and interrupt the sonorous Latin vitalize the immediacy of the action, and the author is caught up in the ceremony no less than the pupil:

> Rung up! Sture þe! Hald up ehnen on heh & honden toward heouene. Gred efter sucurs: Deus, in adiutorium meum intende. Domine, ad adiu. Veni, creator spiritus. Exurgat, deus, & dissipentur inimici eius. Deus, in nomine tuo, saluum me fac. Domine, quid multiplicati sunt? Ad te, domine, leuaui animam meam. Ad te leuaui oculos meos. Leuaui oculos meos in montes. Ʒef þe ne kimeð sone help, gred luddre wið hat heorte. Vsquequo, domine, obliuisceris me in finem? Usquequo auerteris faciem tuam a me? & swa al þe salm ouer. Pater noster. Credo. Aue Maria, wið halsinde bonen o þin ahne ledene. Smit smeortliche adun þe cneon to þer eorðe, & breid up þe rode steaf, & sweng him o fowr half aʒein helle dogge.
>
> (150/12–23)

Another important purpose of the passage is that it draws the anchoress to confession through the keener sense of need of shrift and penance that follows the hard-fought but successful battle.

With somewhat modified intensity but with equal enthusiasm, the *memoria Christi* looms up to remind the anchoress of Christ's torments and strength. The crucifix has served many ends in this chapter, the throttling of the dog the most ingenious, but in this time of rest, it offers peace. Find refuge there, the author says, in the 'clefts of the rock'; like a wounded animal, bloody and spent, 'creep into the holes':

> Muchel he luuede us þe lette makien swucche þurles in him forte huden us in. Creop in ham wið þi þoht. Ne beoð ha al opene?
>
> (151/11–13)

> *Greatly did He love us who allowed such holes to be pierced in Himself that we might hide within them. Creep into them, in thought. Are they not wide open?*

'Go into the rock,' says the prophet, 'and hide yourself in the pits that have been dug out of the earth.'[27] The pits of the earth, of Christ's wounds of the flesh, must serve to complement and rehabilitate many references developed earlier: the pit of the senses where the putrefying animal lies; the pitted sores of disease; the pit in the breast of the pelican, and the pits and snares of the devil. It is at this point that the tropological and mystical nature of the pelican are manifested—in the divine bloodletting that pours life into the young birds from the cleft in the body. The anchoress creeps into the clefts, the sanctuary of the dove:

> Mi culure, he seið, cum hud te i mine limen þurles, i þe hole of mi side. Muche luue he cudde to his leoue culure þet he swuch hudles makede. Loke nu þet tu þet he cleopeð culure habbe culure cunde.
>
> (151/24–27)

> *'My dove,' He says, 'come and hide thyself in the holes in my limbs, in the hole in my side.' Great love He showed to His dear dove in making such apertures. Now see that you whom He calls a dove, have the nature of a dove.*

'See that you whom He calls a dove,' says the author, 'have the nature of the dove, which has no gall.' The Rule has returned, though briefly, to

---

27. Isaiah 2:10, quoted and translated in *AW* 151/14–15. See also St. Bernard's *Sermons*, I, 218–219: 'For against every temptation, against every tribulation, against every kind of necessity, this city of refuge is open to shelter us; "the bowels of the mercy of our God" invite us to enter. Little wonder, then, if *he* does not succeed in escaping from his enemies, whosoever despises such a refuge.'

the *physiologus*, as if directing the reader to reexamine the controlled development of the pelican-bird motif. The dove who seeks out Christ's apertures is protected from the elements and predators by the shield of His Passion, an image so amenable to allegorization that it is made the central theme of the Christ-knight sacrifice in Part Seven. The image has double relevance, for it prepares for the detailed treatment in a future chapter and also serves the immediate need of the anchoress for protective armor with which she returns to the world to renew her war with the devil:

> Al riht swa ʒef þu wult þet te rode scheld & godes stronge passiun falsi þe deofles wepnen, ne dragse þu hit nawt efte þe, ah hef hit on heh buue þin heorte heaued, i þine breoste ehnen. Hald hit up toʒein þe feond. Schaw hit him witerliche. Þe sihðe þrof ane bringeð him o fluhte.
> (151/6–152/11)

And similarly, if you want the shield of the cross and of God's terrible Passion to make the devil's weapons unavailing, do not carry it behind you, but lift it on high above the head of your heart and in front of the eyes of your breast. Hold it up before the devil. Let him see it clearly. The mere sight of it puts him to flight.

After outlining some strong and suitable battle strategy, the chapter rolls quickly to an end, but not without an interesting finish. This arises by way of a little lesson that much comes of little, taught by a woman who set her house afire with a spark:

> Ant nim nu ʒeme hu hit feareð. Þe sperke þe wint up ne bringeð nawt ananriht þe hus al o leie, ah lið & kecheð mare fur, & fostreð forð, & waxeð from leasse to mare aðet al þe hus bleasie forð.
> (153/27–2)

And take heed, now, of how things develop. The spark that flies upward does not set the whole house aflame at once, but stays in one place while its own fire increases, and then it feeds flame to other things and grows greater until the whole house blazes up.

This 'spark that flies upward' provides one of the unexpected turns in the Rule. Just as we await the sudden inflaming of the anchoress with love, or a massive purging of impurities, the reverse becomes the case. The fire belongs to the devil and is destructive; it is fed by anger and wrath and must be quenched only with 'teares weater' and 'iesu cristes blod' before the house is razed. This warning keeps the anchoress alert to the dangers of temptation, particularly pride that spawns confidence. Yet this fire contains the potential of conversion and renewal, which the many references to God's forge reshaping baser materials into a crown bear out. The purifying power of fire, suggested by the scalding waters of tearful prayer, has been temporarily suspended until Part Seven, when in the form of Greek fire it ignites even the enemy with love.

FIVE 'CONFESSION'

There is no sense of victory in 'Confession' as we might expect, since it follows immediately upon a major skirmish. True, the anchoress has beaten off temptations and with Christ's help driven away the devil, but there is little comfort to be found for her pains even at this point. To leap into pride would reverse her gains. The implicit danger of such a fall, no less than the self-deprecating nature of the sacrament, colors the tone and argument of 'Confession'; consolation is within reach but not at hand. The Rule here conforms to its habit of striking out on an unexpected tack, for most of the section is accusatory. The anchoress 'middles' between heaven and hell, saved finally by the efficacy of a true and honest confession. She stands between kingdoms while hell is made visible. And while glimpses of hell are not a new development, it is the first time that the soul of the anchoress is at stake—a sign of the deep commitment at this stage of the Rule.

'Confession' stands as the first part of a tripartite movement that completes the inner Rule. Structurally and sacramentally, 'Confession' prepares for 'Penance' and is antepenultimate to 'Love.' At the same time, it serves transitionally as connector between the reflectively purgative chapters (Parts Two, Three, Four), and the actively purgative (Parts Five, Six, Seven), as this diagram indicates:

OUTER RULE	INNER RULE			OUTER RULE
	REFLECTIVE			
	Custody (II)	Regulation (III)	Temptations (IV)	
Part I		ACTIVE		Part VIII
	Confession (V)	Penance (VI)	Love (VII)	

The conventional pattern of the Rule has been to establish one or more dominant metaphors surrounded and supported by related motifs, all of which grow organically in the course of the chapter and mature rapidly into allegorical 'themes.' As one distinction gives way to another, so the image-spirals rise and fall, and rise again bringing into preeminent play an idea-motif that had been peripheral in the preceding chapter. Such ascending-descending spirals account in part for the inner-outer movement of the Rule and for the restless groping toward completion, a tension only partially resolved and quieted in Part Seven, the approaching culmination of the inner Rule. An unusual, disquieting element of image thinness pervades the orderly arrangement of steps in a full confession. There is comparatively little detail, and elaboration of parts is severely pruned once the discursive opening is out of the way.

'Confession' does not conform to the usual pattern of image development, but the variation is instructive in demonstrating that art can prosper though it remain the handmaiden of religion. After a strong, highly associative opening that seems at first about to spring forward into new treatments of familiar motifs (e.g., the Judith-Holofernes episode, etymologies, battle imagery), the Rule levels off into a bold and frank confession, sparse of ornament, direct and inclusive. This startling departure from established technique does not totally denude the chapter of allegoric substance, for there are always relevant points to be made by way of figurative devices, recurrent images, analogy, and the like. Indeed, the continuity of the confession is strengthened by the sounds and sights of metaphor, but not in the usual way. For once the business of the confession begins, manner never interferes with matter; it is as if the author were following his own precept:

> Schrift schal beo naket, þet is, naketliche imaket, nawt bisamplet feire, ne hendeliche ismaket, ah schulen þe wordes beon ischawet efter þe werkes.   (162/15–17)

> *Confession must be naked, that is, it must be made baldly, not adorned with periphrasis or flavored with courtly expression, but the words used should be according to the deeds.*

Such economy allows him to present the parts quickly; to probe all corners of daily experience in which sin, mortal and venial, can occur;

and to synthesize the power and practice of confession into a single act. The process becomes more than instructional, taking on the nature of paradigm as the author himself seems to be participating in the ceremony. Thus we have the brief justification near the conclusion of the chapter that 'this part that deals with shrift' has relevance for others besides the anchoress.[1]

Finally, there is artistic merit behind the 'settling' of imagery in deference to religious privilege. Allowing for the typically dense quality of the early segments of 'Confession' (which are connected by texture to 'Temptations'), the gradual diminution of metaphoric language results in *rest*, a critical pause before continuation and resolution of the image spirals. Thus the first three parts of the inner Rule build upon each other, achieve a plateau in Part Five, 'Confession,' and then yield their allegorical motifs to intense, exacting development in the remaining sections.

The theme of 'Confession' is reparation and reconciliation. The background in time and place, a battlefield; the foreground—future time and place—hell. Our protagonist has committed a serious offense against his family and suffers loss; he has aggravated a wound, so that it festers; he has been taken prisoner and is to be hanged. Spiritual murder, physical dissolution, death, hellfire—these are the motifs that emerge during the practice of confession. The future is pulled into the present to heighten the threat; hell is made visible while the memory of the devil's court of 'Temptations' is revived, the anchoress having just come through that experience. Because she is human she sins in thought or deed (thus is the battle continually enacted), wounds herself spiritually, and compromises her soul. Even before 'Confession' begins, she has committed an offence and has suffered a wound. All that remains is to die—unless, of course, she makes reparation through a full and honest confession. The results of the confession are reconciliation and restoration of hope. So the final segments of the chapter give way to images of growth and fecundity— a marked change from the grief and sense of loss that dominate the first half.

1. 'Mine leoue suṣtren, þis fifte dale þe is of schrift limpeð to alle men iliche; for þine wundri ȝe ow nawt þet ich toward ow nomeliche nabbe nawt ispeken iþis dale.' (175/2–5).

'Confession has many powers,' begins the author, and these work against the devil and within ourselves. The projection outward of the devil (the actual distinction made between the province of anchoress and that of devil) is indication of the major change, enacted in 'Temptations,' in which the devil was expelled, routed, exorcized from the anchorhold within (and without) with Christ's help. He remains on the fringes of the castle, the battleground. But 'confession' will finish him off—it 'cuts off his head and drives away his army.' The memory of battle with the animal-sins and the devil is rekindled, and the symbolic stroke to the head of the devil connects the anchoress to Judith, who cut off the head of Holofernes, the devil of hell. Judith, whom the author had cited earlier as the model anchoress, now takes on another dimension based on an etymological reading of Judith as 'confession.' The allegorical equation of Judith and anchoress is even more solidly affirmed by the dramatic landscape of the surrounded citadel, the enemy lying in wait, and the final liberation of the land through Judith's act: 'þet is to seggen, þe sunfule is delifret' (154/17–18).

In describing the power of confession against the devil, the Rule relies almost exclusively on biblical accounts of major victories of God's party, moving from Judith and Holofernes to incidental mention of Judas Maccabeus (154/18) and on to Juda (who, like Judith, means 'confession,' 155/24). Confession goes forth like Juda, who put to rout Canaan and carries the banner before God's armies, the virtues.

The introductory segment, then, serves three purposes. It pulls forward the exemplary Judith in her role as anchoress and confirms the efficacy of confession. It defines the allegorical ancestry of the anchoress even more specifically than in 'Regulation' and 'Temptations,' joining her to God's army. And by sustaining the sense and drama of battle of the preceding chapter, it prepares for the spectacle of hell.

But these victories fall within the *power* of confession; insofar as the full confession is yet to be made, they are merely potential victories, promises of things to come. That the author does not return to biblical-allegorical figures at the end should not be surprising, since he has moved into anagogue by then, concentrating on the aftermath of battle, reconciliation. Confession has six powers. The first three, which operate against the devil, have been disposed of in the exegetical account of Judith, Holofernes, Juda, etc. The three that remain work from within and cleanse the soul. Spiritually, confession washes away impurities and restores man to innocence 'as clean and as fair and as rich' in soul as he was before he sinned. The 'fruit' of the power of confession is reconciliation of God and sinner. Not only is the reconciliation at hand when confession concludes, but the imagery of flower and arbor completes the promise made in this segment:

> Þe þridde þing is þet schrift deð us seoluen þe frut of þes oþre twa & endeð him baðe, þet is, makeð us godes children. (155/21–156/23)

> *The third thing which Confession does to us is the fruit of these two others, completing them, and that is that it makes us children of God.*

Most of the chapter is given over to the sixteen parts of the practice of confession, each exploring the occasion of sin and the rewards at Judgment. At first the confession is characterized by the union of method and necessity drawn against a background of gaping hell. In this way, the alternative to full confession emerges immediately to motivate the sinner. Hell is made visible, its flaming mouth waiting to swallow up the damned; the terrible judgment of God is called down, unremitting in severity—justice without mercy. Within this projection into the future, the advancing revelation of Last Things almost overpowers the doctrinal exposition. But in the terrors of hell laid bare are contained sufficient lessons to impress upon the anchoress the absolute necessity of full and frank confession. While a strong homiletic character dominates the early parts, the dramatic momentum gradually recedes as confession swells, absorbing the anchoress (and perhaps the author himself) into a confrontation with sin.

The first of the sixteen particulars of confession is its accusatory nature: 'Schrift schal beo wreiful' (156/11). The sinner must hold herself fully responsible, and not defend herself by blaming others, in the manner of Adam and Eve, each accusing the other: 'Adam þurh eue, & eue þurh þe neddre' (156/15).[2] The pit of hell, the ominously recurring figure

2. 'There are many ways of making excuses in sins. For he who excuses himself may say, I did not do it; or, I did it indeed, but it was right; or, if wrong, it was not very wrong; or, if very wrong, it was not with bad intent. If nevertheless he is convicted of it, like Adam and Eve, he attempts to excuse himself on the ground that he was beguiled by someone else.' St. Bernard, *Steps of Humility*, p. 215.

found in 'Custody of the Senses', is made a reality here as it waits to receive the unshriven soul:

> Bineoðen us ʒeoniende þe wide þrote of helle. Inwið us seoluen ure ahne conscience, þet is, ure inwit forculiende hire seoluen wið þe fur of sunne. Wið uten us al þe world leitinde o swart lei up in to þe skiwes.
>
> (157/16–19)

> *Beneath us there will yawn the wide throat of hell. Within ourselves will be our own conscience, consuming itself with the fire of sin; about us, the whole world flaming with dark flame up into the skies.*

The compromise will be amended on the last day; the sins left unconfessed will act as the accusers then, compounded by the clamor of the conscience. Patient and merciful Christ will have no pity: 'lomb her liun þer.' (157/10).

In boldness of language and emotion, the author's treatment of the Last Judgment departs measurably from the cursory approach of earlier chapters. The presentation here is intended to instruct and purge simultaneously, to carry anchoress and author alike into a future time when pain and sorrow come forth to extract penance that had been withheld on earth.

The same pattern continues into the second segment, 'Schrift schal beo bitter,' beginning with the soul in a state of sin, moving into a hypothetical projection of a state of loss (bereavement, in this case) and ending in a reaffirmed hope for grace.

Even as the terrors of hell are made visible, the theme of reconciliation begins to build. The author develops parallel motifs of loss and winning which keep the human element active while confession is practiced. Separation, estrangement, death of a beloved child or parent delivers the warning of the painful loss of God. The sinner, as the instrument of loss or death, becomes the murderer. The sorrow of loss and death is compounded as he is brought to the docket and condemned. Confession of guilt, repentance in tears and shame, wash away his corruption, and he is saved from death.

'We are children of God.' Twice the Rule has made a special point of this commonplace; first, when confession washes us clean and gives back

to us what we had lost: 'Schrift wescheð us of alle ure fulðen, ȝelt us alle
ure luren, makeð us godes children' (154/27–28); again, when confession
restores the soul to health, makes it fair and rich, and gives us 'þe frut of
þes oþre twa & endeð ham baðe, þet is makeð us godes children' (156/22–
23). The impact of bitter confession increases as we trace the separation
and reunion of parent and child. The sorrow of the man who has lost his
family and friends all in the space of an hour is compared to the greater
loss of the heavenly family when he murders by spiritual sin. Such a one
alienates himself from the holy saints and the angels of heaven, but what is
worse:

> His children, sone se he sunegede deadliche, deiden alle clane, þet
> beoð his gode werkes, þe beoð forloren alle. (159/6–160/8)

> *As soon as he has sinned mortally, all his children have died outright, that
> is, his good works, which are all lost.*

The child in this context is the victim, as the pelican's young (her good
works) had been in 'Regulation.' But, less remotely, we remember the
relation of parent and child in 'Temptations,' where the father applies the
rod because he loves and the mother comforts her child's fears. The child
who had been dear to the father by this spiritual murder is changed into
'a child of the devil of hell' ('he is him seolf biwrixlet & bicumen of godes
child þe deofles bearn of helle'),[3] With the loss of this child, the mother's
grief is multiplied:

> Make bitter man as wif deð for hire child þe nefde bute him ane &
> sið hit biuoren hire fearliche asteoruen. (160/14–16)

> *Make bitter lamentation as a woman does for her child when she had only
> him and she sees him die suddenly before her eyes.*

The sinner alternates in the role of mother and child. First with sin she
slays her parents and siblings (the holy saints); then she is the bereaved
mother whose child has died before her eyes, suggesting Mary looking

---

3. Anticipated in *AW* 44/17–20, where the liar's tongue is said to be a cradle for the
devil's child.

upon her son's Passion.[4] Though the Rule does not go so far as this, the allusion to the anchoress as a spiritual Mary is impressive, and not unique to this chapter.

To the first example of bitter confession, which has involved the loss of God the Father and the spiritual family, the author adds the second. The figure of the condemned man about to be hanged or burned alive for a 'terrible murder' continues the theme into retribution. By the murder of God's spouse, the soul, the 'wretched sinner' (now addressed vocatively as *you*), condemned to hang in everlasting fire, strikes a bargain with the devil, a compact with sin:

> He ʒeoue þe sunne, & tu him þi sawle & ti bodi mid al to weane &
> to wontreaðe, world abuten ende.   (160/26–28)

> *He gives you sin, and you give him your soul and your body too, to its*
> *own pain and misery, world without end.*

The Rule has made frequent use of the figure of the prisoner since his first appearance in 'Custody', where the occasion of a 'secular' crime is the opening of the pit into which the animal falls. The anchoress will be charged at a future time: 'Heo is gulti of þe bestes deaðe biuoren vre louerd & schal uor his soule onswerien adomesdei' (Nero 25/24–26). The prisoner reappears in 'Regulation' as part of the lesson on patience, but there is promise of release as ransom is gathered:

> A mon þe leie i prisun, oðer ahte muche rancun, ne o nane wise ne
> schulde ut bute hit were to hongin ear he hefde his rancun fulleliche
> ipaiet, nalde he cunne god þonc a mon þe duste uppon him of
> peonehes a bigurdel forte reimin him wið & lesen him of pine, þah
> he wurpe hit ful hearde aʒeines his heorte?   (66/17–23)

> *If a man had either to remain in prison or else pay a high ransom,*
> *except to be hanged, would he not be very grateful to anyone who threw*
> *a bag of money at him, with which he could settle the debt and set himself*
> *free from suffering, even if it were thrown violently against his heart?*

4. See particularly 'Custody' (60/16–22), on the threefold piercing of Christ's body (affliction of touch): 'þis stiche wes þreouald, þe ase þreo speren smat him to þe heorte. Þe an wes his modres wop & te oþres maries . . . '

The alternative of the ransom is death by hanging, in purgatory or hell:

> For wið ute cwitance up of þis prisun nis nan inumen þet nis anan
> ahonget, oðer i purgatoire oþer i þe pine of helle.   (67/2–4)

Conversely, imprisonment and hanging in imitation of Christ is a
reasonable extension of the metaphor. The figure of the prisoner has
served to show the value of suffering as, for instance, in 'Custody,' where
the prisoner is Christ Himself, scorned, humiliated, and hanged;[5] and in
'Regulation' in the martyrdom of Sts. Andrew and Stephen and Lawrence.[6] Christ as felon is suggested in 65/24–26:

> Efter alle þe schendfule pinen þet he þolede oþe longe friniht, me
> leadde him ine marhen to hongin o wearitreo, & driuen þurh his
> fowr limen irnene neiles.

> *After all the ignominious tortures that He suffered during the long night*
> *before the Friday, He was led out the next morning to be hung upon a*
> *felon's gibbet, and iron nails were driven into His four limbs.*

He is reviled and tormented in 97/28–98/17 of 'Temptations':

> Ouer alle oþre þohtes, in alle ower passiuns, þencheð eauer
> inwardliche up o godes pinen, þet te worldes wealdent walde for
> his þrealles þolien swucche schendlakes, hokeres, buffez, spatlunge,
> blindfeallunge, þornene crununge . . . his swete bodi ibunden
> naket to þe hearde pilar & ibeate swa þet tet deorewurðe blod ron
> on euche halue.   (97/28–7)

> *Above all other thoughts, in all your sufferings, think always within you of*
> *the sufferings of God, and that the Ruler of the world was willing to suffer*
> *for his servants such ignominy, derision, blows, being spat upon, being*
> *blindfolded, being crowned with thorns . . . having His sweet body bound*
> *naked to the hard pillar and so beaten that the precious blood ran down on*
> *every side.*

5. See 56/7–63/5.
6. *AW* 65/10–15.

Christ and Judas are compared in 147/11–13:

> Ba weren ahonget, ah Iudas for his gult; Iesu wið ute gult for his muchele godlec wes ahon o rode.
>
> *Both were hanged, but only Judas for his guilt. Jesus, guiltless, out of His great goodness, was hung upon the cross.*

'Whose companion will you be?' the Rule asks in 'Temptations.' But the choice is not easily settled, as the events of 'Confession' prove.

Now that the figure of prisoner emerges as dominant in a context of judgment and sentence in Part Five, his condition is that of the abject, unredeemed sinner (for he has lost through persistent sin all affinity to Christ and the spiritual family), and he stands condemned to hang on the burning gallows for all eternity. The severity of the judgment is heightened by the knowledge of irretrievable loss:

> A mon þe hefde al þe world o walde, & hefde for his cweadschipe forloren al on a stunde, hu he walde murnin & sari iwurðen. Þenne ahest tu to beon hundret siðe sarure þe þurh an heaued sunne forlure þe riche of heouene, forlure ure lauerd þet is hundret siðen—ȝe, þusent þusent siðen—betere þen is al þe world. (160/1–6)
>
> *If a man had had the whole world in his power, and had lost it all in a moment because of his wickedness, how he would mourn, and how he would turn to grieving. You, then, should grieve a hundred times more, who by one mortal sin lost the kingdom of heaven, lost Our Lord who is a hundred times, yes, and a thousand thousand times better than all the world.*

In tone and circumstance this passage approaches the grief of the parent at the child's death in 159/6 ff. ('his children sone se he sunegede deadliche deiden alle clane, þet beoð his gode werkes') and, in addition, the language of 'bitter confession' 159/18–2: 'ȝef a mon hefde ilosed in a time of þe dei his feader ant his moder, his sustren & his breðren . . .'; moreover, it sweeps into this spiral (the single example of extended image development of 'Confession') the next illustration of loss—the child who betrays his guardian and wars against his father, the king. The 'beloved

son' joins the enemy, grieves his father and ruins himself.[7] The heavenly
Father, translated along with the child and the guardians to a human,
chivalric setting, admits pity and forgiveness; the son and sinner may
make reparation and so be restored to favor: 'Vre lauerd deð toward us
as me deð to uuel deatter. Nimeð leasse þen we ahen him & is þah wel
ipaiet.' (161/25–26).

The contrapuntal playlet of the fierce and pitiless judgment on the
Last Day yields finally to the closing, equally intense demand for payment of a blood debt, yet one of such enormous dimension that whatever
is given is only a token of what is owed. So God accepts less than His due,
as a father generously cancels his child's debt:

> We ahen him blod for blod, ant ure blod þah aȝein his blod þet he
> schedde for us were ful unefne change. . . . Ant ure lauerd nimeð
> ed us ure teares aȝein his blod, & is wilcweme.   (161/26–3)

> *We owe Him blood for blood, and even so, our blood for His blood, which
> He shed for us, would be a very unequal exchange. . . . And Our Lord
> accepts our tears from us in exchange for His blood, and is well pleased.*

The shedding of tears (as of blood, which washed away the sins of the
world) makes confession bitter, and God is satisfied. The anchoress will
be spared tears at the Last Judgment because she has wept bitterly at
confession. The bath of tears or of blood (the human and divine atonement), related here to a bloodletting, is to be taken up again in Part
Seven, when with a baptism in blood the mother saves her child from
death, immediate and everlasting.[8]

The unity of theme in the practice of bitter confession is sufficiently

7. Service in the devil's court had been elaborated in 109/3–112/11, as part of the
personification of the Seven Deadly Sins. The nourishing of the devil's child is an
incidental motif, beginning as early as 'Custody' 44/17–20: 'Þe deouel is leas & leasunge
feader. Þe ilke þenne þe stureð hire tunge i leasunge ha makeð of hire tunge cradel to þe
deofles bearn & rockeð hit ȝeornliche as his nurrice'; also, in 110/14–16: 'Þe slawe lið &
slepeð o þe deofles bearm as his deore deorling.' In 'Confession' the devil's child is
identified as the unredeemed sinner: 'Ȝet up on al þis ilke he is him seolf biwrixlet &
bicumen of godes child þe deofles bearn of helle.' (160/8–10).

8. *AW* 201/2–202/24, the third of the four loves of this world, anticipating the Christ-
knight sacrifice.

strong to provide a moral base for future development of image motifs, such as the fetid wound and the condemned man. The analogies contained in the examples of loss are sketched here:

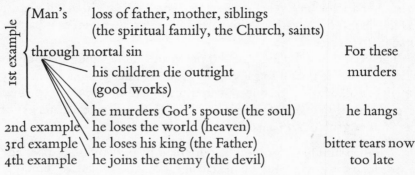

Man's	loss of father, mother, siblings (the spiritual family, the Church, saints)	
through mortal sin		For these
	his children die outright (good works)	murders
	he murders God's spouse (the soul)	he hangs
2nd example	he loses the world (heaven)	
3rd example	he loses his king (the Father)	bitter tears now
4th example	he joins the enemy (the devil)	too late

The next segment, 'Schrift schal beon ihal' (161/8), carries forward the element of tears, which had completed the 'bitter' confession. The setting has changed, shifting from the grand scale in which kingdoms are lost and retaken to a humble house where the poor widow sweeps up the dust into small piles. The connection of 'poor widow,' anchoress, and bereaved sinner of bitter confession is obscured by the change in tone and action, and the lesson conveyed that the sinner must clean his conscience by first purging himself of great sins, and then of lesser, is more obtrusive than lessons of the past. But the Rule is bringing another application of the need for confession into the anchorhold, as it has done on many occasions with exactly the same terms and bustle of homely life.[9] The confession is broadened with the outpouring of tears, for like the poor widow, the anchoress sprinkles the water of tears upon the 'dust of lihte þohtes' lest it fly about and blind the eyes of the heart.

Moreover, the pernicious wounds that threaten the life of the soul pursue the sinner into 'Confession,' in the example of the man with so many wounds that he neglects to show them all to the doctor. In keeping

9. The sins treated as household nuisances occur in 'Temptations' 107/18–20, the scorpion of lechery that is to be shaken out with confession and killed with penance; also, in 110/23–111/9, the devil's 'cinder-jack,' who sweeps together heaps of ashes. In 129/9–12, dust and grit hold together against puffs of wind. Here the example of strength in union is to be followed by anchoress.

hidden the least of them 'he deieð up on as he schulde on alle.'[10] The possibility of cure now lies within his reach, however, in the frank confession of all sins, great and small, even those of childhood. Citing the holy man saved from disease by so complete a confession, the author brings the lesson home to the privileged world of the anchoress. The matter ends with the expected exhortation to 'look into the corners of the heart' and (like the poor widow who sweeps dust into piles), push out the smaller sins after the greater.

Naked confession is to be stripped clean, the sin shamelessly exposed. (We recall how one wound untreated caused the death of the whole man.) The author rejects fine rhetoric and fancy phrases that mitigate the offense, as his own violent language shows when he lashes out at sexual sin:

> Spec hit scheome schendfulliche ant tuk hit al towundre alswa as þu wel wult schende þen schucke. Sire, ha seið þe wummon, ich habbe ihaued leofmon, oðer ich habbe ibeon, ha seið, fol of me seoluen. Þis nis nawt naket schrift. Biclute þu hit nawt. Do awei þe totagges. Vnwrih þe & sei, Sire, godes are! Ich am a ful stod meare, a stinkinde hore. (162/18–163/26)

> *Speak of its shame with obloquy and strike it violently just as you would want wholeheartedly to injure the devil. 'Sir,' a woman will say, 'I have had a lover,' or she will say, 'I have been foolish about myself.' This is not naked confession. Do not wrap it up. Take off the trimmings. Make yourself clear and say: 'Sir, God's mercy! I am a foul stud mare, a stinking whore.'*

10. An echo of St. Bernard's warning: 'For what is the use of confessing some of the sins and hiding others, endeavoring to purge a part of thy conscience and to leave the remainder in filth? . . . Thou must fully expose thy wounds if thou desire to have them healed by the doctor.' *Sermons*, III, 454. Confession and penance as analogous to the cure of infection was an inevitable development once the correspondence of physical-spiritual disease became evident. By the twelfth century, parallel medical procedure and sacrament had been worked out, as in the commentary of Alain de Lille: 'Compunction, therefore, stirs up, confession accuses, satisfaction strengthens; compunction searches out the occasion of the disease, confession manifests it, satisfaction cures it . . . . Compunction punctures the ulcer, confession forces out the pus, satisfaction applies the poultice. Compunction finds the wound, confession lays it open, satisfaction restores health.' *De sex alis cherubim*, PL 210, col. 275.

Bold though the author demands the confession be, and nakedly though he would have the fact of sin revealed, he cannot bring himself to name the sin. Nakedness in sin, nakedness of confession, nakedness throughout most of the segment—in the paucity of images, the absence of allegory—all yield for the moment to the practice and procedure of naked confession as he explores the six facets (person, place, time, manner, circumstance, frequency) of the commission of sin. The special 'perspective' of the segment is the interdependency of form and content, for the recitative dominates, not the imaginative. The spoken word stripped bare of ornament (rare in the Rule) is bitterly frank in exposing sins of deed and of thought as well. The Rule leaves no room for excuses or neglect; the 'how' of naked confession has been scrupulously detailed, and if sins lay concealed from her confessor, the anchoress can expect that they will be bared before the three kingdoms of earth, hell, and heaven for all to see and then tied around her neck as a noose is fixed to a thief. The resurgence of imagery brings back the figure of the condemned man about to be hanged; but now he is more loathsome because his 'foul purulent sores,' his sins, are revealed to the wide world. Here, then, the two motifs meet and combine: the wretched sinner condemned by *disease* to *hang on a gallows*.

The dangers increase as confession is delayed; thus, 'Schrift schal beon on hihðe imaket.' The soul lies in perpetual threat of relapse into sin; so the urgency of the sacrament is emphasized in the 'nine reasons' for speedy confession. Thus we have a list within a list, for we are still within the compass of a 'whole' confession, although the names of categories have changed. Within the unit, the figure of the devil as creditor of the sinner emerges. He lends sin and exacts usurious interest in punishment:

For sunne is þe deofles feh þet he ȝeueð to okere & to gauel of pine; & eauer se mon lið lengre in his sunne, so þe gauel waxeð of pine i purgatoire, oðer her, oðer in helle.   (166/1–4)

For sin is the devil's money, which he gives out, charging the interest of punishment, and the longer a man lies in his sin, so the interest grows, the interest of punishment—in purgatory, or here, or in hell.

The commerce with the devil, the interest paid 'in purgatory, on earth or in hell' is reduced to the familiar motif of the man assailed by sickness, groaning in pain, unable to purge himself—'grunting more for his stitch than for his sin' (167/11).[11] The punishment exacted here applies as well to the man condemned, the thief who is to pay with his life. But the wound, which has plagued the sinner, is worthy of a groan or two, for it grows worse steadily:

þe wunde . . . eauer wurseð on hond & strengre is to healen.

(167/13–14)

The wound grown so fetid that it will soon allow of no mortal cure merges with the next 'reason,' dominated by the figure of the rotting body of Lazarus, stinking in the grave for four days before Christ raised him up (167/15–20). The author's harried cry—his horror—at four or five years' accumulation of stinking sin has barely time to resound before the dogs are at the body: 'Monie hundes, seið dauið, habbeð biset me' (167/25).[12] Thus, while the author evokes a total effect of the dogs rending the carcass, these descant images are anagogical inversions of the allegorical action at hand—the cudgeling of the dog with a rod as he snaps at food on the table. In 'Temptations' the dog of hell was beaten back with the crucifix. More recently, in the recital of 'naked confession' there is at least an allusion to the beating ('Spec hit scheome schendfulliche ant tuk al towundre alswa as þu wel wult schende þen schucke'). Here, it is the rod of the tongue in confession that strikes him down, beats him into submission:

Ah, ananriht, beat, beat, beat, ananriht. Nis þing i þe world þet smeorteð him sarre þen deð swuch beatunge.   (168/10–12)

---

11. 'When pain binds the limbs and grief oppresses the sense, a man can scarcely think of anything else. Therefore, if you wish to be secure, do penance while you are sound.' Hugh of St. Victor, *On the Sacraments*, p. 412.

12. 'The third dead is Lazarus. There is a dreadful kind of death, it is called evil custom. For it is one thing to sin, another to make a custom of sinning. He that sins and is forthwith corrected, soon comes to life again. . . . But he that has accustomed himself to sin, is buried, and it is well said of him, *He Stinketh.*' St. Augustine, 'Homily XLIX,' *Homilies on St. John* (Oxford, 1876), II, 651.

Not only must sin be purged as a boil is lanced to rid the body of corruption (and the pounding rhythms of the author's language bring to mind physical disciplines to quiet the flesh), but it must be quickly done through speedy confession before the rottenness spreads, infecting healthy parts. One sin follows upon another, as we had seen demonstrated as far back as 'Custody of the Senses.'

The Rule has developed the motif of the wound to the point of dissolution of the body. Presumably, with confession having advanced this far, slow recovery is in sight, for the Rule takes a curious turn now. The pivot is Lazarus. His example has brought the body to the grave—into the grave and out! He has also returned the Rule to biblical passages and the world of Jesus. The author's call for humility and noiseless performance of good works in 'Schrift ah to beon eadmod' is conveyed through the image of the wound and the Pharisee who parades what is sound 'þa he schulde habben unwihen hise wunden' (168/24). There can be no cure for him as he hides what is unclean. But humble confession (like the publican's) transforms odious sores into graces:

> Eadmodnesse is ilich þeose cointe hearloz, hare gute feastre, hare flowinde cweise þet ha putteð eauer forð.   (168/26–27)

Humility is like those crafty rogues who always parade their running sores.

The paradox is startling, the turn wholly unexpected. Like the beggar who cleverly shows his deformities to the rich man in hope of moving him to pity (and generosity), so must the sinner 'wið seli truandise' open his sores to Christ's sight and so win Him by 'showing forth his cancer.' The tone and imagery are hardly delicate, but they are intended to emphasize the abject, even disgusting state of the body warped by sin. So, to win the aid of the Physician, confession is to be humble and importunate:

> Wið þus anewil ropunge halseð efter sum help to þe wrecche meoseise, to lechni wið þe seke to healen hire cancre.   (169/12–14)

Thus, with insistent demands, entreat some help for the creature who is sick, so that she may have a physician and her cancer be healed.

Implored this way, Christ cannot withhold His pity, who seeks the slightest reason for giving.

The cure is begun with a symbolic bloodletting, familiar from 'Regulation' as a way to purge the body of disease and restore the life of the soul. Red shame in confession, typified in 'Schrift ah to beon scheomeful' by the passing of the Israelites across the Red Sea 'þet wes read & bitter,' is the way to pass into heaven. Red is the color of life; the red face in confession is a sign that the soul that has been wan has been restored to life: 'icaht cwic heow & is irudet feire,' (169/11–12). Blood, humiliation, sacrifice—partial cures at best even when faithfully enacted by the anchoress. We must wait for Part Seven and the shedding of the blood of a red man, Christ, before total cure is possible.

The gradual change that has been taking place in the course of the confession is that the further inward the sacrament moves, the more determined and contrite the penitent becomes, the easier is his access to God's mercy. This new development, subtly assuming form during the process of naked confession, takes on impetus in humble confession where Christ's generosity begs to be released. Finally, the terrible prophecy of accusatory confession ('lomb her liun þer') succumbs to the promise of mercy: 'Ah his mearci toward us weieð eauer mare þen þe rihte' (170/22).

The bounds of divine mercy and justice are qualified in the two converging particulars of confession, 'Schrift schal beo dredful' and 'Schrift schal beon hopeful.' These directives establish the attitude of confession: hope not unmixed with fear: 'Ah hope & dred schulen aa beon imengt togederes.' The opposites of these, the two vices of despair and presumption, wait to entrap the 'poor animal' who darts like the hare from dogs to the snare. Despair and presumption (the extreme conditions of the diseased man of 'Temptations') are compared to cruel thieves ('grimme robberes') who rob God of mercy on the one hand and justice on the other. The image clearly is of Christ suspended between the two thieves; the cross, a judgment-throne; the robbery on both sides, the one thief (despair and presumption) who mocked and was lost, the other thief (hope and fear) who believed and was saved. The one thief robbed Him of mercy; the other, who robbed Him of his justice, won His mercy, though he deserved less.

Examples of the penalty of presumption—the leap into pride of Satan and then of Adam and Eve, the destruction of whole cities and of the world—are balanced by proofs of Christ's immeasurable mercy, His 'unimete milce.' So, St. Peter, who denied Him, was forgiven; so, the thief, who knew Him, was saved. The figure of the condemned man has become symbolic proof of mercy granted because of a 'feier speche' (full confession). The parallel figure of accusatory and bitter confession had gone to the gallows utterly lost. But the power of confession is such that for the contrite sinner who practices the sacrament in the manner described by the author, God's pardon is assured.

And so, anchoress, if she will come this far in the performance of confession, will not only save herself from the gallows and restore her young (her good works) as the pelican had, but, like the good thief, will secure a place for herself in Paradise. The remaining particulars of the practice of confession are concerned largely with procedural details.

We come then to the end, rewards, promises of ineffable sweetness. Truthful confession ('Schrift ah to beon soð'), which encloses a call for moderation against the offense of excessive humility, is completely barren of imagery, but it provides a link by touching on those things pleasing to God to the next segment on voluntary confession ('Schrift ah to beon willes'), which is heavily colored with phrases and images from Canticles.

The extending of grace is God's prerogative entirely; therefore, confession must be voluntary and not drawn out as if against the will:

Hwen godd beot hit te, reach to ba þe honden, for wiðdrahe he his hond, þu maht þrefter lokin.   (173/5–7)

When God offers it to you, reach out to it with both hands, for if He should withdraw His hand, you might look for it later in vain.

Once again, the anchoress has been urged to receive God's comfort willingly.[13] But what is noteworthy is the change in relations between

13. The same warning against the pride of delay or refusal occurs in 'Temptations,' 134/11–14; 'Ne nawt ne schule we forsaken þe grace of godes sonde, ah þonkin him ӡeorne leste he wreaðe him wið us & wiðdrahe his large hond & þrefter wið to muche wone abeate ure prude.'

God and sinner from the first parts of confession to the last, where the privilege of choice, wise or foolish, is granted to the anchoress who has grown worthy of God's generosity. We have only to compare the imagery of accusatory and bitter confession with the language of this segment to measure her progress. The wounds have closed:

Mi flesch is ifluret, bicumen al neowe.   (173/13–14)

'My flesh has flowered, has become completely new again.'

For þe eorðe al unnet, & te treon alswa openið ham & bringeð forð misliche flures.   (173/15–16)

For earth and trees open in all freedom to send out their many flowers.

Culures unlaðnesse & oþre swucche uertuz beoð feire i godes ehnen, & swote i godes nease smeallinde flures. Of ham make his herbearhe inwið þe seoluen, for his delices. . . . beoð þer forte wunien.   (173/18–21)

The mildness of a dove and other like virtues are beautiful in God's eyes, flowers which to Him smell sweet. Make of them His arbour within yourselves, for it is His delight . . . to dwell there.

Within the promise of renewal there converge reminiscences of the sweetness pleasing to God in 'Custody':

Hope as a sweet spice in the heart—
  Ah hwa se cheoweð spice ha schal tunen hire muð þet te swote breað & te strengðe þrof leaue wið innen.   (43/25–29)

The sweet voice and fair face—
  Ich ihere mi leof speoken. He cleopeð me. Ich mot gan. Ant ȝe gan ananriht to ower deore leofmon & meaneð ow to his earen þe luueliche cleopeð ow to him wið þes wordes . . . Hihe þe heonewart, & cum to me, mi leofmon, mi culure, mi feire, & mi schene spuse.   (52/19–26)

The earth and trees of 'Regulation' where the bird had set her nest were signs of life and growth. In 'Confession' the trees flower in token of spiritual health. In 'Temptations' the refuge of the dove was Christ's wounds. Now, borrowing the verse from Canticles 2:12: 'The flowers have appeared in our land,' the author adds the suggestive 'Of ham make his herbearhe inwið þe seoluen' (173/20), into which Christ may come. This special arbor, this nest, waits to receive Christ, and the mystery is conveyed in the blending of English and Latin:

> Of ham make his herbearhe inwið þe seoluen, for his delices, he seið, beoð þer forte wunien. Et delicie mee esse cum filiis hominum.
>
> (173/20–22)

With this, we turn to 'Penance,' *dead bote*, the critical inner reparation.

SIX 'PENANCE'

Whether martyred by a hard life into the company of the saints or crucified 'night and day upon God's cross,' the anchoress becomes more than
Christ*like*; symbolically, she becomes one with Christ. Penance, the
successor of confession, prepares the soul for grace and finds the heart
inured to sacrifice for the sake of good works.

We begin with anagogue, Part Six having been conveyed there by the
graduated movement of 'Confession,' the preliminary and purgative
element of the sacrament. Satisfaction is about to be made simultaneously
by anchoress and Christ, both of whom were brought to the cross in
'Confession.'

The vital connection of parts is repeated in the language of the opening
sentences, which, though it expands almost identical lines from the end
of 'Confession,' clearly shows the conversion from literal to anagogic
penance:

Al þet god þet tu eauer dest & al
þe vuel þet tu eauer þolest for
þe luue of iesu crist inwið þine
ancre wahes, al ich engoini þe,
al ich legge up o þe i remission
of þeose & i forȝeuenesse of
alle þine sunnen.

('Confession' 176/1–177/4)

Al is penitence, ant strong
penitence, þet ȝe eauer dreheð,
mine leoue sustren. Al þet ȝe
eauer doð of god, al þet ȝe
þolieð is ow martirdom i se derf
ordre, for ȝe beoð niht & dei up
o godes rode.

('Penance' 177/13–18)

*'I enjoin and impose on you, for the
remission of these sins and for the
forgiveness of all your sins, all for
the good that you ever perform and
all the harm that you ever endure
for love of Jesus Christ within your
anchoress's dwelling.'*

*All that you ever suffer, my dear
sisters, all is penance, and hard
penance. All the good you ever do
and everything that you suffer in
such a hard 'Order' is martyrdom
for you, for you are night and day
upon God's cross.*

The change of role of the anchoress reflects the allegorical history of the
condemned man who has passed through the terrors of human and divine
judgment and glanced at heaven. Now, the language and imagery of
suffering and martyrdom are introduced into the anchorhold itself,
where all good that is done and all hardship borne is continual penance.

The Rule has gradually developed the theme of desirability of martyrdom, citing throughout the exemplary conduct of the saints, of Mary,
and of Christ, exhorting the anchoress to imitate the patience and humility of the martyrs, insisting that the sanctity of her mission be preserved
at whatever cost. Related to this is the motif of the prisoner in his several
roles as hostage, thief, murderer, and finally, as demonstrated in 'Confession,' as a penitent, sharing Christ's disgrace and saved by 'a few good
words': 'O þe þeof o rode þe hefde aa iliued uuele in a stert hwile hefde
ed him milce wið a feier speche' (171/16–17). In 'Penance' the distinction
between the types is wiped away:

> As ȝe scottið wið him of his pine on eorðe, ȝe schule scotti wið
> him of his blisse in heouene.   (177/19–21)

*As you share His suffering with Him on earth so you will share His joy
with Him in heaven.*

The cross is the most significant figure in 'Penance,' as the symbol not
only of suffering but of the penitent's special role in Christ's Passion.
That the recluse 'whose joy should consist completely in God's cross' is
numbered among the elect of God is a truth already in evidence when
the author digresses into the 'sentences' of St. Bernard on the three kinds
of men 'of godes icoren': the pilgrim, the dead man, and the man that is
crucified.[1] The calculated interruption of the chapter at this early point
has merit beyond the obvious authority of patristic exegesis. In the free
rendering of St. Bernard's sermon, the author is able to recapitulate
events and ideas that have occurred in previous chapters and make some
anticipatory remarks about Part Seven, 'Love.' And as the highest degree
of divine election—the man hanged of his free will on the cross—is the
last of the three to be discussed, the momentum generated by the preliminary subjects makes a more forceful impact. Each step or degree is

1. 'De peregrino, mortuo et crucifixo,' *Sermons*, II, 107–111.

more exalted than the last, each has special relevance to the experience of the anchoress, each ends in a symbolic death.

We might look at this unit as a record of the author's technique. Thus the first member of the triad, the pilgrim on the way to a shrine, is analogous to the anchoress whose journey leads to heaven. But hers is the superior way, for she travels diligently, ignoring the pleasures and distractions of the wayside 'to finden godd seolf & alle his hali halhen liuiende i blisse.' Yet even the determined pilgrim can stumble along the way or give himself up to a pleasant diversion and not arrive home at all. Who, then, the author asks in a rather sweeping rhetorical thrust that touches the ingenuous, who could be better than good pilgrims? who purer? who less attached to the world? 'Hwa beoð betere þene þeos?' Those who are dead, is his reply, dead and hidden with Christ, ready to spring up with Him 'like the dawn after the darkness of night':

> Ant ȝe schulen wið him springen schenre þen þe sunne in to eche blisse.
> (179/15–16)

> *You shall rise with Him, fairer than the sun, into eternal joy.*

The 'dead' life is one unperturbed by accidents or corruption of the flesh 'þah he ligge unburiet & rotie buuen eorðe.' This paradoxical death to the world assures mastery over the senses and inward feelings. It is at once the means and the end of the religious life. Anger, vainglory, envy, malice are overcome:

> Preise him, laste him, do him scheome, sei him scheome. Al him is iliche leof.
> (179/18–19)

> *Praise him, blame him, do him shameful injury by word or deed—all these things please him equally.*

This singular death that quickens life in man or woman becomes the way by which Christ enters into physically inert flesh, for 'God lives in the heart of whoever is dead in this way.'

Though he is working with Bernard's sermon, the author has refashioned the text to make it conform to his practice of overlayering of phrases and imagery so that a continuum is created, one part passing into the next. Thus the series of questions beginning with 'Hwa is þenne skerre & mare ut of þe world þen pilegrimes' (175/9-6) and ending with 'Hwa beoð betere þene þeos?' (179/9) actually concludes the first example of the good pilgrim, but is placed within the discussion of the second, on the dead life hidden with Christ.[2] Yet even this symbolic death connoting total dedication and self-denial goes begging before the third and highest degree, the man who is crucified:

> Crist me schilde forte habben eani blisse i þis world bute i iesu cristes rode mi lauerd, þurh hwam þe world is me unwurð, ant ich am unwurð hire as weari þe is ahonget.   (180/3-6)

> *Christ forbid that I should have any joy in this world except in the cross of Jesus Christ my Lord, because of whom the world has no value for me and I have as little honour before the world as a criminal who has been hanged.*

The body rendered insensate by death to the world is renewed on the cross by an act of penance. The rule leaves no doubt that at this stage the only purposeful theme is the crucifixion, which the anchoress must suffer as bitter penance:

> For al hare blisse is forte beon ahonget sariliche & scheomeliche wið iesu on his rode.   (180/24-26)

> *For all their joy lies in being crucified in pain and dishonour with Jesus on His cross.*

The motif of hanging on the gallows, then, pursues the anchoress into 'Penance' where the act is penance indeed, but totally changed in nature as the anchoress has changed. An offense against the world would send the common thief to his death; but to be hanged *sariliche, scheomeliche*, to suffer *i scheome & i wa* bring the anchoress to the high pitch of her progress —pain and dishonor—and the Rule to the central premise, the ascent to God through toil and humility.

2. The first degree of the elect extends from 178/4 to 178/27; the next begins on 178/27; 'Nv beoð þeose gode, ah ȝet beoð þe oþre betere,' but regresses immediately into praise of the pilgrim before it is developed separately.

To convey the special sense of her 'elevation,' the author takes three mystical symbols of the upward ascent and entry into Paradise: the ladder, the wheel and the fiery sword (181/7 ff.). Less obvious in the rendering of these images is the persistence of more mundane conditions of labor and humility which exist side by side with mystical symbolism. While the mystical wheels spin furiously across the heavens, the feet of the anchoress are standing on terra firma. The vital movement of images from the arduous climb up the rungs of the spiritual ladder to the rapt advance of the fiery chariot, its wheels red, hot, spinning upward, tends to obscure the more dramatic mounting of the cross in red blood and pain occurring simultaneously.

Arranged into images, the spiraling attitude of the symbols builds in this way:

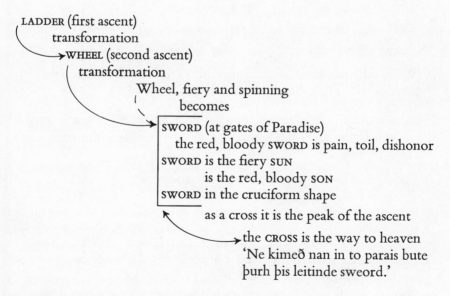

LADDER (first ascent)
    transformation
      →WHEEL (second ascent)
        transformation
            Wheel, fiery and spinning
                becomes
              →SWORD (at gates of Paradise)
                  the red, bloody SWORD is pain, toil, dishonor
              SWORD is the fiery SUN
                  is the red, bloody SON
              SWORD in the cruciform shape
                    as a cross it is the peak of the ascent
                    →the CROSS is the way to heaven
                      'Ne kimeð nan in to parais bute
                      þurh þis leitinde sweord.'

The ladder is assimilated into the wheel which, hot and spinning, merges with the image of the sword—each gradation representing an ascent up to the entry of Paradise. The sword, by its flame and motion, is the sun; by its shape it is a cross; by its purpose it is an instrument of death or pain. None may enter Paradise but by this flaming sword, this cross.

Examining the passage thematically, we see that shame and suffering are, 'as sein Beornard seið,' the two sides of the ladder that leads to heaven, the rungs being the virtues. By this ladder, David, 'þah he king were' and 'godes deorling,' climbed   up: 'Bihald, quoð he, & sih min eadmodnesse & mi swinc.' The initial ascent in labor and humility is equated with the ladder, but in the author's expansion of *swinc* and *eadmodnesse* are contained the elements of the next stage of the ascent. So—

> þes twa word . . . swinc & eadmodnesse—swinc i pine & i wa, i sar
> & i sorhe; eadmodnesse aȝein woh of scheome þet mon dreheð
> þe is itald unwurð.   (181/16–18)

'These two words' which were, in connection with the ladder, labor and humility now become pain and shame, the very substance of the appositive qualifier. Pain and shame so joined together form the wheels of Elijah's chariot:

> Wa & scheome ifeiet to gederes beoð helyes hweoles þe weren
> furene, hit teleð, & beren him up to parais.   (181/23–24)

Elijah's wheels, which carried him up to Paradise, were made of fire. From this figure springs the image of fire, hot and red, that afflicts the body as it purges:

> Fur is hat & read. Iþe heate is understonden euch wa þet eileð
> flesch. Scheome bi þe reade.   (181/25–26)

The revolving wheel, an instrument of such penance as martyrs endure, is of short duration on earth ('ouerturneð sone, ne leasteð nane hwile'). But when it has carried the chariot to the gates, the wheel becomes the Cherubim's sword—flaming, spinning, hot, and red.

The transformation of the red sword into the red cross represents the critical apodosis, when the symbols are 'humanized' and come to rest in the present, in the anchorhold and in the mortal body of Christ. The two routes or approaches to Paradise, whether through symbols or designation, have always been but one, that of toil and sorrow. The ascent has been upward to the arms of the cross:

Ne kimeð nan in to parais bute þurh þis leitinde
sweord þe wes | hat & read. | (181/2–3)

And nes godes rode wið his deorewurðe
blod irudet & ireadet

forte schawin on him seolf

þet pine, & sorhe, & sar schulden
wið scheome beon iheowet? (182/5–7)

*No one enters Paradise but by this flaming sword, which was hot and
red . . . And was not God's cross made red so that He might show in His
own Person that suffering and sorrow and grief should be coloured with
dishonour?*

Whatever possibilities of further development of such images and shapes
and colors remain are realized in Part Seven in the passages on Greek fire,
the red hanged man; and in the case of Elijah's wheels and the revolving
sword, the figure of the sun, symbolic of divinity, rising to take its place
'o þe hehe rode.'

Pain and dishonor are in no way new themes in the Rule. The pain of
diseased wounds, the dishonor of imprisonment and shameful death,
pervade the work. The anagogic sense of a humiliating death by which
the anchoress is crucified with Christ has a practical application in her
narrow world where she is already accounted dead and has received the
rites of burial. The sacrifices of everyday life, the battles with venality,
and the humiliation she may suffer from time to time are part of a penitential life, and the author must bring this fact into the anchorhold.
Temporal duties, bits and pieces of personal advice, seem a rude deflation
from mystical flights of dying with Christ, but practical matters have a
real place in her world too; there is an outer life as well as an inner.

Thus far, there have been two approaches to the cross set forth. The
first occurred in the recital of the elect of God, the third member—whoever is crucified with Christ—surpassing his companions in sacrifice.
The second approach, a mystical experience, carried the anchoress by
means of Elijah's chariot to the red sword, a symbolic crucifix—and
beyond; in fact, directly to the gates of Paradise.

There is now a third approach presented, which takes the penitent to the cross, through the gates of Paradise, to the Judgment seat itself. But she comes not to be judged—has the anchoress as one 'of godes icoren' anything to fear?—but to take a place of honor where she will judge others. Each of the segments generates motion, by walking, mounting, or coursing through space. But in the last of these progressions, Judgment, she rests. Rest, symbolized by the *seat* of honor in heaven, completes her journey, which, paradoxically, must be made with toil.

Toil and rest, impossible of coexistence in this world or the next, are the moral imperatives. Her toil evolves from the passage of the penitent through a foreign land toward her home, for 'one works away from home, but at home one may rest.' Rest is the reward of successful battle in the world of persistent warfare; rest is the end of the arduous passing: 'reste abit us ed hame in ure ahne lond' (183/9–10).

The strange land where the anchoress as a pilgrim (one of God's elect) finds herself is this world, and her journey is beset with trouble. We know from 'Temptations' that the anchoress has undergone trials of the wilderness on the way to the 'high Jerusalem', as the children of Israel had done before:

> Bi þis wildernesse wende ure lauerdes folc . . . Ant ȝe, mine leoue sustren, wendeð bi þe ilke wei toward te hehe ierusalem, þe kinedom þet he haueð bihaten his icorene.
>
> ('Temptations,' 101/16–20)

The crossing brings her finally to her home:

> Ha schulen, seið ysaie, in hare ahne lond wealden twuald blisse, aȝein twuald wa þet ha her dreheð.   (182/23–25)
>
> *In their own land they shall possess a twofold happiness, for the twofold suffering which they endured here.*

A seat, the author says, signifies rest and ease 'in contrast to the toil that is here.' In heaven the seat of never-ending rest is granted to God's elect, those who, like the anchoress, have passed from a hard and servile life to a place of rest and honor.

The exceptional change in her relation to God from 'Confession' is that she is no longer among the judged (saved or damned), but joins in the act of judgment, a kingly privilege reserved for those elected in patience and humility. A further change is that the will seems now to be fully resigned to this potential elevation even though a period of suffering is to be borne:

> Nis þer nu þenne bute þolien gleadliche.   (183/20–21)
> *There is nothing for us, then, but to suffer gladly.*

Her will and Christ's will are in conformity—ideally, at least. But this very important line does more than merely affirm the anchoress' readiness to suffer. Structurally, it binds together the three approaches to heaven the entire chapter has thus far drawn in the figures of God's elect, Elijah's chariot, and the seat of rest. (We sense in the author's interrupter *þenne* a pause that means to say, *After all I have told you, after all that has been promised you, surely you will accept this cup as your portion.*) The line serves to initiate a series of positive converses that contains within the opposing clauses the inherent dichotomy of earthly deprivation and heavenly reward:

to suffer pain here	to rise in happiness later
to share the likeness of His . . . . death	to share His likeness at the resurrection
to live in dishonor and in . . . . suffering	to be made bright as He was at His resurrection
to let others adorn their . . . . bodies	to be adorned by Him as He was adorned

$$(183/24–184/10)$$

This set of conditions by which heaven is won at the cost of this world acts to summarize medially within the chapter the arguments for earthly dishonor and suffering, such as have been depicted in imagery up to now. Yet within this segment another motif begins to take form out of the very nature of these conditions—the delicate but palpable idea of contractual obligation, of a covenant between man and God in which 'the profit motive' is the incentive. Man enters into an agreement with God whose part is deferred to a future time:

> ʒef we þolieð wið him, we schule blissin wið him. Nis þis god foreward? Wat crist, nis he nawt god feolahe ne treowe þe nule scottin i þe lure as eft i þe biʒete. (184/9–12)

> *If we suffer, we shall also reign with Him. Is not this a reasonable covenant? Christ knows, anyone who will not take his share of the loss as he will later of the profit is not a good nor true companion.*

Is not this what the anchoress has been offered in language appropriate to a religious community? The Rule wavers between scriptural eschatology and divine participation in human affairs—of bargains struck and promises cemented. If God cannot win her with a flaming sword, He will win her another way. The course of this new development leads ultimately to the verbal commitment of the Christ-knight in the next chapter, Part Seven, where the exact terms of the 'covenant' are set forth.

Finally, the entire passage has a purpose beyond firming the anchoress' commitment to a life of hard penance; beyond bringing to a halt the series of image motifs that have been building. The passage is transitional between her readiness to suffer and her participation with Christ crucified. She has, in a sense, mounted the cross with Him, as the next segments reveal.

There is much activity generated by the shift to the cross, but the focus on Christ is symbolic and exemplary. The major images are not of Christ's dying, but of fragments of the act—of Christ's body, the head, the limbs, the sweat of death (and life), the garments rent and divided.

The singular responsibility of man to suffer with Christ rises from the figure of God as the Head, and the company of religious as His limbs, joined organically in enduring the trial of sickness and crisis:

> Hwen þe heaued sweat wel, þet lim þe ne swet nawt, nis hit uuel tacne? He þe is ure heaued sweatte blodes swat for ure secnesse. (184/18–20)

Is it not a bad sign, if the head is sweating well and one member does not sweat at all? He who is our head sweated a sweat of blood on account of our illness.

Christ has drawn to Himself the agonies of the festering wound that has plagued the diseased man (or woman) of the Rule; His 'sweat of blood'— the critical fever of the body's struggle to survive the infection—affects the whole body, limbs and all. Sweating is a sign of life; if a 'dry' member exists, it must be cut away from the body and so lose the head, Christ. This is not a new tack in the Rule; the author had dealt with the suffering of Christ's limbs and the sweat of blood as early as 'Custody,' when in an emotionally charged passage he equated the outpouring of sweat to a bloodletting:

On oðer half swa largeliche & swa swiðe fleaw þet ilke blodi swat of his blisfule bodi, þet te streames urnen dun to þer eorðe. Swuch grure hefde his monliche flesch aʒein þe derue pinen þet hit schulde drehen; þet nes na feorlich wunder, for eauer se flesch is cwickre, se þe reopunge þrof & te hurt is sarre.   (60/9–61/15)

And then, that bloody sweat flowed so freely and in such quantity from His blessed body that it ran in streams to the ground; His human flesh felt such apprehension at the cruel torments it was about to suffer; and that is not a strange or astonishing thing, for the more living the flesh, the sharper the sensation and the hurt.

The incomparable life of Christ's flesh ('Euch monnes flesch is dead flesch aʒein þet wes godes flesch') makes His pain more intense, but in His bloodletting lies the promise of health:

Þus lo þe hale half & te cwike dale droh þet uuele blod ut frommard te unhale & healde swa þe seke.   (61/1–3)

Thus the living, healthy part drew out the bad blood from that which was diseased, and so healed that which was sick.

The relevance of these passages to the anchoress who has come so far in her spiritual progress that she is 'joined' to Christ as is a limb to a torso, is quickened by her dedication to a life of continuous penance. The bloodletting awakens her flesh, restores her health, makes her whole again. But she must be willing to sweat. Sweating is a sign of life; the limb that does not sweat is dead and must be cut away:

> Cwemeð he nu wel godd þe þus bilimeð him of him seolf þurh þet
> he nule sweaten?   (184/25–26)

By not participating with Christ in this redemptive act, the religious not only proves herself moribund, but protracts Christ's pain. The healthy part must sweat the more for the poisoned limb: 'Ah in al þe world þe wes o þe feure, nes bimong al moncun an hal dale ifunden þe mahte beon ilete blod, bute godes bodi ane þe lette him blod o rode' (61/25–27).

Sweat is the key. By this Christ entered heaven, in the toil and pain of sacrifice. *Swinc* and *pine* bring the Rule firmly back to the qualifications of the highest degree of election, those whose joy is to be on the cross 'forte beon ahonget sariliche & scheomeliche wið iesu on his rode.' What of Peter and Andrew? What of Lawrence and the maidens who have gone to their deaths in great suffering? This is the price of heaven. The road to martyrdom of the saints that in early chapters seemed merely exemplary is now made accessible to the anchoress who is willing to pay the price.

The justification of voluntary sacrifice is cast in the familiar person of 'cunning children of rich parents who deliberately tear their clothes to pieces in order to get new ones':

> Ant heo weren ilich þeose ӡape children þe habbeð ӡape feaderes
> þe willes & waldes toteoreð hare claðes forte habbe neowe.
>   (185/12–14)

Although the motif of the indulgent parent contributed strongly to the allegorical structure of 'Temptations,' the clever ploy of these 'ӡape children' suggests the passage in 'Confession' in which the torn smocks and festering sores of crafty beggars woo alms from the rich man (Christ).

The garments of 'Penance' are the flesh, rent and torn. The new raiment to replace these rags will be given by God 'ure riche feader i þe ariste of domesdei hwen ure flesch schal blikien schenre þen þe sunne'

(185/16–17). The 'ariste of domesdei' repeats the promise of 183/24 ff. on the resurrection of the body bright and shining as His own:

> Ȝef we beoð iimpet to þe ilicnesse of godes deað, we schulen of his ariste.

The paradox of the transfigured *curtel* that increases in worth with every tear heightens the distinction between worlds, between what is accounted dishonor and suffering here and what will be honored in heaven as tried and proven metal. Also to be considered is the implicit connection of the 'mutilated and rent flesh' ('tolaimet & totoren') with the recent dismembering of Christ as Head. Now, however, the tearing of her garments (suffering, mortification) joins the anchoress to Christ as a limb participating with the Head in the bloodletting. Christ's body is kept whole, and the individual member, though torn, remains joined to it in common suffering.

A further expansion of the garment imagery, the most imaginative by far, reintroduces the allegorical warfare. Lacerated flesh has the power to terrify the devil; such skin is worthless and repulsive, for it is torn to pieces like an old garment. So, when the tattered shreds of garment are hoisted up as God's banner to proclaim a life of hardship and penance, the devil is frightened away. He enters the castle only when his own signs of ease and fleshly indulgence are posted.

The devil has not been a destructive power in the execution of penance, but his presence on the fringes must keep the anchoress watchful always. 'Al þis lif is a feht,' the author has warned, quoting Job 8:1. The devil's weapons are ease and comfort—strategic weakness on the battlefield (and destructive to the penitential life):

> Me mot ute swinken; ed hame me schal resten. Ant nis he a cang cniht þe secheð reste i þe feht & eise i þe place?   (182/5–7)

> *Away from home one must work, and at home, one can rest. Is it not a foolish knight who looks for rest in the course of the battle and for ease in a place of combat?*

The conflicting demands of ease and hardship bring the Rule to the midpoint of 'Penance,' where the argument of justification begins. The stern regimen of denial, toil, and mortification seeks a more convincing rationale than the shedding of one set of garments for another, even though the martyrs stand as examples of the painful exchange. The series of objections and rebuttals in defense of the penitential life that now commences examines the soundness and efficacy of the discipline and takes anchoress as student or catachumen deeply into the sacramental act through Christ's Passion, in which His humanity is most carefully and deliberately stressed.

Thematically, the remaining parts of the chapter are given over to a rather orderly rendition of the Passion, from the onset of Christ's apprehension to the entombment. The author has been building to this end in the numerous references to pain and dishonor, in the symbolic mounting of the cross and in the images of Christ as Head. All segments have striven to justify the rigors of this difficult way of life no matter how the reader reacts personally to the imagery and symbolism. The demands are clear: the penitent's choice must be patient sacrifice, repression of the flesh, submission to the will of God. The example of the saints is insufficient. Christ must provide the motivation, the means, and the end. Thus the author gives the rest of the chapter to Him. He performs the penance; He makes satisfaction.

The formal argument justifying this life begins on 185/9. Even the language of dialogue of pupil and master has the ring of scriptural 'cross-questioning' between Jesus and the disciples:

Me leoue sire, seið sum, & is hit nu wisdom to don se wa him seoluen?

'But, dear master,' someone will say, 'is it wise, now, to do such injury to oneself?'

This is the first challenge to the markedly extravagant demands the Rule has made on the body, most recently in the allegorical interpretation of flesh as 'ure alde curtel'—ragged banners hoisted up in victory. The *wa* of the pivotal question may refer as readily to this passage as to earlier ones on toil and dishonor. The change in the Rule's tone and approach suggests a reaction against hard penance generally even though the immediate images of mutilation and death strike most vividly.[3]

The recurrent, unifying image is the *cup*, first as containing a remedy for sickness, the alternative being death; then the cup simultaneously symbolizing to Christ His approaching ordeal and actually containing the 'bitter gall' served Him on the cross. Finally, in the climactic segments, the washing of the body and the entombment, the potion of bitterness becomes the measure of sweet spices and aloes.

The first reply to the challenge to austerity embodies narratively the anxieties of Christ, the crucifixion, the grief of those standing at the cross. The human analogy of the father punishing the child corresponds to the divine anger devolving upon the Son. The formal reply that initiates the dramatic action begins with the example of two men, both sick, who take different cures. The wise man drinks a potion of bitter herbs and saves himself. The bitter cup of the cure is analogous to the poisonous drink offered Christ 'for ure secnesse':

Godd for ure secnesse dronc attri drunch o rode, ant we nulleð nawt bittres biten for us seoluen.   (186/17–19)

God, because of our illness, drank a poisonous drink upon the cross, and we refuse to bite into anything bitter ourselves.

The prolonged malady must find its cure in suffering, not in comfort: 'Ne wene nan wið este stihen to heouene' (186/20–21).

The unsparing vengeance of God falls down even upon the head of His Son, who was made sinless but took on flesh like ours 'þet is ful of sunne,' for which:

Godd feader almihti, hu beot he bitterliche his deorewurðe sune.   (186/26–27)

How bitterly did God the Father Almighty strike His dearly beloved Son.

---

3. The initiative of the defense is the correlative construction of 185/7–8: 'Oðer þeo beoð canges þe weneð wið lihtleapes buggen eche blisse, oðer þe hali halhen þe bohten hit se deore.' From this proceeds the example of the saints and mutilated maidens, torn flesh as banners, etc., which kindles the argument of justification.

The striking out of the pelican against its young is suggested by the death of the innocent Son. But a more definite equivalent is the chastising of the child by the parent, the loving father who applies the rod to the child though it grieves him. The multiple metaphors of suffering and hardship converge here in the tormented, humanized Christ, before His hour had come, pleading with the Father:

> Ant he þe nefde nawt of sunne bute schadewe ane wes . . . se sorhfulliche ipinet, þet ear hit come þer to, for þe þreatunge ane þrof swa him agras þer aȝein þet he bed his feader are. Tristis est anima mea usque ad mortem. Pater mi, si possibile est, transeat a me calix iste. Sare, qð he, me grulleð aȝein mi muchele pine. Mi feader, ȝef hit mei beon speare me ed tis time.   (186/2–9)

> *And He, who had nothing of sin but its shadow only, was . . . grievously tortured, that before these things took place He was so filled with apprehension, as they hung over Him, that He begged His father for mercy. My soul is sorrowful even into death. My Father, if it be possible, let this chalice pass from me, 'I am in grievous torment,' He said, 'at My great suffering that is to come. My Father, if it may be, spare me now.'*

In Christ's pleas and fear, we have penance enacted—prayers and entreaties to God by the Son in His own behalf and in behalf of the anchoress, joined to Him in suffering and pain and willing to be crucified with Him. The distinction between actual and symbolic sacrifice is made manifest in Christ's singular act of mounting the cross and thereby deflecting from mankind the terrible anger of the Father:

> Þus ure beatunge feol on him, for he dude him seoluen bitweonen us & his feader þe þreatte us forte smiten ase moder þet is reowð-ful deð hire bitweonen hire child ant te wraðe sturne feader hwen he hit wule beaten.   (187/17–20)

> *Thus our chastisement fell upon Him, for He put Himself between us and His Father, who was threatening to strike us, as a mother full of pity puts herself between her child and the stern, angry father who is going to strike it.*

The severity of the Father, the compassion of the Son continue the spiral of parental discipline, but with the addition now of the compelling element of mercy. The third figure to emerge from the highly emotional passages of prayer and meditation on the Passion is the Virgin. Her role as merciful intercessor is a simple inference from the 'moder þet is reowðful deð hire bitweonen hire child ant te wraðe sturne feader'. Though the Rule uses the simile naturally enough to enforce our understanding of Christ's compassion, by this device the author introduces Mary into the steps of the Passion.

The anchoress does not suffer penance *as* Christ, but with Him. When she stands on Calvary, she does so as Mary, as the Virgin who brought forth Christ from the 'nest of the heart.' Her penance is the anguish of personal participation in the Son's death. The oblique reference to the Virgin in the lines following those cited just above more clearly involves the anchoress in suffering and salvation:

> Þus dude ure lauerd iesu crist ikepte on him deaðes dunt forte schilden us þer wið . . . Hwer se muchel dunt is hit bulteð aʒein up o þeo þe þer neh stondeð. Soðliche hwa se is neh him þe ikepte se heui dunt, hit wule bulten on him ne nule he him neauer meanen.
>
> (187/20–25)

> *He Himself took the death blow in order to protect us from it . . . When anyone deals a heavy blow there are repercussions on those standing near. Truly, there will be repercussions upon anyone who is near to Him who received such a heavy blow, and he will never complain.*

The strong blow (of the stern father) not only strikes the mark, but 'hit bulteð aʒein up o þeo þe þer neh stondeð.' The effect recoils against Mary and St. John—*þeo þe þer stondeð*—in grief, and the penitent who suffers *for his luue þe underueng se heui dunt*. The suffering that begins with Christ devolves upon those standing near, and finally upon the anchoress, who, by her proximity to, as well as distance from, the cross is saved from the blow—*þe deofles botte i þe pine of helle* (187/27–28).

The intensity of the passage has diminished with the introduction of secondary figures, particularly the anchoress, whom Christ has saved from the devil's blows. Having retreated then from the events of the

Passion, the Rule resumes its examination of why it is necessary to suffer a hard and bitter life.

For those who ask how God's love is served by self-inflicted pain, the author offers an exemplum of the husband's pleasure in learning that his wife has grieved for him in his absence, that she grows thin and pale from thoughts of love (187/6). So, the Spouse of the soul is pleased when He is mourned and will hasten to her all the faster 'with ʒeoue of his grace.' The gift is bestowed only where body and soul have been cemented by rugged discipline and by tenderness of heart.

Structurally, the section on dangers of indulging the body which emerges out of the challenge to discipline is intermediate between two halves of Christ's penance, the one treating the Passion, the other the entombment. The restraining and subduing of the body are connected thematically to the Passion; the bitter spices of mortification with which Christ's body was anointed will be developed within the context of the entombment.

With words of caution that no one is to deceive herself into thinking that her life may be soft, the Rule takes up the subject of outer penance. Almost at once the comfort of the body is rendered inimical to the health of the soul in the figure of the pot boiling over with meat and drink. The pot of steaming food, the pot of the belly that boils over to inflame the flesh, is almost instantly transformed into 'poisons' that infect the body. Within the return to the familiar afflictions of the body, the medicinal salves, herbs, spices of the cure begin to congregate. But just as the re-entry of the ailing sinner is merely incidental and exemplary, so the 'gingiure,' 'zedual' and 'clowes de gilofre' of his diet and the herbs of physic are transitional. They link the *calix* of Christ's plea and the cup of bitter gall to the washing of Christ's body with unguents and spices.

The cure of spiritual sickness lies in prudent neglect of the flesh, prudent because wisdom and moderation, 'þe moder is & nurrice of alle gode þeawes,' must preserve the body from overabuse, which taints the soul with bitterness. The decoction of spices and herbs, bitter but salutary condiments to heal the wounds of disease, now contracts into the myrrh and aloes and unguents brought by Nicodemus and the three Marys to anoint Christ's body.

With this return to the crucifixion, the Rule moves inward to interior bitterness, for out of bitterness 'awakeneð swetnesse, her ʒet i þis world, nawt ane in heouene' (190/27–28).

The role of spice, first as the bitter ingredient of the cure of mankind (we recall 186/17–19: 'Godd for ure secnesse dronc attri drunch o rode, ant we nulleð nawt bittres biten for us seoluen'), then as the cure of personal sickness, now as a preservative of the body, brings the Rule to the final stage of 'Penance.' Out of bitterness will come sweetness.

An indication of the ascendancy of the motif of spice from the bitter cup to the myrrh and aloes is sketched here:

bitterness
$\left\{\begin{array}{l}\text{Christ's poisonous drink}\\ \text{Godd for ure secnesse dronc attri}\\ \qquad\text{drunch o rode (186/17–18)}\\ \text{'Transeat a me calix iste' (186/7)}\end{array}\right.$

transitional exempla
$\left\{\begin{array}{l}\text{St. Agatha}\text{—}\textit{salves}\\ \text{the Virgin}\text{—}\textit{electuary}\text{ against}\\ \qquad\text{ginger, zedoary, gillyflower}\end{array}\right.$

100 measures of myrrh and aloes
þet beoð bittre speces & bitacnið
bittre swinkes & flesches pinsunges (189/17–18)

ANOINTING OF THE BODY

sweetness   Of þes twa bitternesses awakeneð
swetnesse

The spices and unguents brought by Nicodemus and the three Marys introduce these women and their signification as bitterness joined to hope, struggle, and peace.

The three Marys correspond to consecutive stages of the anchoress' progress in the Rule and, more locally, to her ascent to God through the bitterness of penance. Structurally, they parallel the three kinds of men 'of godes icoren'—St. Bernard's types—with which 'Penance' began, thus striking a balance at both ends of the chapter. And just as the pilgrim, the man who is dead and hidden, and the man who is crucified symbolize respectively higher stages of election, so the three Marys symbolize different degrees of bitterness in being separated from Christ.

The first Mary, Mary Magdalene, signifies repentance joined to the hope of divine forgiveness. Her appearance (or reappearance) as the sinner saved has been anticipated by her entry into 'Confession.' There, Christ's pardon is predicated on her interior penance:

> Vade & amplius noli peccare. Ga, qð ure lauerd to a sunful wummon, & haue wil þet tu nult sungi namare.   (174/10–12)

> Go, and sin no more. *'Go,' said Our Lord to a sinful woman, 'and resolve to sin no more.'*

The second Mary betokens the bitterness of confrontation with sin, of wrestling with temptation:

> Þis wreastlunge is ful bitter to monie þe beoð ful forð i þe wei toward heouene.   (190/16–17)

The struggle with temptations persists even into 'Penance,' where her advances on the road to heaven are compared to the flight from Egypt of the people of Israel who fought bitterly against the Pharoah, 'þet is, aȝein þe deouel' (190/24). Victories over him are decisive, but short-lived: 'Sone se he haueð þe an ouercumen, ikepe anan an oþer' (190/27–191/28).

But the third kind of bitterness 'i longunge toward heouene & i þe ennu of þis world' brings the holy life to the threshold of heaven. The third Mary, Mary Salome, 'for Salome spealeð pes,' is bitter against the world because it keeps her from heaven, from God. She has peace within her heart and so is impervious to the wars that rage about her. The third Mary surpasses the others, for in her longing for God, her 'reste of cleane inwit,' and her bitterness toward this life, she is like the wife grown thin and pale with grief at her husband's absence. That God reciprocates this love we know from the assurances earlier that 'the spouse of the soul,' like the husband who is pleased that his wife longs for his return, will 'hasten to her more quickly with the gift of His grace':

> Alswa ure lauerd þet is þe sawle spus þet sið al þet ha deð þah he hehe sitte, he is ful wel ipaiet þet ha murneð efter him, & wule hihin toward hire mucheles þe swiðere wið ȝeoue of his grace oðer fecchen hire allunge to him to gloire & to blisse þurh wuniende.
>
> (187/8–13)

Bitterness, then, 'rules at every stage' of the inner life.

The segment ends with the strengthened reminder that ease and comfort of the world are not to be desired by those who are with God. From sorrow will come pleasure; from a hard life, a joyous resurrection; from bitterness, sweetness. The reversal of qualities follows the pattern of earthly-heavenly succession begun in 'Confession,' the first half of the sacrament.

Bitterness cannot be the end. Like toil and suffering, it must find its rewards beyond the grave—and does, figuratively, in the spiritual spices that anoint Christ's body. An etymological reading of Mary as 'bitterness' enables the author to unite the anchoress and the three Marys in the buying of sweet-smelling spice and anointing of Christ:

> Ah neomeð nu ȝeme, mine leoue sustren, hu efter bitternesse kimeð swetnesse. Bitternesse buð hit. For as þet godspel teleð, þeose þreo maries bohten swote smeallinde aromaz to smirien ure lauerd. Þurh aromaz þe beoð swote is understonden swotnesse of deuot heorte. Þeos maries hit buggeð, þet is, þurh bitternesse me kimeð to swotnesse. Bi þis nome marie nim eauer bitternesse.[4] (191/12–19)

> *But notice now, my dear sisters, how sweetness follows the bitterness. The bitterness pays for it, for as the Gospel says, these three Marys bought sweet-smelling spices with which to anoint Our Lord. By spices, which are sweet, is signified the sweetness of a devout heart. Remember always that this name, Mary, means 'bitterness'.*

The sweetness for the anchoress is a devout heart warmed by the savor of God—by the presence of God in the bower or nest of the heart. Such spices inflame the heart (not, presumably, the 'pot of the belly').

The tangential experience of anchoress and the Marys in physical contact with Christ is no sooner begun than it is reciprocated:

> Þeo beoð cuminde to smirien ure lauerd þe me þoleð for his luue, þe strecheð him toward us as þing þet ismired is, & makeð him nesche & softe to hondlin.   (192/22–24)

---

4. The author derives this etymology from Hebrew *marah*, 'bitterness,' noting the connection to Merari (Judith's father): 'for þis nome marie as meraht & merariht . . . spealeð bitternesse' (190/4–5).

The bitter things which we suffer for His love come to anoint Our Lord, who reaches out toward us like one who has been anointed, and makes himself soft and sweet to touch.

The coming together of bitterness and tenderness is joined to the question 'Ant nes he him seolf reclus i maries wombe?' (192/24–25); and this sparks a set of inner-outer movements that prepare the way for the entry of love in the form of the Christ-knight of the next chapter. The nest of the heart, the heart within the body, the anchoress in the anchorhold, Christ as recluse in Mary's womb—all converge here in the description of the 'narrow dwelling' of the anchoress and the narrow dwelling of Christ in Mary's womb.[5]

The Rule carries the mystical union of anchoress and Mary a step further, joining the anchoress to Christ in a life that begins in a cramped place:

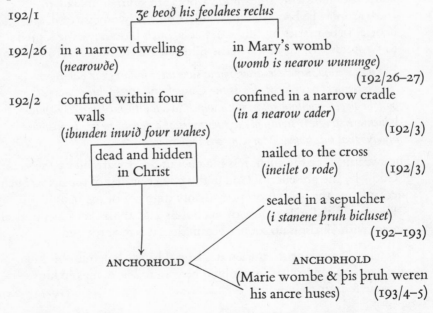

192/1   *ȝe beoð his feolahes reclus*

192/26   in a narrow dwelling   in Mary's womb
          (*nearowðe*)   (*womb is nearow wununge*)
                                                (192/26–27)

192/2   confined within four   confined in a narrow cradle
          walls   (*in a nearow cader*)
          (*ibunden inwið fowr wahes*)   (192/3)

          dead and hidden   nailed to the cross
            in Christ   (*ineilet o rode*)   (192/3)

                                       sealed in a sepulcher
                                       (*i stanene þruh bicluset*)
                                                        (192–193)

          ANCHORHOLD   ANCHORHOLD
                                       (Marie wombe & þis þruh weren
                                        his ancre huses)   (193/4–5)

5. Christ's 'narrow house' was often treated by the Church Fathers. St. Bernard speaks of His entering 'the close prison of a Virgin's womb' (*Sermons*, III, 225). Also in the *Sermons on Canticles*, II, 393, 'Was not the sepulchre a little bed? Was not the manger a little bed? And the Virgin's womb, was not it also a little bed?' The Rule had discussed

Christ and anchoress have been joined together at every stage of 'Penance.' Her participation in the sacramental rite and in a larger sense the penitential life of a religious was drawn against the greater penance performed by Christ. By striking belatedly this analogy of anchorhold-womb-sepulcher, the Rule thrusts her into the tomb with Christ—and out!

The 'two houses' of the anchoress are her body, and girdling that, the outer house of the anchorhold, which is 'like the outer wall about the castle.' Christ's two walls are Mary, whom He left without scar, and the tomb, which opened without break. Christ and anchoress both leave their walls 'wið ute bruche, & leaf ham ba ihale' (193/9):

Anchoress in spirit   Christ in body
wið uten bruche & wem of his twa huses   (193/10–11)

(body / anchorhold)   (Mary / sepulcher)

Christ's egress in body assures her own 'when the spirit goes out in the end.'

The language and imagery of Canticles—intelligible signs of her election—raise her up to the mountains, a new height in her ascent. The hills encountered in 'Regulation' and 'Temptations,' no longer beset by debilitating winds, now promise to become the 'dunes i hehet toward

---

Christ's cramped birthplace and the foot of earth into which the cross was sunk in 'Temptations,' 133/15 ff., as part of a meditation on covetousness. St. Gregory describes His passage from heaven to the Virgin's womb, to the manger, to the cross, to the sepulcher, to heaven, as a series of leaps: 'Veniendo quippe ad redemptiones nostram, quosdam, ut ita dixerim, saltus dedit. Vultis, fratres carissimi, ipsos saltus agnoscere? De coelo venit in uterum, de utero venit in praesepe, de praesepo venit in crucem, de cruce venit in sepulcrum, de sepulcro rediit in coelum.' *Homiliae in Evangelica*, ed. H. Hurter (Paris, 1892), II, 230–231.

The Rule takes up the leaps of the Bridegroom upon the mountains (Cant. 2:8) as its next subject. Gregory introduces Christ's leaps with the citation from Canticles: 'Ecce iste venit saliens in montibus, et transiliens colles,' and then continues into the 'leaps' noted above. Gregory is quoted in the Rule on 194/1–2: 'Luuest tu me? Cuð hit, for luue wule schawin him wið uttre werkes. Gregorius: Probatio dilectionis, exhibitio est operis.' Cf. *Homiliae*, p. 233: 'Si quis diligit me, sermonem meum servabit. Probatio ergo dilectionis exhibitio est operis.'

heouene'; not in pride, however, but in humility and through humiliation:

> Mi leof kimeð leapinde, he seið, o þe dunes, þet is, totret ham,
> tofuleð ham, þoleð þet me totreode ham, tuki ham al to wundre,
> schaweð in ham his ahne troden, þet me trudde him in ham,
> ifinden hu he wes totreden as his trode schaweð.   (193/7–194/11)

> *'My love comes leaping,' she says, 'upon the mountains, that is, he treads*
> *them underfoot, making them vile, allows them to be trodden on, to be*
> *outrageously chastised, and shows on them his own footmarks, so that by*
> *them people might follow him, and discover how he was trodden upon, as*
> *his traces show,'*

In this striking paradox inspired by Canticles, the 'swete luue boc,' the
mountains are trodden underfoot, impressed with the Bridegroom's
footsteps, humbled by the weight of the love. The hills, smaller and less
estimable, cannot rise high enough to receive His foot. But His step upon
the mountains shows the willingness of the anchoress to suffer shame, to
bear upon her body 'iesu cristes deadlicnesse' (194/26–27). Such a weight
is as nothing, for love lightens it '& softeð & sweteð.' The leaping is proof
of the promise made earlier that the Husband, pleased that His wife grows
pale and thin in His absence, will hasten to her with 'gift of His grace.'

'Penance' completes its circle with a return to a citation from St. Paul,
similar in tone and language to the opening statement 'Al is penitence,
ant strong penitence, þet ȝe eauer dreheð':

> Alle wa, qð he, & alle scheome we þolieð, ah þet is ure selhðe, þet
> we beoren on ure bodi iesu cristes deadlicnesse, þet hit suteli in us
> hwuch wes his lif on eorðe.   (194/25–27)

> *'We suffer,' he said, 'all tribution and all shame, but that is our happiness,*
> *to bear upon our body the mortification of Jesus Christ, so that in us there*
> *may be made plain the kind of life that was His on earth.'*

We have come far since the sacrament began in 'Confession.' There
the penalties in hell of a sinful life were clearly marked out and heaven
merely glanced at until the process of confession was completed and the

resolve to sin no more professed. The repentant thief joined Christ on the cross, where the promise of Paradise was made. In 'Penance' the Passion is annealed to the sacramental act so that the sorrow and hardship of Christ are made analogous to the performance of penance by the anchoress. Within this frame, heaven is secure, and comforts and pleasures are rejected as part of a covenant to share in Christ's life on earth and in heaven later.

The casting of the final segment of 'Penance' into a discourse on love implies that satisfaction has been made and prepares firmly for the next part, in which love comes as a sacramental sequence of penance. The offering of sacrifice will be undertaken and performed by the Christ-knight in his death for love. God reciprocates love for love. *Probatio dilectionis exhibitio est operis*. The Christ-knight must keep his pledge.

SEVEN 'LOVE'

Studios mentibus Verbum sponsus frequenter apparet, et non sub una specie.
So Bernard of Clairvaux opens his thirty-first sermon on Canticles pro-
posing to treat of the various ways Christ appears to the soul in its need:
as Bridegroom, as Physician, as a rich, indulgent Father whose larders are
filled with food and wine.[1] To these descriptions of the soul's experience
of Christ as it moves steadily toward union, the author of the Rule adds
another—that of the knight come in full panoply to free the beleaguered
lady from her enemies. Even in an age when allegory was a familiar and
inspired means of conveying spiritual truth through human and natural
form—from ecclesiastical stone to animal physiology—when the Word
Made Flesh seemed the most palpable evidence of the divine intention
behind the physical presence, the invention of a Christ-knight come to
woo the disdainful lady in courtly language and manner is a striking
innovation.

Although it is not possible to insist that the three sisters for whom the
Rule was intended knew romance literature and the idiom of courtly
love, the colorful, dramatic details of the 'wooing' of the lady here and
the many references to courts and castles in other parts of the Rule make
it very likely that this was so. Romance literature, though essentially profane in its secular approach to the matter and manner of love, was not
unknown to the cloisters even in the twelfth century. Aelred of Rievaulx
is found bemoaning the fact that a certain novice dreams more of Arthur's
legendary exploits than is fitting, and that he sooner sheds tears for
Arthur than Christ.[2] The author of the Rule seems not to share Aelred's

1. *Sermones in Cantica*, PL 183, col. 940, commenting on Canticles 1:7: *Indica mihi
diliget anima mea, ubi pascas, ubi cubes in meridie.*

2. Aelred tells of the complaint of a novice that stories of a certain Arthur easily
brought him to tears. See *Speculum Caritatis*, PL 195, col. 565. F. M. Powicke, in his
edition of Walter Daniel's *Life of Aelred* (Oxford, 1951) assumes that Aelred knew
Arthur's legendary history and was repelled by the influence it exerted on the young.

distress at the subversive influence of romance. Rather, he finds it a felicitous way to divert the worldliness of aristocratic tradition to spiritually edifying channels. To convert the best chivalric behavior into parable is to demonstrate the applicability of Christ's love for the soul in every human (or idealized) situation, to exploit profane literature, and especially to use—perhaps exhaust—the religious potential of chivalric idealism that had taken hold of the imagination. But this scrupulously conventional description of his purpose does no justice to the powerful effect the Christ-knight exemplum exerts upon us.

The Church itself had widened the arena that made possible the coming together of militant Christianity and chivalric *deboneirte*. The fusion had its beginnings in the eleventh century in the determination of the Church to control the barbarism of feudal warfare by at least diverting it into service against the enemies of Christendom. A century later the Church was forced to brake the engine it had set into motion, to halt the widespread plundering by the knights of Christ who had gone off to free the Holy Land.[3] St. Bernard's *De laude novae militiae* (1125), addressed to the Templars, is an early attempt to define the duties and responsibilities of the knight; and the emphasis is on humility and sanctity of purpose, as if the young order needed a diplomatic reminder of their monastic origins to curb their aggressiveness.

Of course, to speak of the knight at all is to bring to mind a kind of courtliness, a *gentilesse* that betrays how deeply we have fallen under the spell of later romance tradition. The rough, uncouth, often brutal horse soldier has yet to be humanized, civilized by literacy, idealism, and good manners. To that end, the influential *Policraticus* of John of Salisbury defines the role of knights as instruments of the Church—as the temporal half of the two-edged sword by which God's will is to be executed.[4] In his elaboration of the qualities and qualifications of the true knight, John

---

The source of the stories was probably Geoffrey of Monmouth; however, Breton conteurs had also penetrated the northern reaches of England. See Roger Sherman Loomis, 'The Oral Diffusion of the Arthurian Legend,' *ALMA* (Oxford, 1959), pp. 52–63.

3. Sidney Painter, *French Chivalry* (Ithaca, 1940), pp. 66–68.

4. Painter, p. 71. It is in the sixth book of the *Policraticus* that an order of knight-soldiers as an arm of the Church is proposed. The disciplines of soldiery are mitigated by enthusiasm for their divinely-sanctioned office: 'But what is the office of the duly-

confers upon the secular order of chivalry the obligations of service to God and the Church. When such ideas of Christian chivalry were turned into the vernacular and found their way into the literature of the court, the underlying idealism penetrated the mind and will of the illiterate knighthood.[5]

In literature the fusion of heroic adventure and a higher purpose of religious piety was an inevitable and natural development in an age given to allegorization, when deeper meanings were assiduously sought in art of all kinds. Courtly romance and lyric provide examples of the accomplishments of the virtuous knight stirred by spiritual forces. Chrétien de Troyes had successfully blended the two in *Perceval* and introduced the mystical Grail which combined old magic with new mystery, a union so felicitous that it arrests the imagination into our own time. The emergence of interest in the history of the Holy Grail gave sanctity and purpose to the hitherto earthly, often frivolous exploits of the knight; and the popularity of the Grail romances, particularly in the thirteenth century, attests to the enduring pleasures of combining adventure and religious symbolism. Chrétien and his continuators proved that sacred and profane could complement each other in the same work. Indeed, the task of copying and composing certain kinds of romances fell to the monasteries. Under their direction, romance continued to take on a religious character, and the best deeds of noble men continued to be interpreted as spiritual experiences—courtly idealism turned to the service of God. No wonder, then, that writing in an age when romance traditions were 'in the air' and allegorization was a habit of thought, the author of the Rule created the Christ-knight.

---

ordained soldiery? To defend the Church, to assail infidelity, to venerate the priesthood, to protect the poor from injuries, to pacify the province, to pour out their blood for their brothers (as the formula of their oath instructs them), and, if need be, to lay down their lives. The high praises of God are in their throat, and two-edged swords are in their hands to execute punishment on the nations and rebuke upon the peoples, and to bind their kings in chains and their nobles in links of iron.' *The Statesman's Book of John of Salisbury*, trans. John Dickinson (New York, 1963), p. 199.

5. Through such works as Stephen of Fougères' *Livre des manières* (12th c.), some of John's ideas of knighthood may have become available to the nobility. See Painter, pp. 72–74.

St. Bernard speaks of the form in which the Bridegroom appears to the soul as varying according to need and readiness. The purer the soul, the sweeter the tryst. His thirty-first sermon on Canticles is quoted here in part to show the similarity of approach of Bernard and the author of the Rule:

> The Word, Who is the Bridegroom, often appears to faithful souls; but always, in this life, He does so under some appearance. For we are no more able yet to see Him as He is, than we can see the sun really only as it lights up other things, such as air, a mountain, or a wall. Our bodily eyes, moreover, have this power of sight because they, alone of all our members, have a certain inborn affinity with light; and if they are disturbed and lose that likeness, they can no longer see. In the same way the man who is enlightened by the Sun of Righteousness, that enlighteneth every man that cometh into this world, is able to see Him in proportion to the degree of his enlightenment, because that constitutes a certain likeness to Him. The likeness is, however, not yet perfect; therefore he can by no means see Him as He is.
>
> *His Majesty is therefore to be approached, not rashly but with utmost reverence; and we must seek Him, not from place to place but from stage to stage of spiritual purity. For the purer the soul, the closer will it come to God; and when we are wholly pure, then we shall have arrived. . . . The psalmist tells us from his own experience, the sign that marks the coming of this sort. 'There shall go,' he says, 'a fire before Him, and burn up His enemies on every side.' This fire of holy longing must always precede God's visitation in a soul, to burn up its impurities and so prepare His place.*[6]

Bernard speaks then of the union of the Bridegroom and the soul as being arranged by the good angel—a friend of the Bridegroom, the *ami*, the *confidant* 'whose special business it is to promote this secret intercourse between Him and It.' As he watches it takes place, 'he dances with delight

6. *On the Song of Songs*, trans. 'A Religious of C.S.M.V.' (London, 1952), pp. 88–89; in *PL* 183, col. 940.

in sharing of its joy.'7 This faithful friend knows no jealousy, for he finds happiness in his lord's advantage. 'He goes and comes between Beloved and beloved, presenting Him with the outpourings of her heart and bringing back His gifts; he urges one and reconciles the Other. And sometimes, though not often, he actually effects their introduction, drawing her forward or bringing Him to meet her; for he is a member of the household, well known to the palace; every day he sees the Father's Face, and he fears no repulse.'8

The language and conventions of this suggestive passage are those of romance literature; the 'special friend,' no mere human emissary, is the Holy Ghost. But Bernard must defend his metaphor against misapplication by those who would confuse mystical love with sensual love (a danger inherent in the analogy) by insisting on the purely spiritual commingling of soul and Word. The inpouring of God is a spiritual act upon the soul already burning with love. Such a soul will demand more than mere appearance, for 'the more interior His operation is, the happier it will be. For He is the Word: He does not merely sound in ears, He enters hearts. . . . He does not beat upon our ears, but woos our hearts.'9

God appears to the soul according to its need. He comes sometimes as Bridegroom 'and this experience, granted from time to time even in our present pilgrimage, crowns all the heart's desire.' To those enfeebled souls who need His ministrations He comes as Physician with salves and unguents: 'Those in like cases know well that the Lord Jesus is a doctor Who heals the contrite-hearted and remedies their sickness.' He comes at other times as a Companion by the way who relieves the weary journey with delightful conversation; or as the wealthy Father, 'Whose house is stored with food for all the family.' And finally He comes 'as a mighty King, Who wants to show His timid bride the riches of His winepresses and barns, His gardens and His fields, so that she may desire them and He leads her at least into His secret chamber.'

It is in Bernard's sermon that the language of romance, of Provençal lyric and *fin amour*, are wedded to the special love between God and the

7. Ibid., p. 89.

8. Ibid. Compare this member of the household with love the steward, who serves the Father in Part Seven of *AW* (197/22–25).

9. *On the Song of Songs*, p. 89; in *PL* 183, col. 942.

soul. The inspiration and idiom of carnal love are unmistakable, evocative, but there is a preciousness about spiritualizing these familiar figures
which impairs the grand design, a perception of divine love enraptur-
ing the soul.

The imprint of Bernard's sermon is upon the Christ-knight allegory.
The author of the Rule could have turned to several of the Church
Fathers or to Scripture for the initiative of such characterizations, if he
were content to deal with Christ as Physician, Father, or Companion, as
Bernard does. The Rule goes beyond Bernard's formulaic rendering of
the mystical union. It goes beyond by not going so far—that is, the mysticism does not obscure the allegory. The lady's devotion is enjoined upon
her by the extraordinary chivalry of Christ, who offers Himself sacrifi-
cially to the individual soul as proof of His love service. Our author,
eclectic in his sources and pragmatic in his approach to how they could
best be used, was not refashioning a sensual love lyric to convey the
mystery. The Christ-knight, after pleading his case for the lady's
devotion, after presenting 'reasons' to support his claims on her love,
threatens with unexpected militancy to wrest it from her or to punish
her if she remains aloof or proves recusant. He does not propose to lan-
guish from *mal d'amour* but, having struck a bargain, demands that the
lady meet the terms. That she finally may fail, deny her love, is part of
Christ's pain in His Passion. She is in default when she becomes guilty of
tepidity or pusillanimity.[10] She violates the terms of the 'contract.'[11]

The Rule uses the conventions and figures of romance only so that
they may dissolve and fall away before the better love, one that trans-

10. The Rule's polemic against faint love begins with the offering of *eisil* to Christ.
The problem is a serious one for the religious, who must find within themselves the
capacity to love God in sufficient measure to merit the sacrifice. Étienne Gilson throws
light on the intent of the allegory when, in answering charges that Cistercian mysticism
encouraged the growth of the courtly love tradition, he dismisses sentimental suffering
of the lover as totally alien to the reciprocal love of God and man. Love of God is never
unrequited; and if the mystic suffers, it is not because God does not return love but
because man himself does not love enough to attain union, *The Mystical Theology of
St. Bernard*, trans. A. H. C. Downes (New York, 1940), pp. 181–182.

11. This continues the 'covenant' of true companions of 'Penance,' 184/9–12. At the
end of Part Seven, the denial is understood to underlie the complaint of the laborer
whose wages have been withheld.

cends human commonplace but may be understood (or perceived) as analogous, although infinitely superior to, the attractive idealizations of earthly love and attachments, one that fires the soul with increasing ardor the nearer it draws to consummation in a licit union. This love is to be reciprocal, unqualified, and unhesitating in its submission, or the price paid in Christ's blood becomes too high—at least to human understanding. The eagerness of Christ to overpay for value of goods received creates surprise in the Rule:

> Me lauerd, þu seist, hwerto? Ne mahte he wið leasse gref habben arud us? ʒeoi, iwiss, ful lihtliche; ah he nalde. For hwi? Forte bineomen us euch bitellunge aʒein him of ure luue þet he se deore bohte.
>
> (200/13–16)

> *'But why, master?' you will say. 'Could he not have delivered us with less pain?' Yes indeed, quite easily, but He did not want to. Why? So that we might not have any excuse for not giving Him our love, when He had bought it so dearly.*

The final section of Part Seven, by returning to the idiom of commerce, of biblical quotation and application, removes love from chivalric romance to the less spectacular, agrarian world in which Christ lived and died, to the fields of the rich merchant, to the hills and vineyards of Canticles.

There are four definable concentrations in Part Seven, each unified by a dominant series of images. The first introduces motifs and ideas of the garden and marketplace; the imagery is picked up again and expanded in subsequent segments. The second opens the Christ-knight allegory and is concerned mainly with the wooing. The third develops out of the knight's sacrifice and deals with the crucifixion. The fourth concentration examines the physical properties and moral signification of Greek fire, urine, and sand, and concludes with proof of the sovereignty of love.

The author sets forth at once the contrast of flesh and spirit, pulling forward the suggestion of 'Penance' (by repeating the final sentence of Part Six) that the hardships and mortifications of penance must be endured as preliminary stages of perfection, but are as nothing when compared with love:

> Seint pawel witneð þet alle uttre heardschipes, alle flesches
> pinsunges ant licomliche swinkes—al is ase nawt aʒeines luue þe
> schireð & brihteð þe heorte.   (195/1–5)

Does the growth of love depend first of all on a predisposed heart rather than a disciplined one? Apparently, the heart must be inclined to accept regulation before it can receive love; the realizing of love can occur only in a hospitable climate. The opening passages introduce the pervasive set of images that are developed into and become controlled by the major figure—body and soul in tension reconciled finally by love, transformed into light by the Word.

The heart is where love must be planted. With a citation from 'þe hali abbat moyses,' the author initiates the idea and contingent image of 'cultivation of the heart' as though it were the common earth through which the crop must be nurtured and raised:

> Al þet wa & al þet heard þet we þolieð o flesch, & al þet god þet
> we eauer doð, alle swucche þinges ne beoð nawt bute as lomen to
> tilie wið þe heorte. Ʒef þe axe ne kurue, ne spitelsteaf ne dulue, ne
> þe sulh ne erede, hwa kepte ham to halden?   (196/15–19)
>
> *'All the suffering and all the hardship that we suffer in the flesh, and all
> the good we ever do, all such things are but implements with which to
> cultivate the heart.' If the axe did not cut, nor the pikestaff pierce the
> ground, nor the ploughshare plough, who would want to keep them?*

The idiom of the farm and fields (where love is grown), the rich stores of food laid up in the house of heaven (where love is the steward), and the weighing of goods in St. Michael's scales (where love is finally measured)—such imagery of the garden and marketplace establishes the immediate setting of Part Seven and provides a context for the references to the parable of the workers in the vineyard later in the chapter. Not only does the physical embody the spiritual in the allegory of the knight's wooing of the lady, but it informs all the images in the critical section in which love must wrest the soul out of its earth almost against its will. The 'swote & schir heorte' is the means and the end—the heart purged of bitterness, having come through trial.

The paraphrase of the Abbot Moses (which elaborated the sentence of St. Paul) strengthens the link of penance and love and allows the author to specialize the language even further. He moves from a general statement on the penitential life ('Al þet wa & al þet heard þet we polieð o flesch') to an analogy of the garden ('swucche þinges neo beoð nawt bute as lomen to tilie wið þe heorte'). This, then, is the first application of 'licomliche swinkes' of Paul's sentence, that of cultivation of the earth (analogously, the heart) to bring forth fruit. The vocabulary now is borrowed from farming: *lomen, tilie, axe, kurue, spitelsteaf, dulue, sulh, erede*. Who would love these objects for themselves and not for what they can produce? asks the author, amplifying through agricultural images the statement with which he began Part Seven, that love, and not outer hardships 'schireð & brihteð þe heorte.' Mortification of the body is a tool 'to tilie wið,' to make the heart 'schir & of briht sihðe.'

From the outset of Part Seven we are confronted with such piling up of ideas and images, a gathering together of phrases, repeated expressions, and cross references into a highly concentrated yet flexible unit that levels off temporarily, long enough for the author to wrench out a prominent image with which to begin the next spiral. This has been a technique applied by the author throughout the body of the Rule to connect themes and 'distinctions' as well.

The pattern of repetition and derivative theme typical of this section is established at once, and lends itself to the kind of partitioning of phrases and subdivisions sketched below. The peculiar hortatory quality of the Rule (and this chapter particularly) is explained in part by the closeness of repetends to each other:

FIRST STATEMENT

alle uttre heardschipes
alle flesches pinsunges
   ant licomliche swinkes

AL is ase nawt aȝeines luue þe

SCHIREÐ & BRIHTEÐ þe HEORTE.

(bodily labors—
   'licomliche bisischipe')

Ah, SWOTE & SCHIR HEORTE is
   god to ALLE þinges.

DEVELOPMENT

Si linguis loquar	þah ich cuðe
Si tradidero	þah ich dude
Si distribuero	þah ich ȝeue
	AL were ispillet.
(195/8–196/15)	

(There follows a recapitulation which serves as
transition to the
agricultural images.)

TRANSITION

  al þet wa
  al þet heard   ALLE swucche þinges
  al þet god

lomen to tilie wið þe heorte
(implements with which to
cultivate the heart)

SECOND STATEMENT

	þet
	godd te reaðere þiderward loki
(God will look upon	mid his grace, & makeð þe
the heart so that	heorte SCHIR & OF BRIHT SIHÐE
it may see.)	
	swa
	þe ehnen of þe heorte . . . mei
	cnawen godd . . . gleadien of
	his sihðe.
(196/17–26)	

The phrase 'of his sihðe' concludes the line, but the juxtaposition of 'schir
heorte' in the line that immediately follows creates a joint between all

that has been said of the efficiency of love and the defining of its powers about to come:

> Schir heorte, as seint Bernard seið, makieð twa þinges: þet tu al þet tu dest do hit oðer for luue ane of godd, oðer for oþres god & for his biheue.
>
> (196/26–29)

A pure heart, as St. Bernard said, effects two things: it makes you do all that you do either for the love of God alone, or for the good of others for His sake.

Following his own maxims and those of Churchmen, which he freely uses, the author has been 'tilling the soil' of metaphor and rhetorical device in order to get to the fruit of his labor: a definition of 'schir heorte' as it responds to love—as it must respond to the coming of the Christ-knight:

> Hwet is schir heorte? . . . þet ʒe na þing ne wilnin ne ne luuien bute godd ane, & te ilke þinges for godd þe helpeð ow toward him.
>
> (197/7–9)

What is a pure heart? . . . that you should not desire or love anything except God, and those things which help you towards Him.

> Schirnesse of heorte is godes luue ane. I þis is al þe strengðe of alle religiuns, þe ende of alle ordres.
>
> (197/15–17)

Cleanness of heart is the love of God alone. In this lies the strength of all religious life, the purpose of all Orders.

> Luue fulleð þe lahe, seið seinte pawel. . . . Alle godes heastes, as sein gregoire seið, beoð i luue i rotet.
>
> (197/17–19)

Love fulfils the law, says St. Paul. . . . All God's commandments, as St. Gregory says, are rooted in love.

There now occurs a return to the opening insistence on love's power
and its precedence over all the works of the body. Also, the garden
imagery, which had developed from the metaphor of the cultivation of
the heart, is completed in the figure of St. Michael's scales:

> Alle godes heastes beoð *i luue i rotet*
> (All God's commandments are rooted in love)

> > luue ane schal beon *ileid i seinte Mihales weie*
> > (Love alone shall be put in St. Michael's
> > scales)

alle uttre heardschipes   Þeo þe meast luuieð schulen beo
. . . al is ase *nawt*   meast iblisset, nawt þeo þe
aʒeines luue (195/2–5)   leadeð heardest lif. (197/19–22)
(all exterior hardships   (Those who love most shall
. . . are as nothing   be the most blessed, not those
compared with love)   who lead the hardest life.)

> for luue hit *ouerweieð*

The emphasis on special vocabulary of the garden and market (with
the deliberate play on *weie*) shows the special power of love, reinforces
the statement on the inferior nature of physical hardship, projects and
continues the image of the weighing of produce (love itself the crop
which the 'tools' of physical discipline have cultivated) which will tip the
scales tended by St. Michael at the final reckoning. The image of the
scales and the intimation that love controls them ultimately, so that
Michael himself must submit to love's mastery ('luue hit ouerweieð')
anticipate the emergence of love's sovereignty in the final segment of
Part Seven.

The materialization of love in the figure of heaven's steward ('Luue
is heouene stiward for hire muchele freolec' 197/22–23) completes the
first part of 'Love.' The liberality or munificence of the steward who
keeps accounts and gives freely of her store, withholding nothing, brings
to a temporary halt the correspondence of cultivation of the heart and

tilling of the soil and looks ahead to the sacrifice of the Christ-knight, who spares nothing. The produce of the garden is brought to the table, so to speak, in the person of love, heaven's steward, who gives freely all she has—even herself—for otherwise, God 'would set no store by her service':

> Luue is heouene stiward for hire muchele freolec. For heo ne edhalt na þing, ah ȝeueð al þet ha haueð & ec hire seoluen, elles ne kepte godd nawt of þet hiren were. (197/22–25)

Love personified as the steward is actually a transitional device linking the power of the pure heart (segment one) to the reasons for loving God (segment two). The author's closing comment on the relationship of the body and the spirit reflects his fondness for returning to his original point, after having developed an idea fully. The effect of such 'incremental repetition' is that it acts to summarize and to create circularity effortlessly:

> *opening*
> alle uttre heardschipes . . . al is as nawt aȝeines luue.
> *all exterior hardshipes . . . are as nothing compared with love.*
>
> *closing*
> Þeo þe meast luuieð schulen beo meast iblisset, nawt þeo þe leadeð heardest lif. (197/20–22)
> *Those who love most shall be most blessed, not those who lead the hardest life.*

Within the interval, which has dealt with preparing the heart, much groundwork has been laid for themes yet to be developed.

In the first elaboration of why God is to be loved (the spirit of debate is carried over from 'Penance'), the theme is generosity, God's bountiful gifts. But the similarity of language and clause construction to the recent description of love-the-steward heightens the sense of the rich Father bestowing gifts, as though the author were intent on creating a feeling of fullness. The passages, arranged into clauses, show the correspondence:

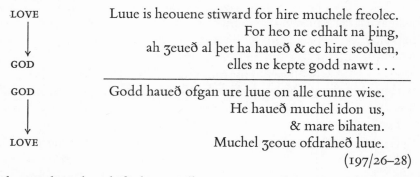

LOVE ⟶ GOD

    Luue is heouene stiward for hire muchele freolec.
              For heo ne edhalt na þing,
    ah ʒeueð al þet ha haueð & ec hire seoluen,
              elles ne kepte godd nawt . . .

GOD ⟶ LOVE

    Godd haueð ofgan ure luue on alle cunne wise.
             He haueð muchel idon us,
              & mare bihaten.
        Muchel ʒeoue ofdraheð luue.

(197/26–28)

The emphasis has shifted to God's generosity. The author has already personified love in terms which suggest God Himself, though the distinction between God and His steward has been carefully made in 'luue is heouene stiward' and is sustained later in the chapter when love appears as a prime mover. The need now is to express the boundless liberality of God, who has cast all under our feet (the gifts of love implied and kept vivid), who gave the world to us through Adam:

Me al þe world he ʒef us in adam, ure alde feader; & al þet is i þe world he weorp under ure fet, beastes & fuheles, ear we weren forgulte.

(197/28–2)

But He gave to us, in the person of our first father, Adam, the whole world; beasts and birds, He cast beneath our feet, before we sinned.

God's gifts do not end with this dominion over the earth—the idea develops directly from the first clause of lines 197/26–27: 'he haueð muchel idon us & mare bihaten.' The 'mare bihaten' suggests Christ's coming (historically, as the new Adam; allegorically, as the knight about to set out on his journey). But what gift to man can be greater than that of excellence over 'all the beasts of the field, birds of the sky and fish of the sea' unless it is restoration through atonement? This is the gift that love will bestow.

The gifts of the Old Testament give way to those of the New; so the 'mare bihaten' is continued and enlarged by lines 197/5–198/7:

He dude ʒet mare; ʒef us nawt ane of his, ah dude al him seoluen.

He did still more. He not only gave us of His possessions, but gave us the whole of Himself.

He gave all of Himself just as love gives all, even herself—'ȝeueð al þet ha haueð & ec hire seoluen' (197/24). Such is love's *freolec*—'for heo ne edhalt na þing.' A similar description of uncontrollable generosity is given by the Christ-knight when he speaks of the man who can withhold nothing ('þe ne con nawt edhalden') because of the holes in his hands.

The boundlessness of love firmly established, the Rule suddenly contracts the abstract into Christ, a citation from Paul serving as transition:

> He dude ȝet mare . . . ah dude al him seoluen.
> Christus dilexit ecclesiam & dedit semet ipsum pro ea. Crist, seið seinte pawel, luuede swa his leofmon þet he ȝef for hire þe pris of him seoluen.
> (198/8–10)

He did still more . . . but gave us the whole of Himself.
Christ loved the church and delivered himself up for it. *Christ, he says, so loved His beloved that for her He gave the price of Himself.*

The author has changed the Latin *ecclesiam* to English *leofmon* (not uncommon in Bernardine tradition), and so changed the scope of the sacrifice to a personal, even intimate gesture of love.

The high price paid by Christ completes the expository argument of why God has deserved our love, and serves to introduce the allegory of Christ's love for the soul, the *leofmon*. The rather severe compression of ideas in this small segment is typical of the effect of the chapter as a whole, for in no other chapter are so many sets of images so closely interwoven or so vividly presented. Nowhere else is the coming of Christ so eagerly awaited, though the end must be His death. And in no other part of the Rule does the author rely so heavily on repeating two or three words— in this case, love, gift, giving—to prepare the reader's attitude.

To summarize, the section beginning 'Godd haueð ofgan ure luue' (197/26 ff.) continues the discussion of the rewards of love expressed through the generosity of God ('al þet is i þe world he weorp under ure fet,' 197/1), and suggests the gift to come in the next period ('he ȝef for hire þe pris of him seoluen,' 198/9–10). Moreover, it asserts through an initial appeal to human reason an unexpected return of love for love, an exchange that implies contractual obligation.

The Christ-knight exemplum, beginning 'A leafdi wes mid hire fan biset al abuten,' brings on the major action of Part Seven; and though it opens somewhat abruptly, its immediate function is to amplify the theme of God's love of the soul, cast here as a metaphor of a king who loved a lady of a foreign land. In the tightly compressed 'forbisne' (as our author modestly calls it) occurs an adventure that has been prepared for in advance by the many references to love's largesse, God's gifts, and the granting to the soul 'the price of Himself.' The promise made by God (the 'mare bihaten') is here realized in part in the expression of the Christ-knight's love and in the reconciliation with the Father sealed with Christ's blood.

The transitional passage fuses old and new, blends scriptural history and romantic gesture; elevates the familiar, homely landscape of garden and farm to an epic setting:

LINKING Crist, seið seinte pawel, luuede swa his leofmon þet
LINE   he ʒef for hire þe pris of him seoluen.

TRANSITION

Neomeð nu gode ʒeme, mine leoue sustren, for hwi me ah him to luuien. Earst, as a mon þe woheð, as a king þet luuede a gentil, poure leafdi of feorrene londe, he sende his sonden biuoren, þet weren þe patriarches & te prophetes of þe alde testament wið leattres isealet. On ende, he com him seoluen & brohte þe godspel as leattres iopenet, & wrat wið his ahne blod saluz to his leofmon, luue gretunge forte wohin hire wið & hire luue wealden. Herto falleð a tale, a wrihe forbisne.   (198/10–18)

Now attend carefully, my dear sisters, to the reason why He should be loved. At first, like a man seeking love, like a king who loved a lady of a far country, who was noble and yet poor, He sent His messengers before Him with sealed letters—the patriarchs and prophets of the Old Testament. Then at last He came Himself and brought the Gospel, open letters, as it were, and with His own blood wrote greetings to His beloved, greetings of love to seek and win her own. There is a story which bears on this, a parable with hidden meaning.

EXEMPLUM   A leafdi wes mid hire fan biset al abuten.

The 'King þet luuede a gentil poure leafdi' thrusts into a feudal setting the pledge of a noble gift to come. The patriarchs and prophets as precursors of Christ move *pari passu* into the language and dress of chivalric romance.[12]

The opening premises of the Christ-knight allegory can be reduced to a series of triads which are continued as the allegory progresses. With this device the vibrating or cumulative movement characteristic of the work is created:

A leafdi wes . . .
    {   hire fan biset al abuten
        hire lond al destruet
        heo al poure   ⟶   inwið an eorðene castel

A mihti kinges luue wes

                                    (passive subject may reflect
      biturnd up on hire   knight's subjugation by
      sende hire { his sonden   love)
                  an efter oðer
                  ofte somet monie   (third qualifying phrase is
                                suspended to carry over
                                the effect of munificence)
      sende hire { beawbelez
                 (baðe feole & feire)
                 sucurs of liueneð   (heo al poure)
                 help of his hehe hird   (lond al destruet)
                                        (fan al abuten)

                                        to halden hire castel

                                           (198/18–24)

12. Bernard's description of the successive stages of the Bridegroom's coming is similar to that of the Christ-knight: 'He comes, He hastens, He draws near, He is present, He looks at her, and finally He speaks; and she takes note of all. He comes to the Church in the angels, He hastens in the patriarchs, He draws near in the prophets . . . Or you may say that He comes in His desire to show mercy, hastens in His zeal to help, draws near to her in His self-humiliation.' *On the Song of Songs*, trans. 'A Religious of C.S.M.V.', p. 180; in *PL* 183, Col. 1050.

The contrast of the worldly situations of knight and lady is striking—she, poor, besieged, imprisoned; the suitor, rich, powerful, generous beyond measure. The irony of the lady's disdain has been anticipated in the general sense of lines 198/7–8: 'se heh ȝeoue nes neauer iȝeuen to se lahe wrecchces,' a line that is most forceful when read aloud. Her unreasonable pride must be humbled and purged before there can be progress toward union. The lady must make an ascent to know God as Christ descended and condescended in order to know man. Christ came as a man and was humbled, a condition enjoined upon Him (in Bernard) by Truth, and in the Rule by a higher reality, love.

The Christ-knight's attitude is at first gentle and unassuming; but in the cumulation of verbs displaying his *deboneirte*, we see a gradually increasing militancy, such as he will demonstrate in the freeing of the lady:

> He com him seolf
> > *schawde* hire his feire neb
> > > ... of alle men feherest to bihalden.
> > *spec* as swiðe swoteliche & wordes se murie þet
> > > ha mahten deade arearen to liue.
> > *wrahte* feole wundres & *dude* muchele meistries
> > > biuoren hire ehsihðe.
> > > > (198/26–2)

> *He came Himself*
> > showed *her his fair face*
> > > ... *of all men fairest to behold.*
> > spoke *so sweetly and with such delight that*
> > > *they might have raised the dead to life.*
> > worked *many wonders and* performed *many marvels*
> > > *before her eyes.*
> > > > (The final clause encloses action and effect of the
> > > > preceding statements)

The clauses are repeated immediately:

> *schawde* hire his mihte (*showed her his power*)
> *talde* hire of his kinedom (*told her of his kingdom*)

bead to makien hire cwen of al þet he ahte (*asked that he might make her queen of all he possessed*)   (198/2–199/4)

The offering and bestowing of these gifts fulfill partially the promise of God to man; but the Rule's intent here is to compare the unsparing generosity of this unique knight to the reckless arrogance of the lady:

Al þis ne heold nawt. Nes þis hoker wunder? For heo nes neauer wurðe forte beon his þuften.   (199/4–6)

All this availed nothing. Was it not strange, this disdain? For she herself was not worthy to be his handmaid.

She dispassionately accepts all while withholding her love, even her gratitude. By assigning all the action verbs to the Christ-knight, the author creates an imbalance deliberately, one that also implies the lady's helplessness. The inequalities so alarming in this all-nothing exchange may be explained by the excesses of chivalric *deboneirte*, but more accurately by the assertion 'luue hefde ouercumen him' (199/6), which qualifies the noun and suggests the mastery has fallen to love: 'ah swa þurh his deboneirte luue hefde ouercumen him.'

Part of the evocative effect of the exemplum is achieved by the summary challenges to the reader: 'Hwet wult tu mare?' (198/26); 'Nes þis hoker wunder?' (199/4–5); and most especially by the pledge of the Christ-knight in which the plea for the lady's favor is made:

Nu þenne biseche ich þe for þe luue þet ich cuðe þe, þet tu luuie me lanhure efter þe ilke dede dead, hwen þu naldest liues.

(199/13–16)

Now I beseech thee, for the love I show thee, that thou shouldst love me, at least after my death has been accomplished, who wouldst not while I lived.

Finally, the author's response to the knight's offer leads into the signification:

Nere þeos ilke leafdi of uueles cunnes cunde зef ha ouer alle þing ne luuede him her efter?   (199/18–20)

Would not this lady be of an evil nature had she not loved him thereafter beyond everything else?

The signification is more than exegesis; it continues the allegory, expands the chivalric ideal and gives definitions. By repeating the imagery of the knight's suit, the author keeps alive the symbolism of the Christ-knight while he introduces the metaphor of the Godhead as a shield pierced on all sides by the foe. A cursory examination of the parallel parts (with signification running above allegory) will show how similar are the phrases and images:

Þes king is iesu, godes sune, þet al o þisse wise wohede ure sawle þe deoflen hefden biset.

ALLEG.   A leafdi wes mid hire fan biset al abuten, hire lond al destruet . . .

Ant he, as noble wohere, efter monie messagers & feole goddeden, com to pruuien his luue & schawde þurh cnihtschipe þet he wes luuewurðe, as weren sumhwile cnihtes iwunet to donne.

ALLEG.   A mihti kinges luue wes þah biturnd up on hire swa unimete swiðe, þet he for wohlech sende hire his sonden, an efter oðer, ofte somet monie; sende hire beawbelez baðe feole & feire . . . He com him seolf on ende.

Dude him i turneiment, & hefde for his leoues luue his scheld i feht as kene cniht on euche half iþurlet. His scheld þe wreah his godd head wes his leoue licome þet wes ispread o rode, brad as scheld buuen in his istrahte earmes, nearow bineoðen as þe an fot, efter monies wene, set up o þe oðer.   (199/25–3)

This king is Jesus, the Son of God, who in just this way sought our soul's love when it was besieged by devils.

There was once a lady who was completely surrounded by her enemies, her land all laid waste . . .

*And He, like a noble lover, after having sent many messengers
and many good gifts, came to give proof of His love, and
showed by knightly deeds that He was worthy of love, as
knights at one time were accustomed to do.*

---

*But a king of great power loved her so much that he sent
messengers to her one after another, and often several
together, with many fair jewels . . . At last he went himself.*

*He entered the tournament, and like a brave knight had His
shield pierced through and through for love of His lady. His
shield, concealing His Godhead, was His dear body, which was
extended upon the cross, broad as a shield above, where His
arms were stretched out, and narrow below, where, as many
think, one foot was set upon the other.*

If we consider the language of the prefatory or transitional passage which
leads into the exemplum (p. 188), we have a third set of like figures, each
adding incrementally to the other until the end is realized. That end is
the death of the Christ-knight.

Even as early as the opening statements of Part Seven on the merits of
bodily hardships, the Rule has been developing implicitly the sacrifice
based on love rather than obedience. Moved to act by love, the Christ-
knight suffers meaningfully: 'al is ase nawt aʒeines luue.' Christ suffers
licomliche for love; love brings about the Passion. Man strives by
flesches pinsunges, and *alle pine & passiun þet bodi mahte þolien* to possess
Christ, who cannot be won except by love. Opposing motives, such
paradoxes as exist in divine and human affairs, are operating here, but the
wills must be made to conform or the sacrifice is wasted. The tension or
stress of uniting the faculties of the soul and the divine will is carried over
into the exemplum in the conflict of Christ-knight and lady.

More subtle than this is the progress of history in Christ's coming and
Passion as the fulfilment of the promise made at the beginning—the Old
Law supplanted by the New—the historical sense of the garden carried
to the next phase, Christ Himself, the knight, come personally after the
patriarchs and prophets (His many messengers) to bring the gospel
written in His own blood. His object is to win the soul, a proud and

undeserving lady, who must be humbled. It is voluntary sacrifice that makes the redemption possible. Christ and the soul must freely pledge themselves:

Ich chulle, for þe luue of þe, neome þet feht up o me, & arudde þe of ham þe þi dead seched.   (199/10–11)

For love of thee I will take this fight upon myself—and deliver thee from those who seek thy death.

The heart that wills to love is the only condition enjoined upon the soul. The knight, already driven by love, prepares to go to his death on this pledge.

The question whether with less suffering He might have redeemed us is posed and answered simultaneously: 'ne mahte he wið leasse gref habben arud us?' (200/13–14). In *arud* (delivered, redeemed), the necessity of the death *o rode* is contained. This movement away from the central allegory does not spur a theological argument; rather, it simplifies the whole issue of why Christ as the Christ-knight had to suffer this way when He could have redeemed the soul with less pain to Himself:

Ah he nalde. For hwi? Forte bineomen us euch bitellunge aȝein him of ure luue, þet he se deore bohte.   (200/14–16)

But He did not want to. So that we might not have any excuse for not giving Him our love, when He had bought it so dearly.

The concentrated activity of the exemplum has relaxed—leveled off at the cross actually while the provocative imagery of the body as a shield is yet to be explored. With his reply that it was our love 'þet he se deore bohte,' the author returns briefly to the idiom of measures and quantities, costs and the marketplace. The original challenge to the value of so costly a sacrifice is met and disposed of when the author draws upon the wisdom of an old saw and applies it to Christ's love: 'Me buð lihtliche þing þet me luueð lutel.' Christ bought us with His blood—'deorre pris nes neauer.' The high cost of the redemption assures the lady's liberation and binds her by her vow to the Christ-knight who 'ȝef for hire þe pris of him seoluen' (200/16–18).

The motif of the marketplace is insinuated rather cleverly into the lesser allegory of Christ's body as a shield pierced on all sides; for though the Rule seems to spring forward into a new theme, the developing imagery is linked to the challenge of so costly a sacrifice. The allegory is organized to carry through the dependence of the lady on the shield (the crucifix), a device of war borne in battle by the human knight. The shield is fashioned out of common materials that the author carefully describes as though he were a purveyor of goods at market hawking a precious thing. Also evident in the passage is a resurgence of triads embodying the analogous shield, body of Christ, and crucifix. These interact within the frame of the knight's sacrifice:

He bohte us wið his heorte blod forte ofdrahen of us ure luue þet costnede him se sare

I scheld beoð þreo þinges

$$\begin{cases} \text{treo} \\ \text{leðer} \\ \text{litunge} \end{cases}$$

Alswa þe $\begin{cases} \text{treo of þe rode} \\ \text{leðer of godes licome} \\ \text{litunge of þe reade blod} \end{cases}$ MEMORIA CHRISTI (200/17–22)

His leofmon bihalde þron hu he

lette $\begin{cases} \textit{bohte hire luue} \\ \textit{þurlin his scheld} \\ \textit{openin his side} \end{cases}$

$\begin{cases} \qquad \text{TO} \\ \text{schawin hire his heorte} \\ \text{schawin hire} \begin{pmatrix} \text{openliche} \\ \text{inwardliche} \end{pmatrix} \end{cases}$

ofdrahen hire heorte

he luuede hire (200/26–1)

This special love brings the Rule to a discussion of the four loves of this world: love of good friends, man and woman, mother and child, body and soul.[13] The segment appears at first to be a departure from the theme of sacrificial death, but as each love is defined and then measured against Christ's love, the relation to Christ-knight becomes clear. The four loves constitute a kind of unit; each elaboration of earthly love and attachment yields before the greater love offered by Christ. The digression—more properly a branch—is finally absorbed into the allegory out of which it arose.

In the first love ('bitweone gode iferen'), the death 'i giwerie' of Christ surpasses all expression of human friendship, for He gave 'his deorewurðe bodi to acwitin ut his leofmon of giwene honden' (200/7–201/9). To this line may be compared the Christ-knight's assurance of help to the lady: 'tu ne maht naneweis wið ute mi sucurs edfleon hare honden' (199/8–9).

The second love, that of man and woman, is also inferior when Christ's love for the soul is considered. He yields to His spouse, for whom He has boundless mercy despite her disloyalty: 'þah þe sawle his spuse forhori hire wið þe feond under heaued sunne.' His love is marked by such constancy as is unknown to men, even favored men. The contrast is more striking when the defection of the disciples, who fled in fear from Christ's side, is recalled:

> Þet þis scheld naueð siden is for bitacnunge þet his deciples, þe schulden stonden bi him & habben ibeon his siden, fluhen alle from him & leafden him as fremede. (199/3–5)

> *That this shield had no sides signifies that His disciples, who should have stood by Him and should have been at hand, all fled from Him and abandoned Him as if He had been a stranger.*

Within the context of this second love of man and woman, the restorative powers of Christ the Bridegroom are emphasized in an antithesis:

> Monnes neoleachunge makeð of meiden wif, & godd makeð of wif meiden. (201/27–28)

---

13. See Geoffrey Shepherd's comments on the classification of loves in *AW*, note 9, p. 59. For a summary of the divisions of loves in the writings of Bernard and his contemporaries, see Étienne Gilson, *Mystical Theology*, pp. 245–246.

The maidenhood of the soul, 'gode werkes & treowe bileaue,' is the pre-condition of the nuptials.

The bath of blood that the mother willingly prepares for her child's cure is the essence of the third love of the world. This figure lends itself readily to analogy with the bath of Christ's blood drawn to cleanse the spouse for the nuptials: 'na þing ne mahte healen us ne cleansin us bute his blod ane.' There is an allusion here to the restored maidenhood of the second love, for the spouse must be worthy of the Bridegroom's 'cleane cluppunges.'

The three baths Christ prepares—of baptism, penitence, and redemp-tion (*fulluht, teares, blod*)—are superior because of their threefold nature. The gesture too is matchless because of the power of Christ's love to endure. Might a mother forget her own child? asks the Rule, as if antici-pating the reader's objection. Whatever the answer, Christ can never forget. He has the remembrance graven into His hands:

Ich habbe, he seið, depeint te i mine honden. . . . Ah ure lauerd, for he nalde neauer forȝeoten us, dude mearke of þurlunge in ure munegunge i ba twa his honden.　　　　　　　　　　　(202/18–24)

'I have painted you,' He says, 'in my hands.' . . . but Our Lord, because He wished never to forget us, put marks of piercing in both His hands, to remind Him of us.

This simply presented progression pulls forward the imagery of the shield as Christ. The 'bath of blood,' repeated in the 'painted hands' (*Ich habbe depeint te i mine honden*), recalls the reddened shield—colored so fair —and the heart itself:

. . . þe litunge of þe reade blod þet heowede hire se feire. (200/21–22) *the painting of red blood which colored it so fair.*

He . . . lette þurlin his scheld, openin his side, to schawin hire his heorte.　　　　　　　　　　　　　　　　　　　(200/27–28) *He . . . allowed His shield to be pierced, His side opened, to show her His heart.*

The Christ-shield imagery has been suspended to introduce the discourse on the loves of the world. Its reappearance in the midst of the third love, apart from its immediate purpose of proving the permanence of Christ's love, keeps alive the allegory and the *memoria Christi* to which the Rule will return shortly.

The fourth love of the world ('bitweone licome & sawle') begins with a play on the word *twinnin* in the treatment of the sorrow of dear friends at the moment of parting:

Þe sawle luueð þe licome swiðe mid alle, ant þet is etscene
iþe twinnunge; for leoue freond beoð sari hwen ha schulen twinnin.

(202/24–26)

The soul loves the body greatly, and this is clearly seen in their parting, for dear friends are sorry when they must separate.

Part of the goal of the passage is to identify the principals. The spouse is the soul; Christ the persistent suitor. There is no deprecation of the body at all in the seventh part of the Rule; and in the fourth love of the world, there is evinced a fondness for the flesh insofar as it is the worldy companion of the soul—the very cloth that Christ put on when He came to woo her. This fourth love is a good love and as natural as the other three. The proof is the promise made of a future reunion of body and soul in heaven.

But Christ's love surpasses all of these, overpowers them. A transitional line reintroduces the allegory:

Iesu cristes luue toward his deore spuse . . . passeð alle &
ouerkimeð þe fowr measte luuen þet me ifind on eorðe. Wið al
þis luue ʒetten he woheð hire oþis wise.   (202/1–4)

Jesus Christ's love for His dear spouse . . . surpasses and triumphs over the four greatest kinds of love found on earth. With all this love He is ever seeking hers in the way I shall describe.

The assertion that He is ever seeking her love brings the Rule to the next progression, a return to the wooing, and closes the middle section of elaboration, amplification, and definition which have emerged from the suit of the Christ-knight. The movement here tends to advance the allegory to the next phase.

Continuity is sustained by opening the actual wooing with the language which had introduced each of the four loves:

Fowr heaued luuen	(200/2, between friends)
Much luue	(201/10, man and woman)
Nu of þe þridde luue	(201/2, mother and child)
Nu þe feorðe luue	(202/24, body and soul)

And now the specific love of the exemplum:

Þi luue, he seið, oðer hit is forte ȝeouen allunge, oðer hit is to sullen, oðer hit is to reauin & to neomen wið strengðe.   (202/4–6)

'Your love,' He says, 'can be given freely, or it can be sold, or it can be ravished from you and taken by force.'

The placing of *þi luue* in initial position points up an interesting paradox in the lady's relation to the knight. This love may be yet another worldly love to be overcome; in this sense, it is a fifth love of the world, one that is inferior to Christ's love. However, *þi luue* conveys a certain uniqueness, and so contrasts to the loves of the world. This love participates in both worlds, for it represents the love of the soul, the lady, being wooed in its earthen castle by an ideal knight who offers salvation.

The detailed pleading of his case by the Christ-knight stands out sharply against the ready unconditional sacrifice of Christ in the elaboration of the four loves of the world. The lady seems unmoved even when the knight reminds her of his generosity in the figure of the man who could withhold nothing so that it was said he had holes in his hands:

Nam ich þinge freoest? For swa me seið bi large mon þe ne con nawt edhalden, þet he haueð þe honden, as mine beoð, iþurlet.

     (202/9–203/11)

Am I not most generous? For people say of a generous man who can keep nothing back, that his hands are pierced; and so are Mine.

The image of the pierced hands appears here for the first time in connection with the Christ-knight but carries over into this phase of the courtship the particulars of the crucifixion—the sacrifice that is about to be reenacted.

The alternative of the free gift of love revives the idiom of the market-place and the figure of the liberality of love, heaven's steward:

> ʒef þi luue nis nawt toʒeouene, ah wult þet me bugge hire, buggen hire? Oðer wið oðer luue, oðer wið sumhweat elles. Me suleð wel luue, & swa me ah to sulle luue & for na þing elles. ʒef þin is swa to sullen, ich habbe iboht hire wið luue ouer alle oþre. . . . ʒef þu seist þu nult nawt leote þron se liht chap, ah wult ʒette mare, nempne hweat hit schule beon. Sete feor o þi luue. Þu ne schalt seggen se muchel þet ich nule ʒeoue mare. Wult tu castles? kinedomes? Wult tu wealden al þe world? Ich chulle do þe betere, makie þe wið al þis cwen of heoueriche. (203/16–27)

> *If your love is not to be given, but you are willing that it should be bought, how shall it be bought? Either with love in return or with something else. Love is rightly sold for love, and for nothing else. If yours is to be sold thus, then I have bought it with love beyond all other. . . . If you say that you will not set its price so low, but would have still more, say what it must be. Set a price upon your love. You will not name so much that I will not give more. Would you have castles, kingdoms? Would you have the whole world in your power? I will provide more for you, make you queen of the kingdom of heaven.*

The series of turns in the Christ-knight's proposal, marked by a gradually expanding generosity and a growing 'ferocity' of tone, are initiated by the conditional ʒef:

$$\text{ʒef} \begin{cases} \text{þi luue nis nawt toʒeouene} \\ \text{þine is swa to sullen} \\ \text{þu seist þu nult nawt leote þron se liht chap} \end{cases}$$

Every doubt settled, every condition met, the knight offers the kingdom of heaven—a rule as queen, sevenfold brighter than the sun. And once again the triads appear, more prominently at this point because of the excited pitch of the 'love terms.' Ornamental phrases and connectors are discarded as the knight gets to the heart of the bargain with table-pounding rhythms:

> nan uuel ne schal nahhi þe
> na wunne ne schal wonti þe
> al þi wil schal beon iwraht (in heouene\
>   & ec   (in eorðe)
>   ȝe & ȝet \in helle.)
> Ne schal neauer heorte þenchen hwuch selhðe þet ich
> nule ȝeouen for þi luue (unmeteliche\
>   (uneuenliche)
>   \unendeliche/ mare.

$$(203/28-4)$$

The great store of gifts, the 'unmeteliche, uneuenliche, unendeliche mare' lavished upon her, fills the text with bounty, with riches pouring forth as if rained down upon the lady: 'Al Creasuse weole . . . Absalones schene wlite . . . Asaeles swiftschipe . . . Samsones strengðe . . . Cesares freolec . . . Alixandres hereword . . . Moysese heale.'[14] After this lengthy elaboration of the 'wedding gifts' (which recall the knight's personal qualities), the coldness of the lady is not only unreasonable, but unacceptable. The irony of her *hauteur* who 'nes neauer wurðe forte beon his þuften' arouses the astonished reproach of the author:

Nis ha to heard iheortet þet a þulli wohere ne mei to his luue turnen?

$$(204/20-21)$$

Is she not excessively hard-hearted who cannot be brought to love such a lover?

The demand of love in return brings the wooing to a close. Of the three ways love is to be given to the Christ-knight—freely, by sale, or through force—two have already been described as part of the bestowal of favors. The first, love freely given, made an appeal to the reason: 'Nam ich alre þinge swotest & swetest?' (203/12); the next, love sold after practical bargaining: 'Ah wult þet me bugge hire?' (203/17). The third way involves a dramatic reversal of the knight's customary courtliness. The

---

14. For the history of this description of the beatitudes from Anselm to Richard of St. Victor, see Geoffrey Shepherd, '"All the wealth of Croesus . . .": A Topic in the *AR*,' *MLR*, 51 (1956), 161–167.

sharp departure from the patience and forbearance of Christ (particularly, in His relation to the four loves of the world), marks a turn in tone in the argument, moving now with militancy and acceleration beyond anything the leisurely development of past segments has led us to expect. It is as if the knight has grown weary of timidity and compromise; as if the gross imbalance of his gifts (which include his life) against hers suddenly erupts in anger. He will save her with or without her consent:

> Lo, ich halde her heatel sweord up o þin heaued todealen lif &
> sawle & bisenchen ham ba in to þe fur of helle. . . . Ondswere nu &
> were þe, ȝef þu const, aȝein me, oðer ȝette me þi luue þe ich
> ȝirne se swiðe.   (204/14–18)

> *See! I hold a hostile sword here over your head to divide life and soul, to
> plunge both of them into the fire of hell . . . Answer Me now and protect
> yourself against Me if you can, or give Me your love that I long for so
> much.*

For who, the author asks, can hide from His heat? The quotation from the psalmist ('Non est qui se abscondat a calore eius,' Psalm 18:17) comes as a response to the lady's reserve, but structurally the 'heat' is pivotal. The third concentration of Part Seven emerges out of the author's substitution of *love* for heat:

> Non est qui se abscondat a calore eius. Nis nan þet mahe edlutien
> þet ha ne mot him luuien.   (204/24–25)

> *There is no one who can hide herself away in order to escape loving Him.*

When he has joined love and heat, the author moves at once into the play on the homonymous sun/son and on the relation of the Son to the sun (over Calvary) where Christ's love has brought Him:

> Þe soðe sunne iþe undertid wes for þi istihen on heh o þe hehe
> rode, forte spreaden ouer al hate luue gleames.   (204/25–27)

> *For this the true Sun was lifted up at noon on the high cross, to send out
> in all directions the burning rays of love.*

The emphatic *undertid* and *on heh o þe hehe rode* is strengthened by the contrast of *under* and *heh*; by repetition of sounds *istihen, heh, hehe*; and by the actual enclosure of Son within the image of *sunne*. The image depends on likeness of sound to fuse together the elements of Calvary, visually and intellectually, in an instant. The figure of the crucified Son spreading 'ouer al hate luue gleames' carries forward the metaphor of radiant sun and calls up the recent elaboration of Christ as shield, particularly in the image of the outstretched arms 'brad as scheld buuen in his istrahte earmes' (199/1). The 'hate luue gleames' of the sun, 'þe soðe sunne,' pour forth heat in order to set fire to His love's heart, to ignite in the earthly heart a 'bearninde luue . . . þet hit bleasie':

> Ich com to bringen, he seið, fur in to eorðe, þet is, bearninde luue
> in to eorðlich heorte.
> (204/1–3)

In quick contrast the noisome, lukewarm love, offensive to Him as He addresses his *leofmon*, recalls the condition which the Christ-knight lays upon the lady before he goes forth to tournament, to love him firmly after his death:

> Ich walde, he seið to his leofmon, þet tu were i mi luue oðer
> allunge cald, oðer hat mid alle. Ah for þi þet tu art ase wlech
> bitweone twa, nowðer hat ne cald, þu makest me to wleatien;
> & ich wulle speowe þe ut bute þu wurðe hattre. (204/6–205/10)

'I would,' He says to His beloved, 'that in loving Me you were either utterly cold or utterly hot, but because you are as it were lukewarm, between the two, neither hot nor cold, you disgust Me, and unless you grow hotter, I will vomit you out.'

The tepid love ('wlech bitweone twa') is abhorrent.[15] Christ's disgust is vividly expressed in 'wleatien 'and 'speowen'—an image and reaction that relate most intimately to the bitter mixture of urine and vinegar to come.

Fire, kindled by two crossed sticks from which 'hate luue gleames' pour down, seals together the third concentration on the death 'o rode' and the fourth on the power and sovereignty of love. The source of the metaphor is the biblical account of the woman of Sarepta of 3 Kings 17, given a new turn in the Rule. The two sticks gathered with the woman of Sarepta are kindling to ignite the heart:

15. 'Moreover, there can be no fellowship between the Spirit and the Flesh, between fire and tepidity, particularly as the Lord is wont to vomit what is lukewarm out of His mouth.' Bernard, *Sermons for the Seasons*, II, 248. The source is Rev. 3:16.

Þeos twa treon bitacnið þet a treo þet stod upriht & þet oþer þe
eode þwertouer, o þe deore rode. Of þeose twa treon ȝe schulen
ontende fur of luue inwið ower heorte.   (205/15–18)

*These two pieces of wood represent the one which stood upright and the
one which crossed it, in the precious cross. With these two pieces of wood
you should kindle the fire of love in your heart.*

The two sticks, upright and crossbar, dissolve into the figure of the
crucifix, the *memoria Christi*. Here the *bihestes* made earlier are realized in
the attainment of Christ Himself, for the outspread arms beckon and
drooping head inclines in the posture of a kiss:

Þencheð ȝef ȝe ne ahen eaðe to luuien þe king of blisse, þe tospreat
swa his earmes toward ow & buheð as to beoden cos duneward his
heaued.   (205/18–20)

*Think how gladly you should love the King of glory who extends His
arms towards you and bows down His head as if to beg a kiss.*

The mystical reading of the woman of Sarepta encloses physically the
mystical kiss of the mouth, the final stage of preparation for contemplative union with Christ. Having conveyed his figures into symbols, the
author retreats, slipping into direct exegetical method to deal with the
vital elements of the allegory. The return to more restrained language of
exposition and development is typical of his style.

Besides suggesting that the author had achieved some degree of contemplation (his personal experience is supported by the reference to the
kiss of peace in Part One), the passage touches briefly the idea of God's
grace as a condition of love. The significant promise that God 'wule
gestnin wið ow & monifalden in ow his deorewurðe grace' as He did the
woman of Sarepta is reminiscent of the opening statements on love and
the cultivation of the heart:' . . . þet godd te reaðere þiderward loki mid
his grace & makeð þe heorte schir & of briht sihðe (196/21–23).

The 'heat of His love,' the 'hot rays of love,' the 'kindling' with two
crossed sticks—all mount cumulatively and peak in the climactic imagery
of irrepressible Greek fire:

Grickisch fur is imaket of reades monnes blod, & þet ne mei na
þing bute Migge ant Sond & eisil, as me seið, acwenchen. Þis

grickisch fur is þe luue of iesu ure lauerd, & ȝe hit schule makien of reade monnes blod, þet is, iesu crist ireadet wið his ahne blod o þe deore rode. (205/25–2)

Greek fire is made from the blood of a red man and cannot be quenched, it is said, except with urine, sand and vinegar. This 'Greek fire' is the love of Jesus our Lord, and you shall make it from the blood of a red man, that is, Jesus Christ, reddened with His own blood on the precious cross.

'Apt if startling' is Geoffrey Shepherd's response to the opening line of the terminal segment of Part Seven. The metaphor is striking indeed, first in the sudden change in tone from the exegetical passage on the woman of Sarepta where this fire is 'kindled'; and then in the arresting conception of Greek fire made of the blood of a red man. The author has taken the image of liquid fire, 'wildfire,' from popular accounts of Crusade warfare,[16] and combined it with a sanguine Christ, for tradition had it that Christ had had red hair and ruddy coloring. The presence of Christ (and the Christ-knight) in a very real physical sense and the sensuousness of the imagery are especially evident at this stage of Part Seven. The uncontrollable wildfire, the bloodied Christ ('ireadet wið his ahne blod o þe deore rode'), the specifics of urine and vinegar that threaten to smother the consuming Greek fire—all converge here into the emotional, highly concentrated repetitions and refinements of the power of the sacrifice. And the pervasiveness of redness (initially the color of fire) provides a definite focus for the Passion, the *memoria Christi*, the affective influence of Christ crossed that kindles the *incendium amoris* between anchoress and Christ, between lady and Christ-knight.

The fire imagery, skillfully introduced in Greek fire, merges with the Son/sun concept and configuration, the hot love beams; the kindling of love with 'twa treon' (which makes of the anchoress a Sareptian 'þet is ontende mid tis grickisch fur,' 205/4) sets the heart aglow. The heart fired with love becomes the dominant image into which all the other figures and emotional qualities flow. It is devotion to the cross—an outpouring of love for the sacrificed Christ, inexpressible and insensible, that frees the heart of earthly weight and enlightens the understanding.

What creates the special effect of these passages is the rapidity of

16. See Geoffrey Shepherd, *AW*, note 11, p. 65, for sources. Urine, sand, and vinegar were effective extinguishers commonly used even in ancient times.

confluent images interrelating, disappearing, recurring—all firmly grounded in physical, sensuous appeals. The emotional response to Christ is love. Direct, intense, lasting.

We may trace the route the author has structured by returning briefly to the first assertion of heat (*Non est qui se abscondat a calore eius*),which occurs at the end of the Christ-knight's suit. The heat predicted there is created within the frame of the woman-of-Sarepta episode and erupts into Greek fire. The crucifixion, the Christ-knight's active sacrifice, is proceeding simultaneously, kindling the fire with red blood—'Greek fire is made of the blood of a red man':

(1) *Wooing*

Non est qui se abscondat a calore eius

(PASSION) þe soðe sunne . . . o þe hehe rode forte spreaden . . . hate luue gleames

$$\left(\begin{array}{l}\text{to ontenden his luue \& his}\\\text{luues heorte.}\end{array}\right)$$

$$\boxed{\begin{array}{l}\text{wlech luue—ich wulle}\\\text{speowe þe ut}\end{array}}$$

(2) *Woman of Sarepta*

'Sarepta means to kindle'

(PASSION) þeos twa treon . . . o þe deore rode

$$\left(\begin{array}{l}\text{ʒe schulen ontende fur of luue}\\\text{inwið ower heorte.}\end{array}\right)$$

(3) *Greek fire*

'made of the blood of a red man'

(PASSION) þe luue of iesu . . . ireadet wið his ahne blod o þe deore rode

$$\left(\begin{array}{l}\text{þis blod . . . schal makien ow Sarep-}\\\text{tiens, þet is, ontende mid tis}\\\text{grickisch fur.}\end{array}\right)$$

$$\boxed{\begin{array}{l}\textit{migge, sond, eisil}\\\text{quench Greek fire}\end{array}}$$

(204/24–205/8)

The heat created by the burning beams (1) ignites (2) and bursts into Greek fire (3), which is turned against the enemy.

To the special uses of medieval 'wildfire' which have been set in operation should be added that of its use defensively against siege, a reading which would satisfy the tendency of the Rule to return to already established patterns. We recall that the lady in her earthen castle is beset on all sides by the foe. Greek fire is the weapon by which she is inflamed with love of God and with which she destroys her enemy, whether it be the world, the flesh or the devil. The terrifying effects of the fire in warfare reinforce metaphorically the power of the Passion to hold off the enemy:

> Þis blod for ow isched up o þe earre twa treon schal makien ow sareptiens, þet is, ontende mid tis grickisch fur þet, as Salomon seið, nane weattres, þet beoð worldliche tribulatiuns, nane temptatiuns, nowðer inre ne uttre, ne mahen þis luue acwenchen.
>
> (205/2–6)

> *This blood, which was shed for you upon those two lengths of wood of which I have spoken shall make you Sarephtans, that is, it will set you aflame with this Greek fire, unquenchable, as Solomon says, by any waters, that is to say, by the tribulations of the world, or by any interior or exterior temptations.*

Yet even as the anchoress is quickening to this spiritual fire, the cautions against extinguishing it begin to build. The depressants, urine, sand, vinegar, not only put out Greek fire, they render the sacrifice wasted:

> Migge is stench of sunne. O sond ne groweð na god & bitacneð idel. Idel akeldeð & acwencheð þis fur.   (205/8–10)

> *Urine is the stench of sin. Nothing good grows on sand, and it signifies idleness. Idleness cools and quenches the fire.*

Sand nurtures nothing but idleness; it cools and quenches Greek fire while other fires—'þe brune of sunne'—begin to flare. Just as one nail drives out another, so 'þe brune of godes luue driueð brune of ful luue ut of þe heorte.' The play on *brune* conveys the figure and force of the paradox. Moreover, the advice to the anchoress to avoid idleness is couched in verbs of activity. 'Sturieð ow cwicliche,' she is told; this will 'heaten ow & ontenden þis fur aȝein þe brune of sunne' (as a physical operation as well as spiritual effect.) The maxim of the nail, juxtaposed with the 'brune of godes luue' driving out the 'brune of sunne,' alludes to the piercing of the hands, the bloodletting by which the holy fire is enkindled.[17]

The Rule deals quickly with the first two members of the group so that it may get on with the elaboration of *eisil*—that which sours the heart with envy and spite, human weaknesses to which even the anchoress may be subject in the unnatural condition of enclosure. But with the *eisil* ('sur heorte of nið oðer of onde'), we are back to the crucifixion, to the sour offering to Christ on the cross, to the pain of bitterness and hate betokened by the vinegar:

> Vnderstondeð þis word. Þa þe niðfule giws offreden ure lauerd
> þis sure present up o þe rode, þa seide he þet reowðfule word,
> Consumatum est. Neauer, qð he, ear nu nes ich ful pinet, nawt
> þurh þet eisil, ah þurh hare ondfule nið þet tet eisil bitacnede þet
> heo him duden drinken. Ant is ilich as þah a mon þet hefde longe
> iswunken & failede efter long swinc on ende of his hure. (206/15–22)

> *When the malevolent Jews offered Our Lord this sour present on the
> cross, it was then that He said those piteous words, It is consummated.
> 'Not until now,' He said, 'have I been made to suffer to the limit'; and
> it was not because of the vinegar but because of their hateful malice,
> symbolized by the vinegar which they offered him to drink.*

The exchange of Christ's body ('dude his deorewurðe bodi,' 200/8, as ransom for the *leofmon*) for 'þis sure present' from the 'sur heorte' of bitterness and anger is to be deplored. The bitter heart, like bitter *eisil*, is an insufferable reward for labor on earth and suffering on the cross. And as he develops this idea, the author skillfully reintroduces the imagery of the laborer in the garden or vineyard:

> Ure lauerd mare þen twa & pritti ȝer tilede efter hare luue, & for al
> his sare swinc ne wilnede na þing bute luue to hure. Ah i þe ende

---

17. The image comes from St. Bernard: 'Let the Lord Jesus be thy heart's delight-driving from it delight in the allurements of the flesh, as one nail drives another.' *Sermons on Canticles*, p. 52.

of his lif, þet wes as i þe euentid hwen me ʒelt wercmen hare deies
hure, loke hu ha ʒulden him for piment of huni luue: eisil of sur
nið & galle of bitter onde. O, qð ure lauerd þa, Consumatum
est. Al mi swinc on eorðe, al mi pine o rode ne sweameð ne ne
derueð me nawiht aʒein þis, þet ich þus biteo al þet ich idon habbe.
Þis eisil þet ʒe beodeð me, þis sure hure þurhfulleð mi pine.

(206/22–3)

*Our Lord for more than two and thirty years had striven for their love,
and wanted nothing in payment for His hard toil except love, but at the
end of His life, as it were in the evening, when workmen are given their
daily wage, see how they paid Him, not with the sweet drink of love,
sweet as honey, but with the vinegar of sour malice, and the gall of bitter
hatred. 'O,' cried Our Lord then, 'it is consummated. All My labour on
earth, all My suffering on the cross have not grieved, have not afflicted Me
at all compared with this, that they should thus receive My gift, all I have
done. This vinegar which you offer, this sour payment, completes My
suffering.'*

The concentration in these passages on the act of love, the incidental but
pointed references to drink, the complaints of suffering, and the direct
references to the laborers in the vineyard act to complete the circularity
of the seventh part, moved, of course, beyond the experience of ordinary
men but not beyond application to the lives of men. The imagery of the
garden, the toil of the laborer, the tools with which the heart is cultivated
are revived here, but it is Christ-made-man through whom these
worldly labors are expressed in language and action most familiar to
men. Christ 'tilede efter hare luue' with 'swinc on eorðe' and 'pine o
rode.' We might compare this cultivation of the lady's heart with the
opening statements of 196/15–17: 'Al þet wa & al þet heard þet we
þolieð o flesch . . . ne beoð nawt bute as lomen to tilie wið þe heorte.'

This is one instance of the parallels in activity, tone, and language joining the beginning and closing sections of Part Seven. The return to a
simple setting not only brings together the labor of Christ for man's love
and that of man for the 'brihte & schir heorte þet is godes luue ane,' but
provides the means of identifying the daily commonplaces of the
material world with the exercise of the Divine Will.

Between the literal-allegorical presentation of concrete images (garden-marketplace, knight-lady, *memoria Christi*) are the intangibles of symbol, enlarging, contracting in rhythm with the imagery; never static but continually activated by significations, allusions, cross-references. The interaction of the moral lesson and transfer of Christ the Laborer into the parable of the workers in the vineyard may be noted in the following way:

> The vinegar offered in wrath and bitterness
>   (alswa ure lauerd mare þen twa & þritti ȝer tilede efter hare luue,
>   & for al his sare swinc ne wilnede na þing bute luue to hure)
> at the end of His life
>   (i þe euentid hwen me ȝelt wercmen hare deies hure)
> was sour spite and the gall of bitter envy.
>   (loke hu ha ȝulden him for piment of huni luue.)   (206/22–26)

Repaid for His labors this way, Christ's sacrifice is the more painful: 'Þis eisil þet ȝe beodeð me, þis sure *hure* þurhfulleð mi pine' (206/2–3).

The 'brihte & schir heorte' has become the 'sur heorte'; and although the references to the Jews has indirectly but powerfully identified *eisil* with their role in the crucifixion (all the more reason for the anchoress to drive out of her heart envy and spite), the force of the argument depends on the ability of *eisil* to quench Greek fire 'þet is þe luue of ure lauerd.' This bitter drink is the very one that cools ardor, the mixture that the pusillanimous religious offers Christ, only to be spat out: 'Ich wulle speowe þe ut' (204/9). In this way opening premises grow organically in the Rule—they come full circle.

The cry *Consumatum est* of 206/17, which, with the offering of the vinegar, signals the climax of the passage, is transformed into a personal expression of futility, of waste, of meaningless sacrifice and humiliation:

> Al mi swinc on eorðe, al mi pine o rode ne sweameð ne ne derueð
> me nawiht aȝein þis, þet ich þus biteo al þet ich idon habbe. Þis
> eisil þet ȝe beodeð me, þis sure hure þurhfulleð mi pine. (206/28–3)

The impassioned complaint from the cross reminds us of the knight's demand that the lady promise to love him more after his death than she did before. The lady, then, is in default; the knight's reward is the 'bitter þonc.' The engaging drama of the Christ-knight exemplum and the pathetic, emotional appeal of the crucifixion come together in the completing of Christ's pain: 'þis sure hure þurhfulleð mi pine.'

Whether the extinguisher of Greek fire be sand, urine, or vinegar, each stands as an alternative to the life the anchoress or lady has chosen for herself. If there is a lapse, if her submission to Christ is not total, then He has died for nothing. It was to save her that He came as the Christ-knight —not to redeem the world in a general atonement, but to offer Himself personally, intimately to her. The lady has shown herself worthy of the knight's favors ('low a wretch' though she may be), just as the anchoress has progressed in her spiritual journey to love. The author's warnings against tepid love, the pusillanimous heart, the quenching of fire, are reminders to her (and to us) of how far the anchoress has come and how deep is her betrayal if she returns His love with a 'bitter þonc.'

The moral imperative of the sacrifice is made eminently clear in the promise of love returned for love: to love Him means to love all, even the enemy. In the triumphant and unexpected turn that reactivates the power of Greek fire, the lady defeats the enemy:

> Me warpeð grickisch fur upon his famen, & swa me ouerkimeð ham.
> (206/7–8)

But the physical, militant act of throwing out Greek fire to consume the enemy is rehabilitated under the force of love, for the fire eats up their malice and kindles their love:

> Ʒef þi fa hungreð, fed him. To his þurst ʒef him drunch. . . . Þus þu schalt, seið Salomon, rukelin on his heaued bearninde gleden, þet is to seggen, þus þu schalt ontenden his heorte forte luuie þe.
> (207/12–18)

> *If thy enemy be hungry, give him to eat: if he thirst, give him to drink . . . Thus, says Solomon, you shall heap burning coals on his head, that is to say, thus you shall kindle his heart into loving you.*

In this way, the anchoress follows Christ's example, extending to the 'enemy' the kind of magnanimity Christ felt toward His tormentors.

The recurrence of the theme of liberality (specifically in the dispensing of food and drink) links this passage to the opening imagery of the cultivation of the heart as though it were earth to bring forth fruit, the 'briht & schir heorte' which is 'luue of godd ane.' Living Christ's example, the anchoress is to give mercy and love to the enemy (even to the backbiters and flatterers of which we have heard much). Otherwise, she completes Christ's pain:

> Hwa se hit bereð i breoste toward wummon oðer mon . . . ha offreð godd þis eisil & þurhfulleð onont hire iesues pine o rode.
>
> (206/5–7)

> *Anyone who bears it in her breast against man or woman . . . is offering God that vinegar and playing her own part in completing the agony of Jesus on the cross.*

Heap burning coals upon their heads (Greek fire tossed into the army of besiegers) and enkindle them with love so that they will repay you in kind—this is the reward of prayer and represents the equity of exchange between master and laborer in the field or the vineyard. But to love as Christ had loved and been a worker in the world ('mare þen twa & þritti ʒer tilide efer hare luue') for an ungrateful master is not an unworthy task after all; for Christ had done so, and He will repay those who do so in His name with just wages at Judgment. The settling of accounts is conveyed in a relaxed, intimate tone suggestive of the aftermath of struggle and serene confidence:

> 'Hwi luuedest tu þe mon oðer þe wummon?' 'Sire, ha luueden me.' 'Ʒe,' he wulle seggen, 'þu ʒulde þet tu ahtest. Her nabbe ich þe nawt muches to ʒelden.' Ʒef þu maht ondswerien, 'Alle wa ha duden me, ne na luue ne ahte ich ham; ah, sire, ich luuede ham for þi luue,' þet luue he ah þe, for hit wes iʒeuen him & he hit wule þe ʒelden.[18]
>
> (207/19–25)

18. The *De amicitia christiana* of Peter of Blois supplies this passage: 'Because you love your friend, he loves you; so it is with the law of friendship; if you love your friend for the love of Christ, that falls within merit. But how much greater the difference and greatness in meriting the grace of God if for the love of Christ, which rules your will, you love your enemy for the sake of God.' *PL* 207, col. 885.

*'Why did you love that man, or that woman?' 'Because they loved me,
Lord.' 'Yes,' He will say, 'You paid what you owed. There is not much
in this for which I can reward you.' But if you can reply, 'They caused me
much suffering, and I owed them no love, but I loved them, Lord, for love
of Thee,' then He owes you that love, because it was given to Him, and
He will give it back to you.*

The sudden personal address by Christ, the power in simplicity of this
verbal exchange brings home the promise that He will reward those who
do good works in His name. This had been the obligation of love earlier,
giving 'al þet ha haueð & ec hire seoluen' (197/24). Throwing 'her
weight' on St. Michael's scales, she will be judged by her good works:

Luue ane schal beon ileid i seint Mihales weie. Þeo þe meast luuieð
schulen beo meast iblisset.   (197/19–21)

By such slow degrees, like the anchoress who must inch her way up to
heaven, the author has brought the Rule back to love. Carnal love, all
ties to the flesh, must fall away. The point no longer is denial of the flesh,
since that implies recognition of existence and conscious suppression.
The flesh must dissolve before Christ may come; this condition is set by
Christ's own words to the disciples that unless He leave them (in body),
the holy spirit, which is His love, may never come into them: 'Ah hwen
ich beofrom ow ich chulle senden him ow' (207/3–4).

The alternatives are clearly and simply stated: earthly comfort or
heavenly, this world or the next—the subject which has been and continues to be the theme of the Rule. The inner Rule is opened and closed
by the same question, we might say, for in 'Custody of the Senses' God
insists upon a decision:

For ne schalt tu nanesweis þes ilke twa cunforz, min & te worldes,
þe ioie of þe hali gast & ec flesches froure, habbe to gederes. Cheos
nu an of þes twa, for þe oðer þu most leten.   (54/2–5)

*For you shall by no means have both these comforts, mine and the
world's, the joy of the Holy Spirit and the comfort of the flesh together.
Choose then one of these two, for the other you must leave.*

At this critical point in the seventh part, in which the choice of one or the other (inner or outer, once again) is left entirely up to the anchoress, so that her submission to the flesh or spirit is voluntary, the Rule returns to the language and imagery of the first segment on the 'briht & schir heorte':

> Schirnesse of heorte is godes luue ane. I þis is al þe strengðe of alle
> religiuns, þe ende of alle ordres.   (197/15–16)

> Cheose nu euchen of þes twa, eorðlich elne & heouenlich, to
> hweðer ha wule halden, for þet oðer ha mote leten; for i þe tweire
> monglunge ne mei ha habben neauer mare schirnesse of heorte . . .
> þet god & te strengðe of alle religiuns & in euch ordre. Luue makeð
> hire schir, griðful & cleane.   (208/10–15)

> *Let everyone choose now between these two, earthly comfort and
> heavenly, to which she will cleave, for she must let the other go, since she
> can never again, if she mingles the two, have purity of heart . . . the
> virtue and the strength of all religions and of every Order. Love makes her
> bright, peaceful and pure.*

Flesh and spirit are irreconcilable in the life of the anchoress. The author has slowly developed this simple doctrinal truth into a perception of Christ bodiless, for even the flesh of Christ must be withdrawn— 'and what flesh on earth was so sweet and so holy as His?'—before love may take possession.

The power of love is now enlarged to a new dimension. While love had served generously at table before, when the several types of sacrifice were yet to be examined, God provided the initiating force: '. . . þet godd to reaðere þiderward loki mid his grace & makeð þe heorte schir & of briht sihðe.' Now love is the master. The Christ-knight has shown himself to be overcome: 'Luue hefde ouercumen him' (199/6–7). Love assumes absolute sovereignty: 'Luue haueð a meistrie biuoren alle oþre' (208/15–16). All that she touches, she makes her own; God Himself is subject to her 'meistrie.'

The allusions to the marketplace reappear, with love the only acceptable means of exchange for good (goods): 'Þu makest wið uten oþer swinc his god þin ahne god' (208/21–22). The line alludes to Christ's 'swinc o rode,' which may be paid for with love; for the power of love is such that if it subjugates Christ, what may it not do to men?

The value of love is measured by what human or material possessions can accrue through it; but the idiom of commerce and barter is merely a figurative device to convey the anagogue of love's sovereignty passing into the hands of the beloved, who may do with Christ what she will:

Luue haueð a meistrie biuoren alle oþre. For al þet ha rineð, al ha turneð to hire & makeð al hire ahne.   (208/15–17)

Deore walde moni mon buggen a swuch þing þet al þet he rine to, al were his ahne.   (208/18–19)

Rin him wið ase much luue as þu hauest sum mon sum chearre. He is þin to don wið al þet tu wilnest.

(208/24–25)

Love has an authority above all others, for all that she touches she wins to herself and makes it all her own.

Many a man would pay dearly for something which made all that he touched with it, his own.

Touch Him with as much love as you sometimes feel for a man. He is yours to do with all that you will.

The Christ-knight yields at the sign of love: 'Streche þi luue to iesu crist; þu hauest him iwunnen' (208/23–24).

The emphasis is on touch, physical and metaphorical. The *streche* alludes to the crucifix and evokes the recent imagery of Christ's pain and, more significantly, the posture of Christ as the Bridegroom:

Þencheð ʒef ʒe ne ahen eaðe to luuien þe king of blisse, þe tospreat swa his earmes toward ow & buheð as to beoden cos duneward his heaued.   (205/18–20)

Think how gladly you should love the King of glory who extends His arms towards you and bows down His head as if to ask a kiss.

Through subjection by love, 'he is þin to don wið al þet tu wilnest.'

The basic imagery, however, remains that of the marketplace, where Christ is being measured against men, where goods are being handled (a possible reading of *rinen*), where His cost is being 'reckoned.' Love has 'put Him on the block,' in a real sense. This is an interesting reversal of the redemption. Throughout the Rule, Christ is said to have bought man with His blood, but at this point it is He who is offered and bought by the anchoress at the cost of the world:

> Ah hwa luueð þing þet leaueð hit for leasse þen hit is wurð?
> Nis godd betere uneuenlich þen al þet is i þe world? . . . Undeore
> he makeð godd & to unwurð mid alle, þet for ei worltlich þing of
> his luue leaskeð.   (208/26–1)

> *But who loves a thing and will part with it for less than it is worth?*
> *Is not God incomparably better than all there is in the world? . . . But he*
> *who loosens his love from God in favour of something in the world, holds*
> *God cheap and values Him all too little.*

The excess of Christ's love is expressed in His willing vassalage. He is not content to make the lady His equal—here the author's timorous accents dissolve suddenly—He makes her His master:

> Ʒet ich dear segge mare—he makeð hire his meistre & deð al þet ha
> hat as þah he moste nede.   (208/3–5)

The analogy of Christ-knight is apparent, but love has gone beyond allegorization. The author's insistence on personal involvement rises in intensity as he himself is caught up in the experience he tries to describe. Language comes pouring out as if it were a channel of Christ's boundless love, as if there were no end to the proofs of His service:

> Ʒet ich dear segge mare   (208/3–4)
> Mei ich pruuien þis?   (208/5)
> Nes þes wið luue ibunden?   (209/20)
> Hwet wult tu mare?   (209/21)

Love binds. Love binds Christ; He may do nothing without her leave. Love is His chamberlain, His counsellor, His spouse. The happiness that the Bridegroom has prepared for His spouse is incomparable: 'Ha is uneuenlich to alle worldes blissen'. And as the author moves to express mystical transcendence, he continues into a realm of experience which for him dissolves into the inexpressible: 'Ha is untalelich to worldliche tungen.'

With the ascendency of love as sovereign of the heart, the master to whom Christ is subject, the inner Rule is brought to an end. We come back to the heart, to the full understanding of the 'swote & schir heorte' and of the relation of lady and handmaiden. This Rule, 'þe leafdi riwle,' is served by whatever serves love and the regulation of the heart: 'Þis luue is þe riwle þe riwleð þe heorte.'

Part Eight, concerned with the outer Rule, with recapitulation and summary, serves two purposes of overall organization. It brings the Rule outward from the highly concentrated, intense discourse on love, thereby providing a gradual relaxing of tension, a 'quieting' of the energy generated by the dense accumulation of images of Part Seven; and structurally, together with Part One, it 'encircles' the Rule so that the outer-inner analogy persists into the work's linear design, the outer encircling the inner.

The author's frank statement of the relative unimportance of external rules shows his flexibility on matters governing the daily exercise of duties and observances, for these may be changed when better ones are provided. It is the inner Rule that is inviolable: 'Aȝein þinges þe beoð biuoren, of ham is lutel strengðe.'

The anchoress is advised to take communion fifteen times a year, and the occasions are named. Dietary restrictions, including fasts and abstention from 'white food,' meats, and fat, are touched upon; but always the author carefully provides for the eventuality of sickness, when greater freedom in diet is permitted and encouraged. She is advised not to take meals with guests outside her domicile, as some others do, for in her 'order' she is dead to the world. From this, the author concludes with good-humored logic:

Me haueð iherd ofte þet deade speken wið cwike. Ah þet ha eten wið cwike, ne fond ich ȝet neauer. (211/23–24)

One has often heard of the dead speaking with the living but I have never found that they eat with the living.

Personal conviction of this symbolic death is the ideal mental condition of the recluse, but the *caveats* that follow betray a certain shortcoming in the actual day-to-day experience, when the temptation to entertain visitors or spend lavishly (even when the motive is earnest generosity) distracts her from the contemplative life. Withdrawal from the world is described by the divergent lives of Mary and Martha, the two sisters of the active and contemplative lives.[1] The anchoress, following Mary, has chosen the better part. Within the segment on the model life 'sitting with Mary in perfect stillness at God's feet,' the author inserts derivative counsels on living frugally on alms donated by others, on quietly distributing whatever pittance remains to the poor, so that the anchoress' good deeds are done in silence: 'Ʒef ha mei spearien eani poure schraden, sende ham al dearnliche ut of hire wanes; under semblant of god is ofte ihulet sunne' (212/23–25).[2]

The outer Rule stresses the need for modesty, prudence, and civility, whether the subject is conduct toward visitors, dining with male guests, or courtesies toward children and servants. The anchoress is cautioned against frivolity and acquisitiveness, and against worldly diversions that might lead to greater offenses. If she must have a pet, let it be a cat only; large animals will make a housewife of her and draw her heart outward: 'Ancre ne ah to habben na þing þet utward drahe hire heorte.' She is not to conduct business with the hope of making a profit, nor allow friends to deposit their possessions in her anchorhold for safekeeping. She must not apply rigorous discipline to her body without permission, for any instrument that hardens the heart is to be avoided:

> Sum wummon inohreaðe wereð þe brech of here ful wel icnottet, þe streapeles dun to þe vet ilacet ful feaste; ah eauer is best þe swete & te swote heorte. Me is leouere þet ʒe þolien wel an heard word, þen an heard here.   (214/15–215/17)

A woman will occasionally take to wearing breeches of hair-cloth tied firmly about her, with the leggings closely laced down to the feet; but a

---

1. The traditional interpretation of Luke 10:38–42, initiated by St. Augustine in his sermons and continued by Gregory and Bernard. For salient excerpts from the writings of the Church Fathers, see Butler, *Western Mysticism*, pp. 157–198.

2. A similar idea occurs in 76/25–27: 'Hercnið nu, leoue sustren, hu hit is uuel to uppin, & hu god þing hit is to heolen goddede.' Most of the points have been taken up in previous chapters, particularly in the colorful description of the animal-sins in 'Temptations.'

*sweet and gentle heart is always best. I would rather you suffered a hard
word well, than hard hair-cloth.*

Besides setting out recommendations on manner of dress, personal
cleanliness and manual labor (nothing more strenuous than needlework
and the repair of church vestments), the author keeps fresh the memory
of the inner Rule so that the anchoress will know that the disciplines of
external rules prepare her for interior comfort. So, the need for peace and
harmony in the anchorhold is conveyed through a reminder of the
dangers of a puff of wind blown by the devil, which extinguishes the fire
in the heart. Failing in this, the devil pulls apart the burning brands with
which the heart is ignited with 'te hali gastes fur'—an allusion to the
crossed sticks used by the woman of Sarepta in Part Seven: '& te hali
gastes fur cwencheð hwen þebrondes þurh wreaððe beoð isundret, for
þi halden ham i luue feaste to gederes' (219/18–20). The author's tactful
solution to the question of dissension in the anchorhold (now that he has
raised this as an issue, he seems determined that the anchoress not regard
it as a personal reproof) is to cast his counsel into advice the anchoress may
give to her servants:

Þis is a þing, witen ha wel, þet is gode leouest—sahtnesse & some—
& te feond laðest. (219/10–11)

*This, let them understand, is a thing most pleasing to God, reconciliation
and concord—and most hateful to the devil.*

Thus, by instructing her servants, the anchoress is herself instructed. Like
their mistress, the maidservants are expected to live on as little food and
wage as is necessary. If they serve well, their reward will be the happiness
of heaven:

Hwa se haueð ehe of hope toward se heh hure, gleadliche wule ha
seruin & lihtliche alle wa & alle teone þolien. Wið eise & wið este
ne buð me nawt blisse. (220/13–15)

*If anyone looks with hope to a reward so noble, she will serve willingly and
bear all hardships and all trials easily. Bliss is not to be bought with
comfort and pleasure.*

The reciprocity of labor and heavenly reward had been the promise of 'Penance.'

The advice that the author passes on to the anchoress concerning treatment of her servants may apply to the relation of author and anchoress as well. If any sins through negligence of the other, who will be called to account on Judgment Day? Who but the anchoress, who neglected to instruct her women well (who, we might add, but the author, had he not taken such pains to write this rule of living)? The summons to teach the Rule with love and gentleness, which the author diligently follows in regard to the anchoress, he passes on to her in her relation with others. We are justified in reading it as an expression of mutual responsibility for the anchoress, and hers for those in her charge:

> Lihtliche & sweteliche forȝeoueð ham hare gultes hwen ha hem
> icnaweð & bihateð bote. (220/2–221/3)

> *Forgive them their faults readily and with kindness when they acknowledge them and promise amendment.*

With a sigh of relief that his Rule has come to an end, the author asks that the anchoress read a little of the book each day, turn to it whenever possible. Otherwise, much time has been put to little use.

So ends the Rule. The battle lines are blurred; the smarting of temptations has dulled. The exhortation to victory has become a memory, and the drama has faded into the day-to-day business of external duties, of prayers, and of mending church vestments.

It is the scribe who has the last word. Relieved no doubt that his arduous task as copyist is over, he asks to be remembered in prayers 'ne beo hit se lutel.' And the closing promise that good bringeth forth good seems more than pious apothegm; it is a reflection on a lesson of the Rule: 'Hit turneð þe to gode þet tu bidest for oþre'—by such prayers all are raised up.

CONCLUSION

The *Ancrene Riwle* has made only one demand upon the anchoress: that she govern her heart according to 'þe leafdi riwle,' in which all God's behests are contained. This is the inner Rule that serves the lady and keeps her free from stain. The inner Rule, in turn, is served by the outer, which deals with external things, the body, keeping vigils, fasting and the like. The distinction between outer and inner Rules is made explicit throughout the author's introduction and is repeated within the body of the text in the organization of the chapters. The outer Rule stands at either end of the inner, encircling it, protecting it, as if it were a body enclosing the soul.

Analogies of this kind are typical of the author's creative method, arising perhaps from his knowledge of biblical exegesis or from his personal intuition of correspondences among aspects of experience. The whole of the inner Rule is in fact, a step-by-step study of and induction into the beginnings of contemplation. It prepares the anchoress for the reception of Christ by teaching her how to perfect her religious life and reflects through the steady inward movement of its parts, the gradual progress of the anchoress toward love, in which the Divine Will is consummated. In this way the Rule is an analogue of the anchoress' growth. Also, because the consecutive stages of spiritual growth form the important organizational principle of the work, it has seemed best, for purposes of this book, to follow the author's example and trace the course of the Rule chapter by chapter.

The inner Rule, the 'lady', is constructed of a continuous series of interrelating motifs that support and often embody the lessons. Despite the pervasiveness of imagery, there are few motifs sustained throughout from beginning to end; but those that exist, running, like thread, in and out of the fabric in patterns of line and color, give shape and direction to the whole. Included in this category are the wounds and sores of disease, the prisoner under sentence of death, the lady's castle under siege, and, most intrinsic of all the major motifs, the allegorical journey from this world to the next.

Lesser motifs which are predominantly developed and completed within a chapter or in one and part of a second are the leap into an open pit, the flight of birds, the forging of a crown, the buffeting of winds, and others listed below. To this set might be added recurrent image clusters which show little dynamic movement but are indicators of what progress the anchoress has made; imagery drawn from Scripture, details of the Passion, and the mystical nuptials belong here.

There are, of course, the highly dramatic encounters between anchoress and the Seven Deadly Sins which do not constitute motifs so much as an allegorical context against which a vital inner struggle is being waged. And on the level of allegory and anagogue there is the Christ-knight exemplum of Chapter Seven which encompasses and completes motifs like the besieged castle and the symbolism of the crucifix and the ransomed prisoner.

The list that follows will recall several of the image schemes in their respective chapters which have been discussed in these pages. Omitted for the moment is Chapter Seven, which stands as the very rare jewel of *Ancrene Wisse*.

Two—*Custody of the Senses*
the animal let loose; the leaps into the pit; the lady under siege; Christ's suffering in the five senses; the wounds.

Three—*Regulation of the Inward Feelings*
the pelican and its young, the eagle, the sparrow; the building of the 'nest of the heart'; the puff of wind and 'falling sickness'; the beckoning of the Bridegroom.

Four—*Temptations*
forging of the crown; discipline of the child and God's game; the wounds of disease; the battle with the Sins; the devil's court; sanctuary in Christ's wounds.

Five—*Confession*
the conduct of Judith; the child of hell; the prisoner led to the gallows; the sores of disease exacerbated.

Six—*Penance*

> the journey of the elect to the cross; the fiery chariot; the oils to
> anoint the corpse; the revival to life of the 'dead and buried';
> the step of Christ upon the mountain.

We need only examine the development of a number of motifs to measure the progress of the anchoress in the cultivation of the heart. Glancing broadly at the allegorical journey, Chapter Two begins with a leap—that of the heart out of the body with all the attendant analogies. Thence the journey begins, to end up high on the mountain that receives the impress of Christ's foot. More specifically, the animal (the heart that leaps lightly out) lands in the pit and dies, or, alternatively, is saved from this leap when the guardians of the heart, the watchmen-senses, are attentive. Movement in the animal world continues into Chapter Three with the bird exempla; on the tropological level, the anchoress is being cleansed of impurities that would vitiate the birth of her spiritual offspring, good works (spiritually, Christ). In Chapter Four, the anchoress joins the company of God's chosen in a trek across a wilderness full of threatening beasts, the temptations. Her position on the hill of holy life at the beginning of the ordeal is a sign of her readiness. Having achieved a second elevated position (a tower), she drives off the enemy. The journey done, she takes refuge among the rocks (Christ's wounds). Chapters Five and Six find her highest among God's elect—those who are to be raised up in symbolic crucifixion with Christ, joining Him in pain and toil. Mystical elements in the fiery chariot that carry the first among God's elect to the gates of heaven yield to the figure of a body raised up in crucifixion. The anchoress by her sacrificial offering is raised to the mountain touched by Christ's foot. The journey that began when the heart leaped out has brought her to a greater understanding of spiritual life.

The wound motif pursues the anchoress almost from the first, striking her heart through the access sins have into the senses. Even though she is seemingly able to recover (Christ's assumption of suffering in His senses in Chapter Two) and to rise above spiritual wounds by disciplining her inward feelings, graver wounds are inflicted in the battle action of Chapter Four, in the castle warfare and the struggle with the Sins in the wilderness. The comforts and remedies are provisional cures. The pain of disease, like creeping sores, threatens the sinner and brings her to her knees. In her willingness to be saved lies the beginning of renewal. Pain gives way slowly to the remedies of the Physician until finally Christ's bloodletting of Chapter Six frees her. As He takes to Himself the suffering of the body, she participates in the general bloodletting as a limb.

Closely related is the theme of the felon, a sometime-thief and murderer, who is brought out of his prison to be judged and hanged. Christ, scourged and sentenced to die on the gibbet, mounts the cross 'like a lamb brought to slaughter,' and the sinner is saved by His intervention, saved also by 'a few good words' of faith and penance (Chapter Five).

The closer the anchoress comes to Christ, withstanding trials, embracing penance, the more willing is He to lay down His life for her. The wounds of the invalid are purged with spices and aloes with which Christ's body is smeared before the entombment. Her resurrection from voluntary entombment in the anchorhold and the release of the soul from the feeble body are assured in Christ's example.

It has always been the Passion, always Christ from the beginning. There is no phase or detail of the crucifixion so small that it cannot be found somewhere in the Rule; or so profound that it cannot be explicated by images and exempla. Yet in this inclining our author is not exceptional; in his dwelling on Christ's humanity he has illustrious precedents in the Bernardine literature that swept his age with enthusiasm, and he owes more than a small debt to Aelred of Rievaulx for the general description of a rule of living and the emotional fervor of the meditations. If there had been a 'dark night of the soul' for him it had settled into a firm and resolute faith and a compassionate understanding of the ways of his world. Men are human, they are flawed; on this earth, he says, there was but one Man who could let blood. This sense of Christ's going to the cross, mounting it with deliberate, purposeful intent strikes this reader truer to the author's attitude than the new pathos that finds its way into the Rule from time to time. Christ is whole, He is healthy, He is chivalrous.

The sacrifice of the Christ-knight, described in exquisitely detailed figures, is the high point of the Rule, bringing to rest, or completion, the spiraling images of the Passion which have been accumulating steadily, the castle-and-siege metaphors, and the promises of the persistent suitor, which until Chapter Seven had been tendered in the language of Canticles.

One might well ask why it is that after two hundred pages of text, the allegory and events of the Christ-knight exemplum—matters that have been touched on every exegetical level often enough to render them familiar if not predictable—should be so fresh and vital. A key lies in the personalization of the principals as they reenact a drama whose parts have been minutely delineated throughout. We have come to know the lady, her circumstances, her *hauteur*; we know the price of her deliverance, the nobility of the knight. We understand his anger when she seems reluctant to be saved, though the cost to her is little enough. The intimacy in the midst of abstraction (even to the most nonspecific of chivalric settings) has been diligently rehearsed in the voice and promises of the Bridegroom of Canticles heard in every section of the Rule.

Another key to the power of the chapter, one typical of the author's style, is his method of handling the Christ-shield metaphor. He builds up, through cumulating images and multiple associations already firmly rooted in the iconography of the crucifixion, a crescendo of rapidly delivered phrases, bits of dialogue and scriptural verse, precepts, and definitions. There is excitement created by verbal animation, telescoping of imagery and emotional pull. We move from the general to the acutely specific. The light imagery that begins rather ingenuously with the figure of a bright and shining heart becomes the true Sun raised up on the cross, throwing beams down to enkindle love in the heart. So the *memoria Christi* on the wall, like a shield hung up in memory of a knight, reminds the anchoress of her debt, protects her from the vulnerable flesh and moves her to love. The light, by conversion in mysticism, kindles *incendium amoris* in spouse and Bridegroom. The Christ-knight, the Son or true Sun, whence this light comes, recedes slightly as the theme of light into fire grows—burgeoning through shifts of emphasis, now delicate and unobtrusive, now striking, until it is asserted with massive acceleration as the theme and center of the work, the *Greek fire*. This is the ultimate weapon, and it is no more and no less than love. This theme dominates the Rule.

Finally, there are groups of images and allusions in the work that are not motifs in themselves but create a certain tone within which moral instruction is delivered. An example of this is the suggestion of sensuality whenever the Eucharist is offered, in the Mass kiss, and in the physical body of the *memento Christi*. Related to these are the intimations of the anchoress as another Mary preparing the nest of the heart to receive Christ.

The dynamic changes in setting and situation so often juxtapose earth and heaven, the anchoress and the bower, that the third world of hell, the kingdom of the devil, seems less of a totally articulated reality than it is. But from the very early chapters there emerges the counteraction of the devil's forces, first in the rather sketchy mention of witchcraft and the black arts through which the anchoress, falling into sin, is transformed into a she-wolf or unicorn; then in the slowly developing social structure of hell where the devil holds court, raises armies, wins the weak and sinful to his party, and threatens to take possession of the prize. This power, the enemy itself, disintegrates in Greek fire.

We are left to speculate on the reaction of the three sisters for whom the author labored so heroically in the creation of his book. What of the denseness of imagery, the evolving patterns of allegory, the spiritualization of argument increasing gradually as the capacity to love grows? If the author's style presented any problems to the anchoress, we must imagine that continual reading of the work wiped these away even as the affective force of the mystical imagery was expanding. Her advantage in approaching devotional prose of this kind was that she shared the religious ideals and attitudes of the author in a manner and to a degree lost to us today. Her needs were satisfied not by the intellectual pleasures of 'search and destroy' dialectic, but by the emotional and mystical response to Christ's divinity and humanity. The presentation of arguments in the Rule is designed to fulfill this need. Eight hundred years later the serious reader is still at it, still searching, still reaching, but from a changed perspective; marveling not at Christ's mastery so much as the author's; moved more by the man's technical skill than his faith, but impressed by both. This was not the kind of immortality he had in mind for himself or the sisters who were to receive this book from his hand; but helpless to demur at the literary honors accorded him, he must remain content to have achieved the best of all possible worlds. To which the author, who has left us not so much as a name, would respond

Preise him, laste him, do him scheome, sei him scheome. Al him is iliche leof.

APPENDIX

THE THIRD MEDITATION OF STEPHEN OF SAWLEY

This meditation corresponds in event with the first Joy of Mary as given in the Rule. They are repeated below in separate columns. Marginal letters denote equivalent sections, summarized here.

(A) Subject of meditation.
(B) Instructions concerning prayers.
(B¹) In Luke II, the *Magnificat* follows (*ad consensum uirginis*).
(B²) The *Gaude, dei genetrix.*
(C) The petition.
(D) The *Ave.*

(A) *Tertia meditatio.* Tertia meditatio considerat Gabrielem archangelum de celis uenientem, uirginem dulciter salutantem, illam salutationem mellifluam formantem, in qua modo totus exultat orbis terrarum. Cogita ergo, dilectissime, et forma in animo tuo quid admirationis, quid deuocionis, quid exultationis

(B) senserit beata uirgo in angeli uisione, in eius allocutione, in noue salutationis exposicione, in ipsius angeli consolatione, sicut potes

(B¹) perpendere ex serie Euuangelii secundum Lucam: MISSVS EST GABRIEL, usque et consensum uirginis, et in hac consideratione dices:

(A) Leafdi seinte Marie, for þe ilke muchele blisse þet tu hefdest inwið þe i þet ilke time þet iesu, godd, godes sune, efter þe engles gretunge, nom flesch & blod in þe & of þe, underfeng mi gretunge wið þe ilke aue, & make me telle lutel of euch (C) blisse utewið, ah froure me inwið & ernde me þeo of heouene. Ant ase wis as i þe ilke flesch þet he toc of þe nes neauer sunne, ne i þin, as me leueð, efter þe ilke tacunge, hwet se biuore were, clense mi sawle of fleschliche sunnen.

(B) Biginne þe aue aþet dominus tecum, as me biginneð antefne, & tenne þe salm, & efter þe salm al ut fifsiðen, uirginis, et in hac consideratione dices:

Tercium gaudium. Gaude, gloriosissima dei genetrix et sanctissima
(B²) uirgo semper Maria, que sola fuisti
digna suscipere noue salutationis
gaudium, tibi celitus per angelum a
deo transmissum.

Tercia peticio. Deprecor te, domina
dulcissima, per illius salutationis
singulare gaudium: da michi
(C) illud aue mellifluum, primum
nostre salutis presagium deuoto
corde et mundis labiis cotidie tibi
offerre, michi ad solacium in omni
temptatione, et tibi ad honorem et
laudem, o clemens, o pia, o dulcis
Maria. Aue, sancta et gloriosa et
perpetua et pia dei genetrix, uirgo
(D) semper Maria, gracia plena,
dominus tecum, benedicta in
mulieribus et benedictus dominus
Iesu dulcis fructus benedicti uentris
tui, amen.

& þus to euch salm, Aue Maria,   (D)
gratia plena, dominus tecum.
Magnificat. Aue maria al ut fifsiðen.   (B¹)

[The rest of the series follows. Each
Joy ends with five *aues*. At the conclusion there are prayers and versicles
in honor of Mary and finally the
Gaude.]

Gaude, dei genitrix, uirgo inmaculata.
Gaude, que gaudium ab angelo sus-   (B²)
cepisti. Gaude, que genuisti eterni
luminis claritatem. Gaude, mater.
Gaude, sancta dei genitrix. Virgo tu
sola mater innupta. Te laudat omnis
filii tui creatura, genitricem lucis.
Sis pro nobis pia interuentrix.

INDEX

Abstinence, 104–105, 116

Adder, 47, 68

Aelred of Rievaulx, 4, 22n, 90, 173–174; *Regula* 4, 17, 18, 226

Agate, 68–69, 123

Air, 59–61, 82

Allegory: a level of interpretation, 12; in battle with Sins, 13; in Bestiaries, 58; of birds, 61, 67; of the game, 96; Seven Deadly Sins, 103, 106; used with anagogue, 116; in Mass passage, 120; in fight with dog, 123; to dramatize the Passion, 125; development in 'Confession,' 128–130; absence of, 140; in rending of carcass, 141; use in figure of condemned man, 148; of indulgent parents, 158; in tattered garments, 159–160; as medieval habit, 173–175; in Bernardine literature, 178; of Christ and the soul, 187; Christ as knight, 189, 192; in Christ-shield, 195; *four loves of the world* as, 196, 198; in Woman of Sarepta, 204; uses of, in 'Love,' 210; movement into anagogue, 216; summary of use in *AW*, 223–224; its vitality, 227; anchoress' understanding of, 228

Anagogue: in bird imagery, 11; in inner Rule, 56; reward of study, 78; movement away from, 116; in reconciliation with God, 130; inversion of allegory, 141; opening of 'Penance,' 147; in crucifixion, 153; love's sovereignty, 215; in Christ-knight exemplum, 224

Anchorhold: in England, 3; life in, 6–8, 114, 220–222; analogies in *AW*, 39, 57; window of, 40; as a confine, 42; as metaphor of castle, 44; curtains in, 48; future rewards of enclosure in, 51; as support of the church, 72; as refuge, 76; residence of devil's court, 105; devil exorcised from, 130; confession in, 138; place of symbolic martyrdom, 148; symbolism humanized in, 152; penitential life in, 153; analogies of 'narrow dwelling,' 168–169

Ancrene Riwle: basis in traditional materials, 3; format of, 4; *AW*, 5; structure, 8–12, 35, 42; image spirals in, 14, 15; inner Rule, 29, 36, 56, 223–224; concrete example in, 34; heart as symbol in, 68; use of penance in, 127–128; author and his book, 222; as spiritual guide, 223–224

Anger: exegetical account of, 10–11; purging of, 13; in act of pelican, 57–61, 64; its destructiveness, 67; agate is deterrant of, 69–70; compared to pride, 73; as puffs of air, 74; sin of the heart, 78, 82, 84; temptations fed by, 126; mastery over, 149; Christ's suffering because of Father's, 161–63; of the Christ-knight, 202, 227

Animal: leap into the pit of, 41, 43–44, 56, 68, 119; its death, 49; use of imagery, 52, 71; rotting of, 53, 56; connection with bird imagery, 58, 61; carnal-spiritual faults in, 61–62; caught and killed, 79; Sins personified by, 82, 82n; in herd clinging together, 114; as devil's mount, 119; slain in pit of senses, 124; trapped by dogs, 143; allegorical representation, 173; Adam's dominance over, 186; recurrence as figure in *AW*, 224–225

Animal-sins: in allegorized battle, 13; crown sign of victory over, 92; described in 'Temptations,' 97–103; remedies against, 109; as force joined with devil, 114, 130; summary of use in *AW*, 224–225

Arrow: in devil's attacks, 44, 45; lust of the eye, 47, 54

Arthur, 173, 173n

Ashes, 104

Assuerus, 78

Atonement: reminder in *memoria Christi*, 70; as figure of bath of blood, 137; God's promise to man, 186; act of Christ-knight, 211

Author: his background, 3, 5; literary abilities, 23; participation in prayer, 123; confrontation with sin, 131; handling of

Urine: in Greek fire imagery, 179; and vinegar, 203; depressant of Greek fire, 205, 207, 211

Vainglory: and loss of good, 73; a spiritual fault, 82; overcome by pilgrim, 149
Venom. *See* Poison.
Vessel, 76
Vigil(s): of Judith, 61–62; food of soul, 72; sorry vigil of sloth, 103; of outer Rule, 223
Vinegar: of faint love, 178n; and urine, 203; depressant of Greek fire, 205, 207–210
Vineyard: of Canticles, 179; parable of workers in, 180; Christ as laborer in, 208–210; rewards of, 212
Visitors: come to dine, 6; hand touching, 11; entertainment of, 220
Vitae Patrum: in anchorhold, 7; example from, 104

Watchmen: senses as, 39; of castle, 44; and Bridegroom, 49
Wheel of Elijah's chariot, 151–153
Widow: Judith a modest, 61; anchoress as, 138, 139
Wilderness: struggle with Sins in, 82, 225; predators of, 97–98; journey through, 103, 106
Wilmart, André, 18–20
Wimple, 7
Wind: as blasts of sin, 41; and precepts on anger, 59–61, 72–73; and flight, 65, 74; dust scattered by, 70, 73; assailing hill, 81,

83, 86, 169; structural link with wound imagery, 82–83; stilled by tears, 112; a destructive force, 115; pride a bag of, 122; use as motif in *AW*, 228
Window: parlor, of anchorhold, 6, 47; and holding school, 7; analogies of, 10–11, hands at, 11, 54; of the eye, 39, 40; fastened and well-locked, 41; black cloth on, 43; as battlements, 45; face turned to, 50
Wolf: of rage, 61; as predator of discord, 114; anchoress as she-wolf, 228
Wounds: five, 23; wind-borne, 61; structural link to wind imagery, 82–83, 86; festering, 82, 129, 141–142; temptations as, 83–85, 87, 111; pelican's, 83, 97; refuge in Christ's, 11, 13, 83, 88, 124, 145–146; too sensitive for cure, 84; and disease of sin, 84–85, 89, 106, 141–142; spiritual, 84n, 107, 129; comforts and remedies of, 86–87; healed, 87; as major image motif, 89, 142, 153; of spear, 91; of battle with Sins, 109; reopened, 121; bring proud man low, 122; hidden, threaten soul, 138–139, 139n; Christ assumes, 157; spices to heal, 164; summary of use in *AW*, 223, 224–225, 226
Wrath: a spiritual temptation, 84; animal-sin described, 99, 101, 103; juggler in devil's court, 103; killed by love, 114; remedies against, 114–116; devil's fire fed by, 126
Wrestling: contest of Christ and devil, 82; Christ's strategy in, 121